I0812700

IMAGES
*of America*

# PENN AND MADISON TOWNSHIPS

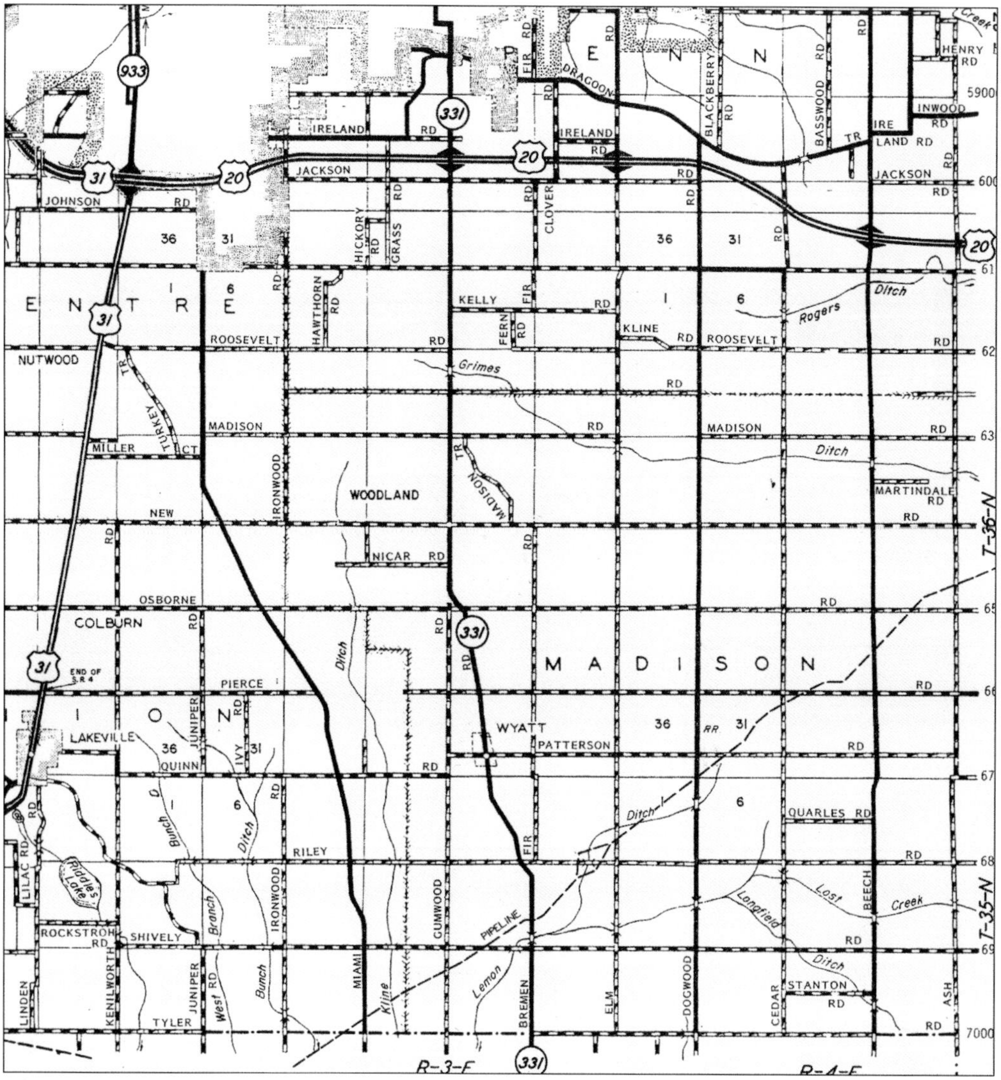


This plot map shows the rural character of Penn and Madison Townships, excluding the city of Mishawaka.

*On the cover:* Captured in 1910 at the Mr. Louis Bollenbacher Homestead in Madison Township on a beautiful summer day are, from left to right, Annie Bollenbacher, Nora (Bollenbacher) Martin, Nellie (Bollenbacher) Birk, and Violet Martin. (Courtesy of Jeanette [Battles] Martin.)

IMAGES
*of America*

# PENN AND MADISON TOWNSHIPS

Debra C. Perkins

ARCADIA
PUBLISHING

ISBN 978-0-7385-4072-6

Published by Arcadia Publishing
Charleston, South Carolina

Printed in the United States of America

Library of Congress Control Number: 2006924918

For all general information contact Arcadia Publishing at:
Telephone 843-853-2070
Fax 843-853-0044
E-mail sales@arcadiapublishing.com
For customer service and orders:
Toll-Free 1-888-313-2665

Visit us on the Internet at www.arcadiapublishing.com

*I dedicate this book to the memory of my grandparents, Charles A. Beehler Jr. and Virginia E. (Battles) Beehler, and to the honor of my parents, Paul and Patricia Hubbard.*

# Contents

# ACKNOWLEDGMENTS

Residents past and present of Penn and Madison Townships have been very supportive in my venture. A very special thanks to Lighthouse Imaging (Mike Bennett, Sue Bennett, Eric Szajko, and Michelle Szajko) for their encouragement and assistance with my photographs. Without them this book would not have been possible. A special thanks to Charlie Tredway for also helping with photographs and making things easier. To Anna Wilson, acquisitions editor at Arcadia Publishing, thank you for all your patience and assistance in my venture. To everyone who took the time to locate photographs and share them with me, I send my deepest appreciation. I met some very nice people during my research, and I thank you all for you kindness. To my family, I thank you for your understanding while I was away or on the computer. I could not have completed this dream without your support.

To recognize some of the residents in this area, I would like to especially thank the following: Patricia Hubbard, Paul Hubbard, Rich Mochel, Dora Fredericks, Helen Marker, Jeanette Martin, Vicki Berger, Rosemary Dixon, Dennis Beehler, Fern Beehler, Michael Schalliol, Joyce Schalliol, Bruce Horein, Dorothy Neer, Verdene Hunke, Harold Hunke, Evelyn Salyer, Brad Kline, Lee Kline, Janet Holderbaum, Clifford Holderbaum, Dale Hahn, Judy Marker, John Marker, Susie Pogue, Craig Lechlitner, and many others.

# INTRODUCTION

Within St. Joseph County there are two rural townships, Penn and Madison. Back in the 1840s, these townships were heavily wooded and swampy. The early settlers decided to change this, and today this area has become a very prosperous farming community. In March 1845, the area once known as Penn Township was divided into two townships. The southern portion was named Madison Township, which did not attract settlers until around 1840. Madison's land was heavily timbered, the soil a strong clay, and swamps and low ground met the explorers at every turn. Brave, hardy pioneers recognized the rich quality of this region's soil. Soon sawmills and drainage ditches converted the forbidding terrain into the most valuable farmlands of St. Joseph County. The principle occupations of Madison Township's people have always been in the timber, lumber, and farming businesses. Within Madison, once the only rural area in St. Joseph County with a high school, are two towns: Wyatt in the southwest and Woodland to the north. Wyatt is situated on the Wabash Railroad. Early settlers in the area included the Cline, Bennett, Godfried, Enders, Palmer, Kline, Kiefer, Marker, Conrad, Mochel, Beehler, Loucks, and Birk families.

William and Timothy Moat settled Penn Township in 1828. Penn Township was one of the original three townships in St. Joseph County, created in 1832. Years later, this area was subdivided into Madison and Penn, Harris, and parts of Clay, Centre, and Union. Penn Township remains the largest township in the county. The terrain in the southern part of Penn is quite similar to adjoining Madison, and the St. Joseph River flows through the northern part of Penn. In places, particularly in the vicinity of the river, the landscape of Penn is particularly charming, the finest of prairies. Penn Township's first school was erected in 1832 near the site of present-day Osceola. Baugo Creek is located in the same vicinity. The power of that little stream has been used for milling purposes, both sawmills and gristmills, and the Lake Shore and Grand Trunk Railroads both pass through Penn Township. Other pioneers included the Macy, Byrkit, Ireland, Webster, and Parks families.

One of the three most important towns in the area is Osceola. It received its musical name from the famous Seminole chief, who was taken prisoner by General Jessup in October 1837, a few weeks before the town was platted. The town struggled until the construction of the inter-urban railway from South Bend to Goshen in 1899 and 1900.

Another important town, Wyatt, was platted in March 1894. When the Wabash Railroad came through the heavily timbered area and drained lands turned into fertile farms, the need for a shipping town was evident. Wyatt soon began to grow as settlers erected buildings and started businesses. The third major town in the area, Woodland, has been in existence at least since

1860, but the town was never platted. Woodland has always been a business center and boasted schools, churches, grocery stores, a post office, physicians' offices, sawmills, blacksmith shops, and other typical features of a rural town.

Penn and Madison have always been closely connected. This book hopes to preserve the past for the families' generations that will follow.

# *One*

# FAMILY

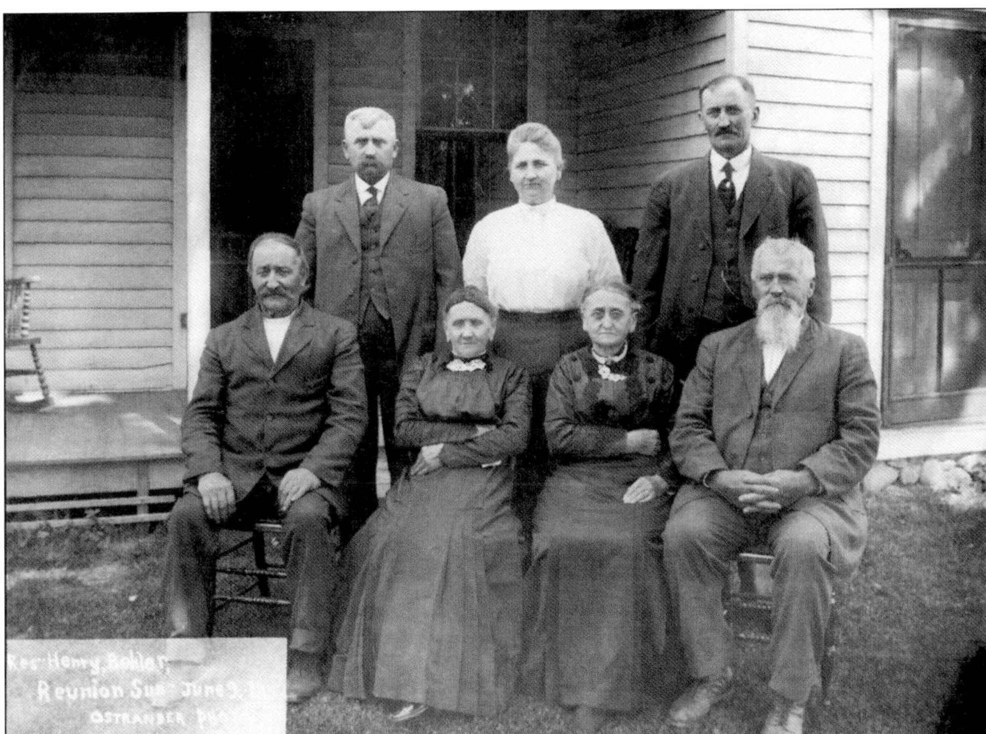

A Beehler reunion was held on June 9, 1913, at the residence of Henry Beehler. Pictured are, from left to right, as follows: (first row) Jacob Beehler, Mary (Beehler) Reinhold, Elizabeth (Beehler) Kelley, and Philip Beehler Jr.; (second row) Peter Beehler Jr., Emma (Beehler) Horein, and Henry Beehler. (Courtesy of the author.)

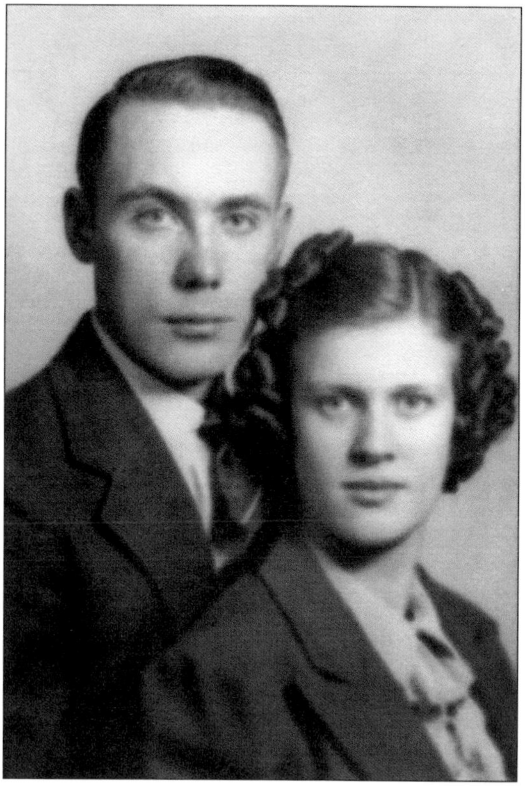

On April 19, 1939, Ralph V. Roeder and Charlotte D. Beehler were married. This photograph is from their wedding day. They made their home on Elm Road just north of Osborne Road, in Madison Township. (Courtesy of the author.)

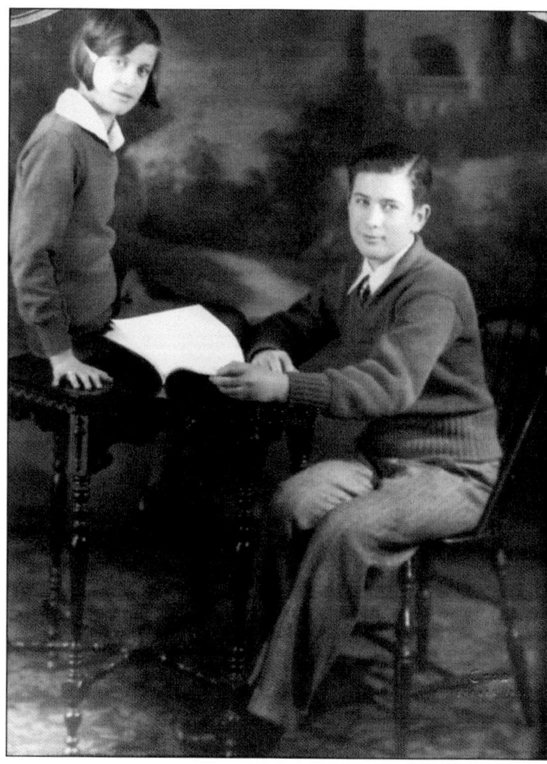

Siblings Charlotte D. Beehler and Charles A. Beehler Jr. are depicted here around 1930 in their preteen years. They are the children of Charles A. Beehler Sr. and Elsie E. (Schalliol) Beehler. Charlotte and Charles grew up on the corner of Osborne and Dogwood Roads. Their parents were born and raised in Madison Township. (Courtesy of the author.)

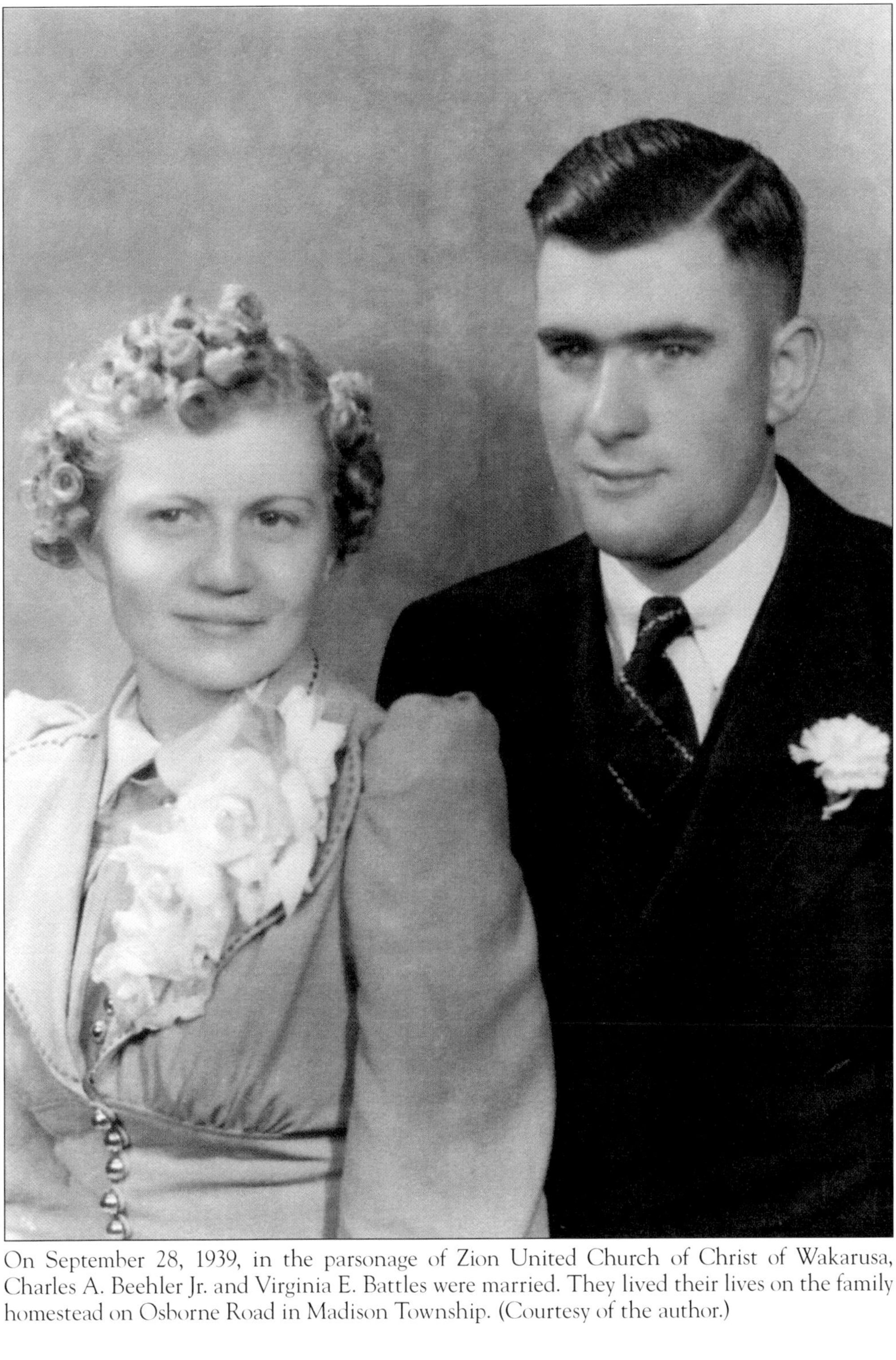

On September 28, 1939, in the parsonage of Zion United Church of Christ of Wakarusa, Charles A. Beehler Jr. and Virginia E. Battles were married. They lived their lives on the family homestead on Osborne Road in Madison Township. (Courtesy of the author.)

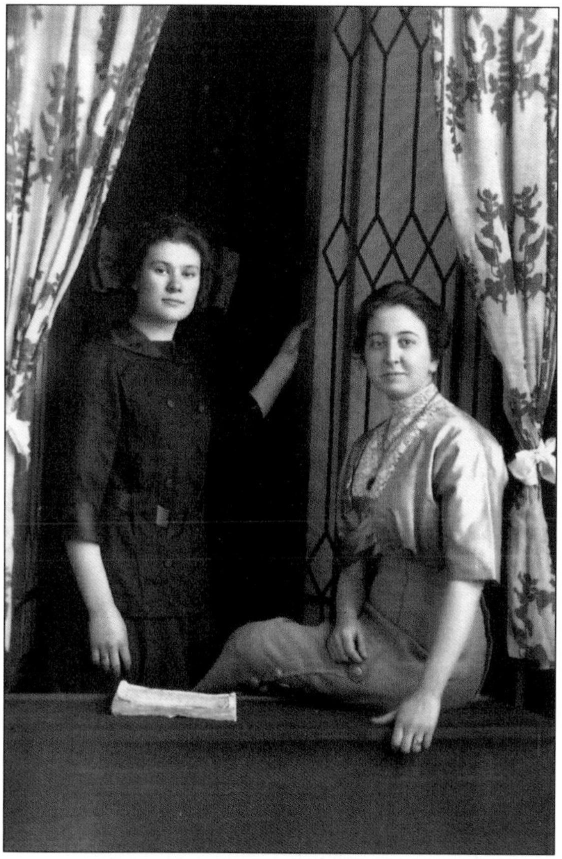

Two cousins share a special moment in this photograph. Elsie E. Schalliol (left) and Estella Hunsberger are pictured here in March 1913. (Courtesy of the author.)

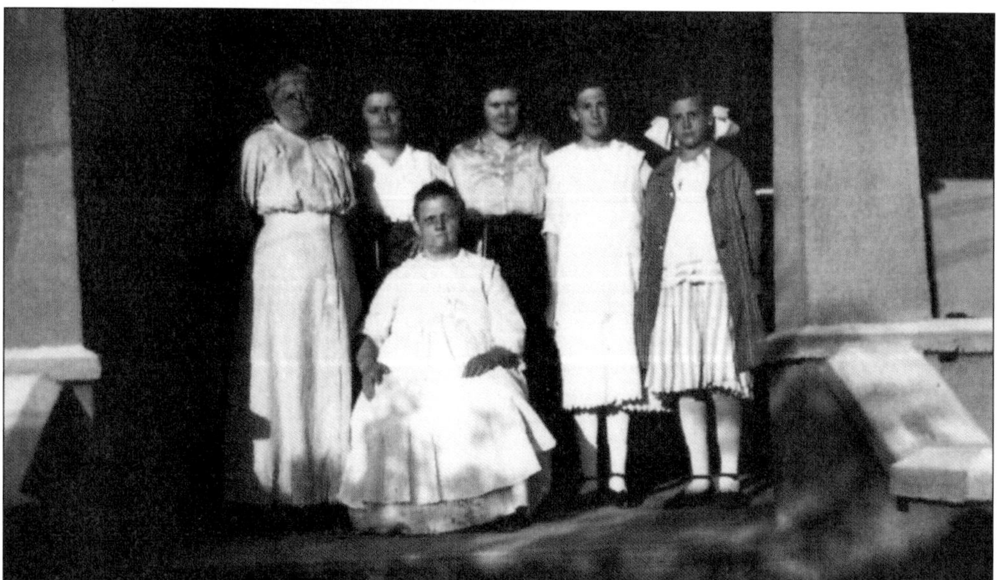

Dorothea S. W. (Bollenbacher) Schalliol, a German native, is shown seated here, with her daughters standing behind her. This picture was taken on the front porch of their home on Beech Road in Madison Township. (Courtesy of the author.)

Pictured in this photograph, from left to right, are Roscoe Schalliol, Earl Robinson, Thaddeus "Tod" Schalliol, and Grover Schalliol (seated). (Courtesy of the author.)

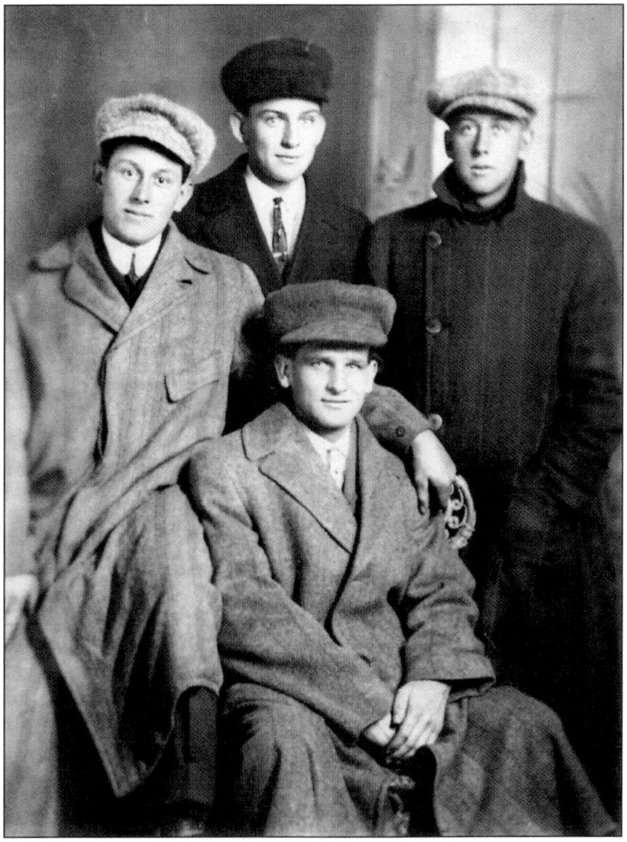

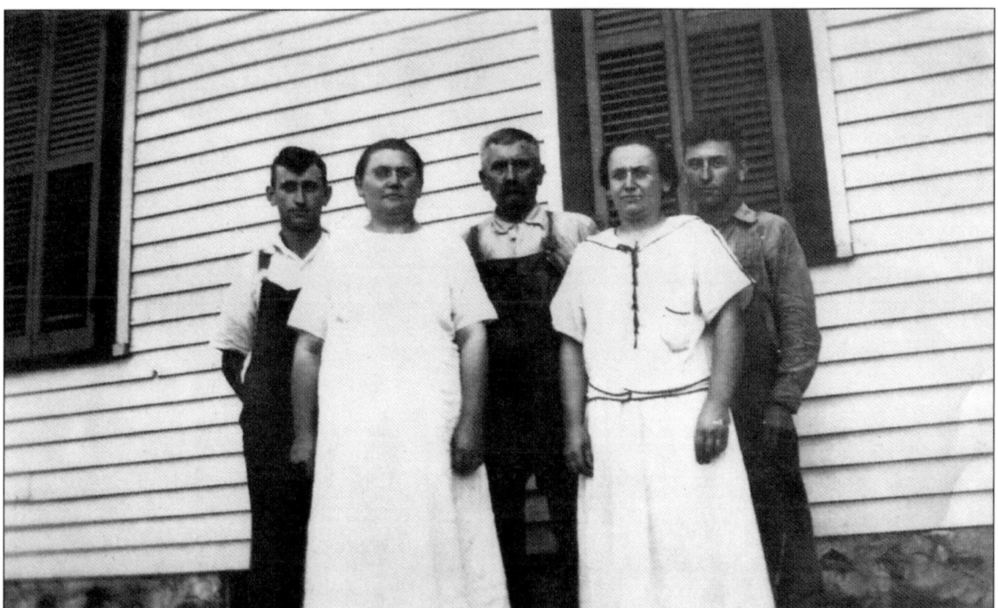

This family picture shows, from left to right, Charles A. Beehler, Matilda Beehler, Peter Beehler, Carrie Beehler, and Warner Beehler. (Courtesy of the author.)

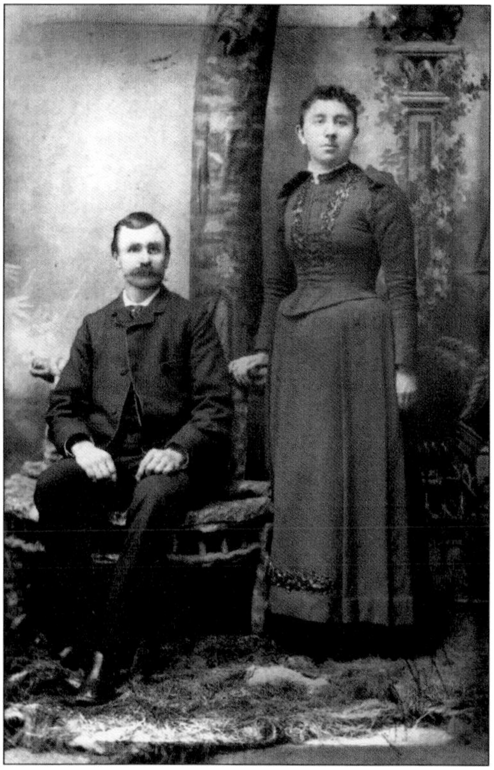

This photograph shows the parents of Cora (Bollenbacher) Myers, Phillip P. Bollenbacher, and Lydia (Kastner) Bollenbacher. (Courtesy of the author.)

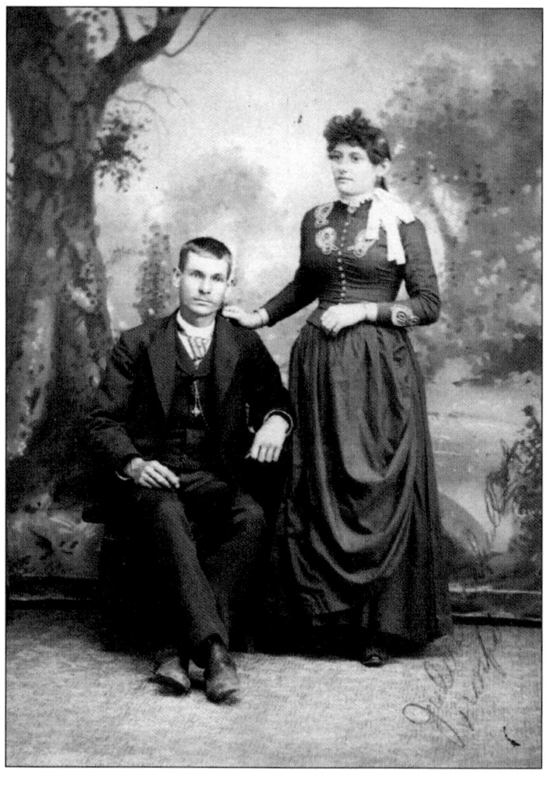

Pictured here are Julius G. Schalliol and Matilda (Harter) Schalliol. They were the proud parents of three children: Roscoe Schalliol, Vern Schalliol, and Dorothy (Schalliol) Fredericks. (Courtesy of the author.)

This photograph features Adam Beehler, son of Philipp Buhler and Anna (Litzenberger) Beehler and a cousin to Peter Beehler Jr. Adam, who married Sarah Bertha Beehler, arrived in the United States from Wurtenburg, Germany, on March 29, 1869. Later, with his cousin Peter as a partner, Adam purchased the mill of a former employer and continued its operation for seven years. At the close of that period, he sold his interest to Jacob K. Beehler and turned to agricultural pursuits. (Courtesy of the author.)

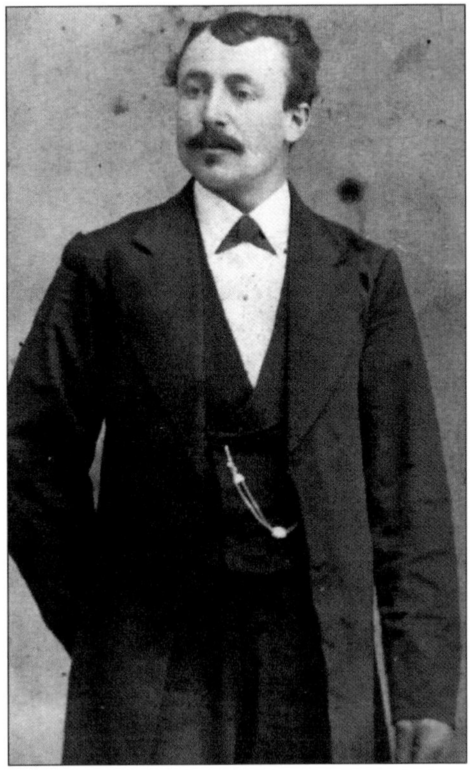

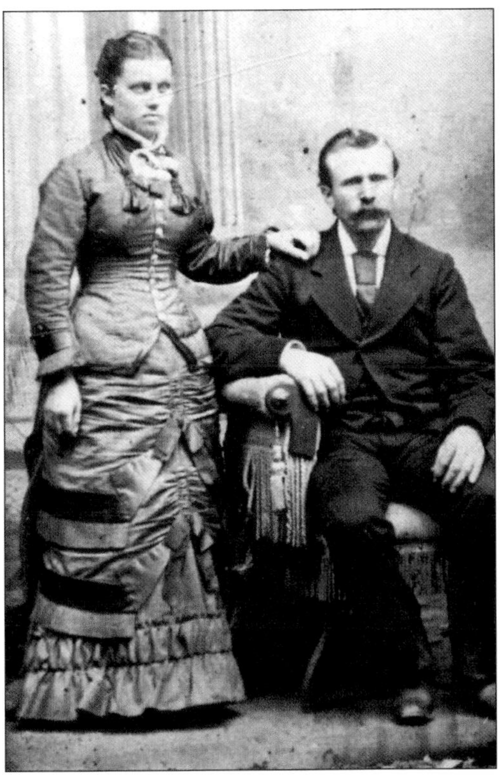

Louis Bollenbacher and Katherina (Hesch) Bollenbacher had their photograph taken to share with their loving family. (Courtesy of the author.)

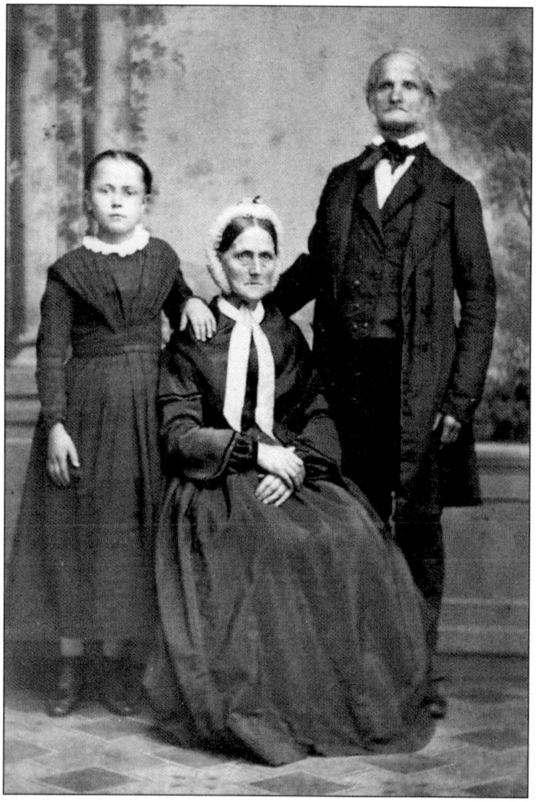

This photograph is of the parents and sister of Sophie (Auman) Bollenbacher. Sophie was the mother of Dorothea (Bollenbacher) Schalliol, Phillip P. Bollenbacher, Louis Bollenbacher, Clara (Bollenbacher) Hahn, and Emma (Bollenbacher) Strope. (Courtesy of the author.)

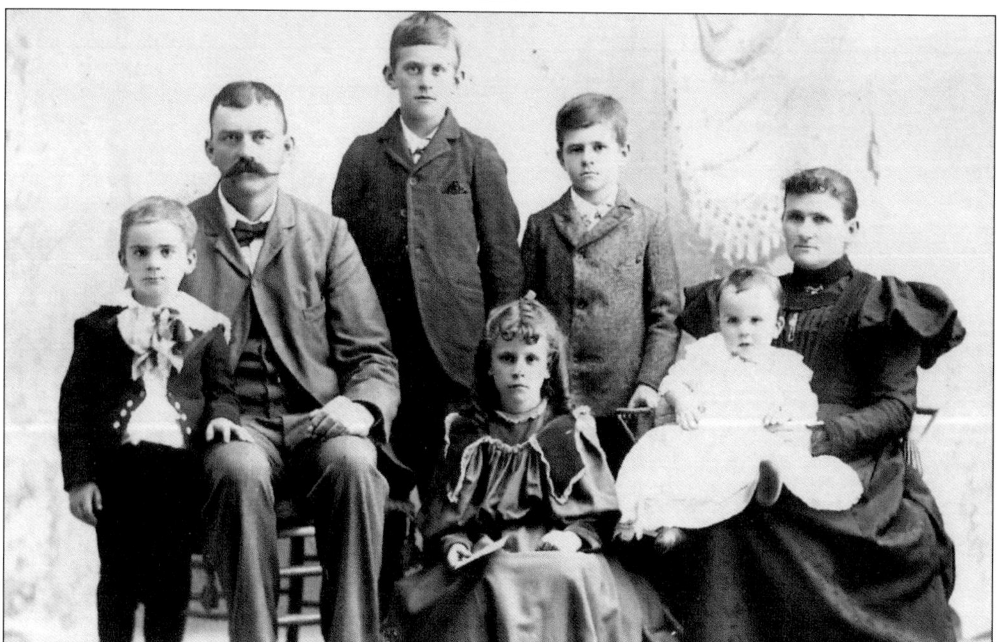

The Frank Hahn family is shown here. Pictured in this photograph, from left to right, are Richard Hahn, Frank Hahn, Elmer Hahn, Louise Hahn (sitting), Walter Hahn, and Clara (Bollenbacher) Hahn, holding Edna Hahn. (Courtesy of the author.)

This is the wedding picture of Charles D. Schalliol and Rosina (Giessler) Schalliol. They were the parents of Wilbur Schalliol, Richard Schalliol, Robert Schalliol, Paul Schalliol, Herbert Schalliol, Edgar Schalliol, and Mary (Schalliol) Mossey. (Courtesy of the author.)

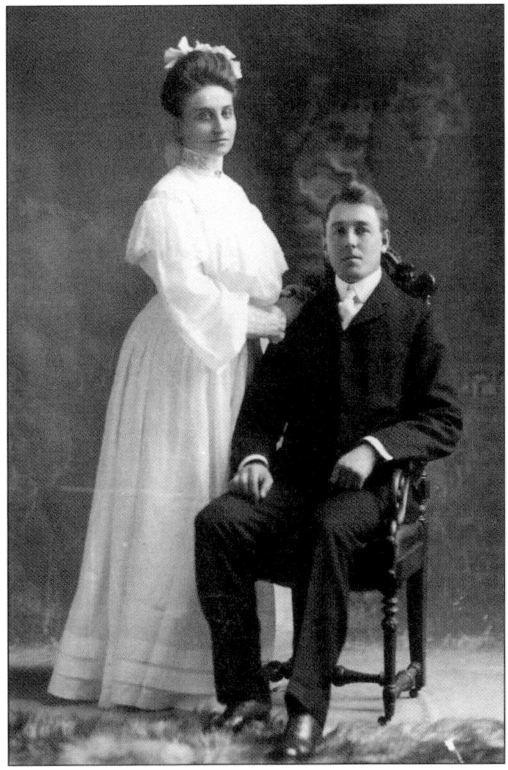

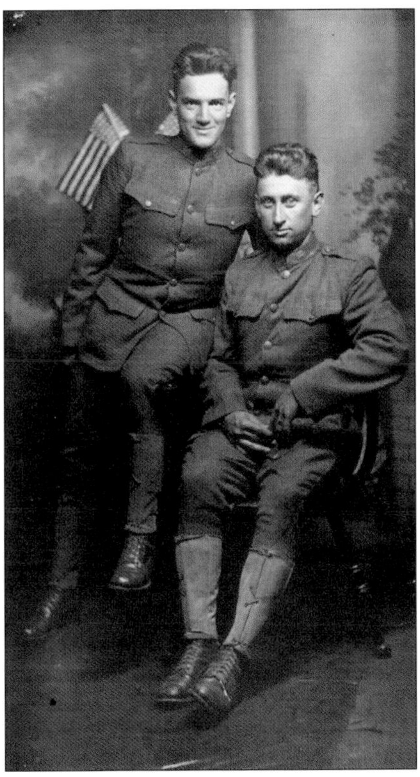

Sam Marker (left) and Charles A. Beehler Sr. were photographed in their army uniforms during World War I. On the backside of the postcard, Charles wrote, "At Logansport, while waiting. We felt just like we looked." (Courtesy of the author.)

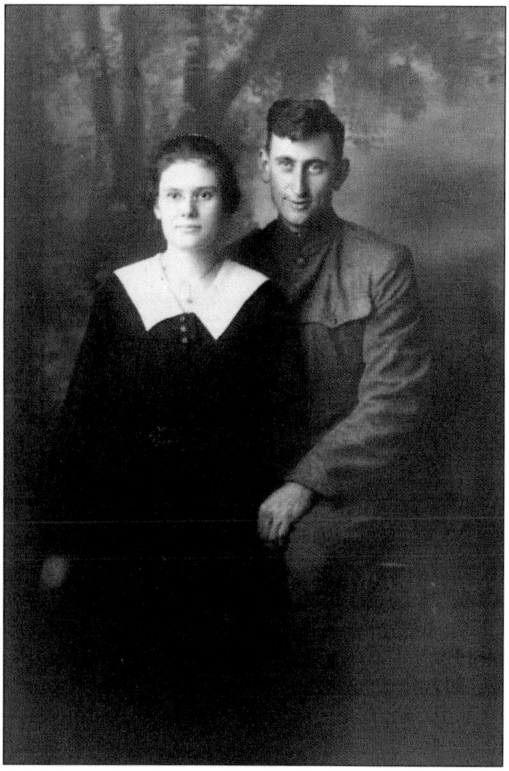

Elsie (Schalliol) Beehler and Charles A. Beehler Sr. were photographed before Charles left for France during World War I. Elsie delivered their first child during the time Charles was abroad. (Courtesy of the author.)

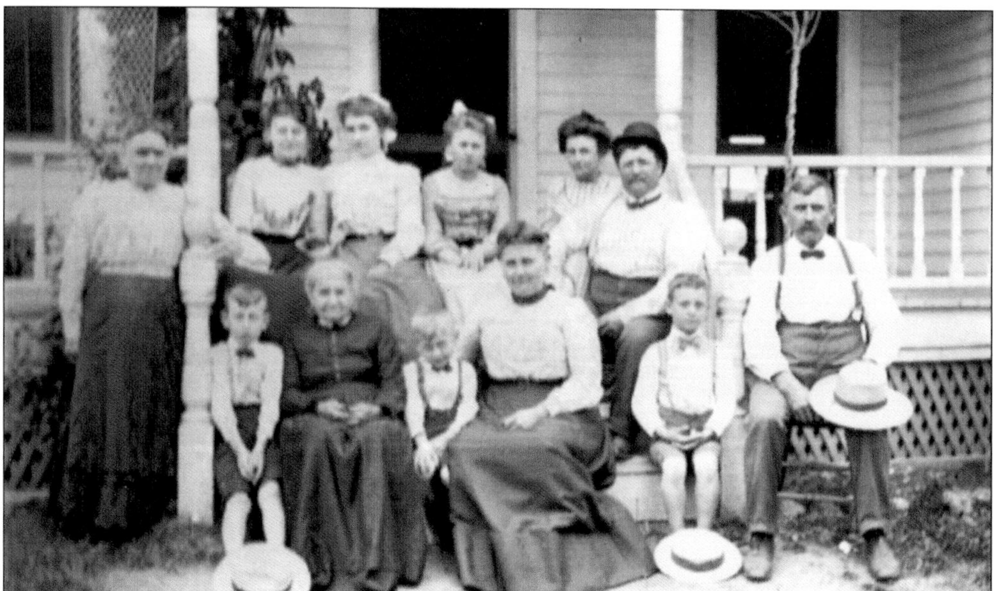

A photograph taken after a get-together features, from left to right, the following: (first row) Charles A. Beehler, Emma (Beehler) Horine, Warner Beehler, Elizabeth (Beehler) Kelley, Otto Kelley, and Peter Beehler Jr.; (second row) Mary (Beehler) Reinhold, Amelia Kelley, Mary Kelley, Minnie Beehler, Ella Beehler, and unidentified. The picture was taken around 1902. (Courtesy of the author.)

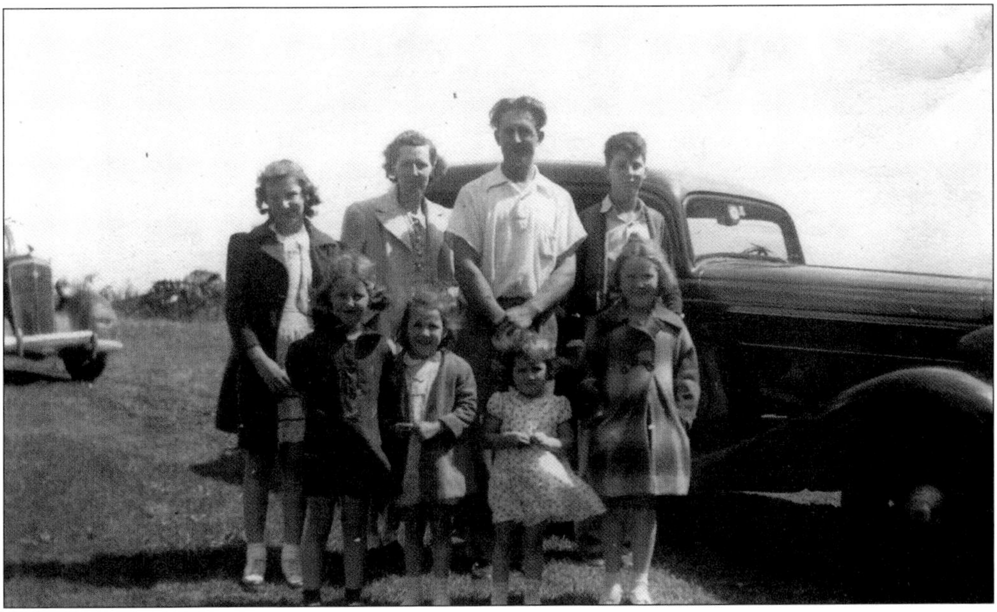

This photograph was taken during an outing. It shows, from left to right, the following: (first row) Alma McClelland, Carol Vandygriff, Janet Holderbaum, and Patricia Graham; (second row) Lois Frick, Florence Kulp, Walter Abbiehl, and Leroy ?. (Courtesy of Clifford and Janet Holderbaum.)

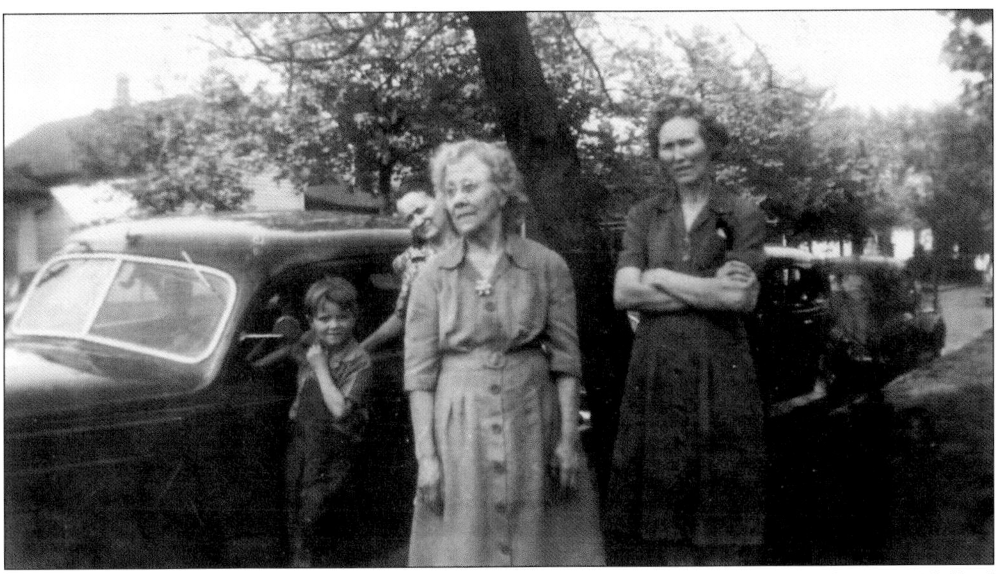

This 1945 photograph portrays four generations. Pictured from left to right are Clifford Holderbaum (son), Marie (Wagner) Holderbaum (mother), Louise Berger (great-grandmother), and Martha (Berger) Wagner (grandmother). (Courtesy of Clifford and Janet Holderbaum.)

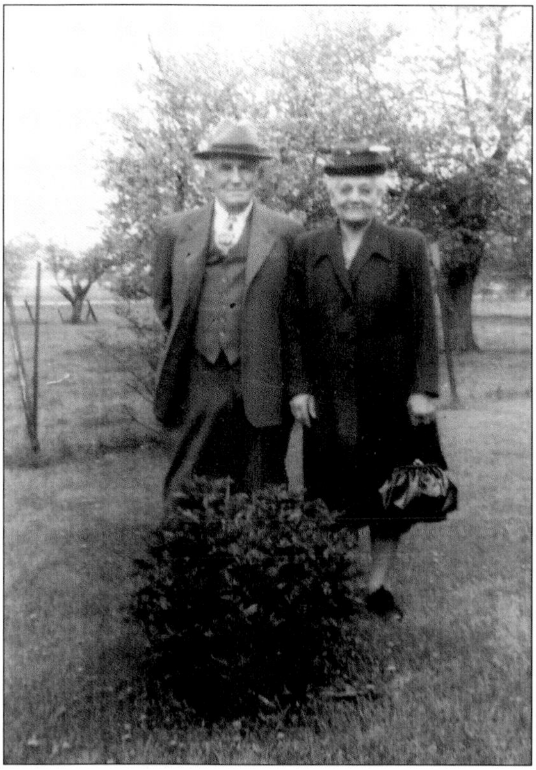

Pictured here are Oliver and Eva Pittman. They were the proud parents of Fern Pittman, Dessie Pittman, Addie Pittman, Russell Pittman, Herbert Pittman, Erma Pittman, and Lester Pittman. (Courtesy of Fern Beehler.)

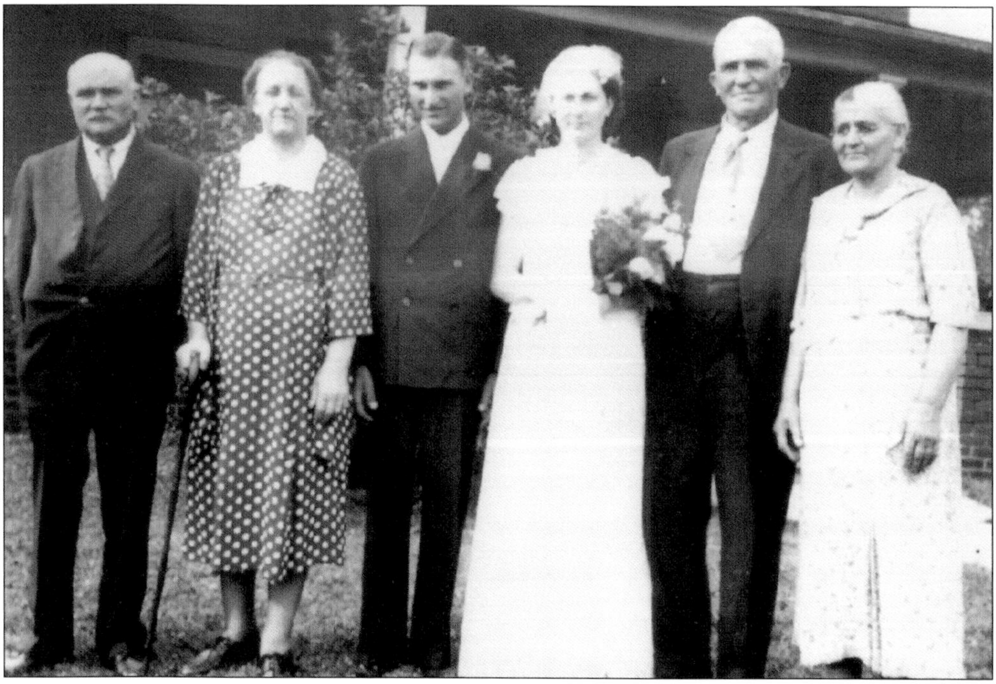

On June 14, 1936, this photograph was taken of , from left to right, Joseph Beehler, Anna (Birk) Beehler, Clayton Beehler, Fern (Pittman) Beehler, Oliver Pittman, and Eva (Manges) Pittman after the wedding of Clayton and Fern Beehler. (Courtesy of Fern Beehler.)

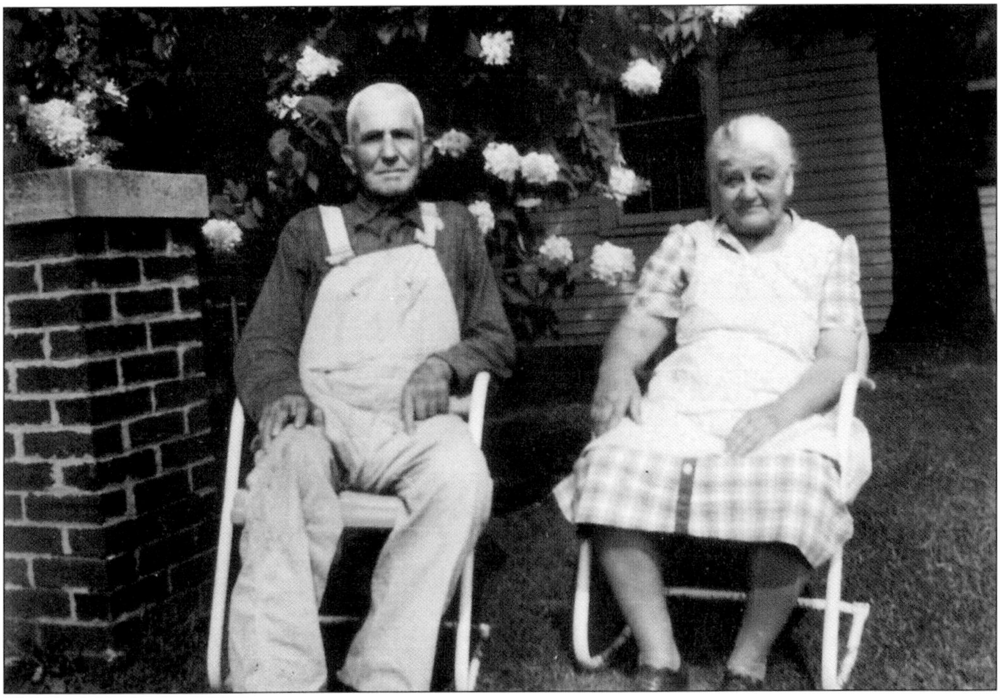

Oliver and Eva Pittman were allegedly the first homeowners in Madison Township to have an indoor bathroom. (Courtesy of Fern Beehler.)

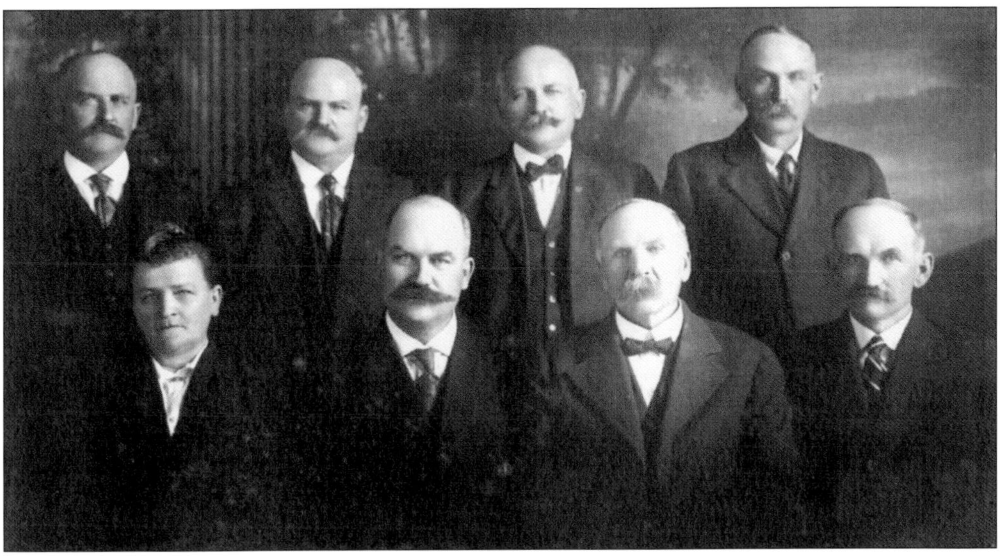

This photograph shows the children of Peter Beehler and Mary (Weible) Beehler. They are, from left to right, as follows: (first row) Sarah Beehler, Charles Beehler, Phillip Beehler, and Peter H. Beehler; (second row) Jacob Beehler, Joseph Beehler, Fred Beehler, and Adam G. Beehler. (Courtesy of Dennis and Rae Beehler.)

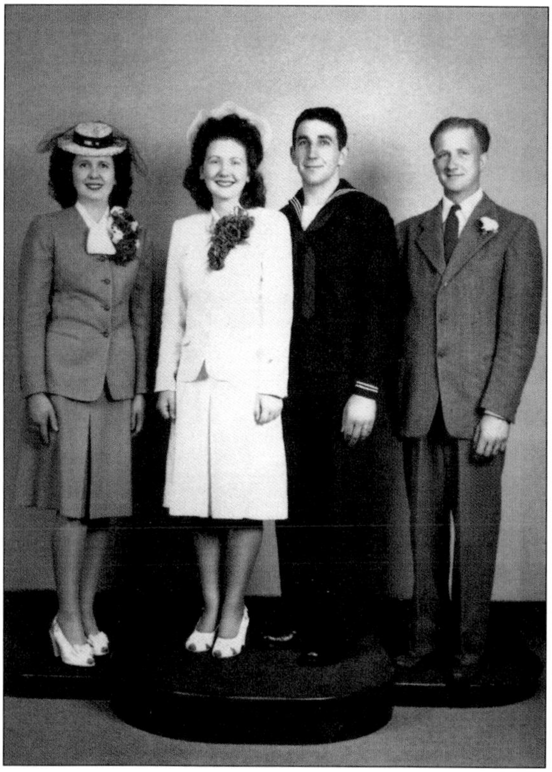

This wedding photograph was taken on June 17, 1945. Pictured are, from left to right, Marion Schrader (maid of honor), Ruby Schrader, Harold Mutti, and Eugene P. Beehler (best man). (Courtesy of Dennis and Rae Beehler.)

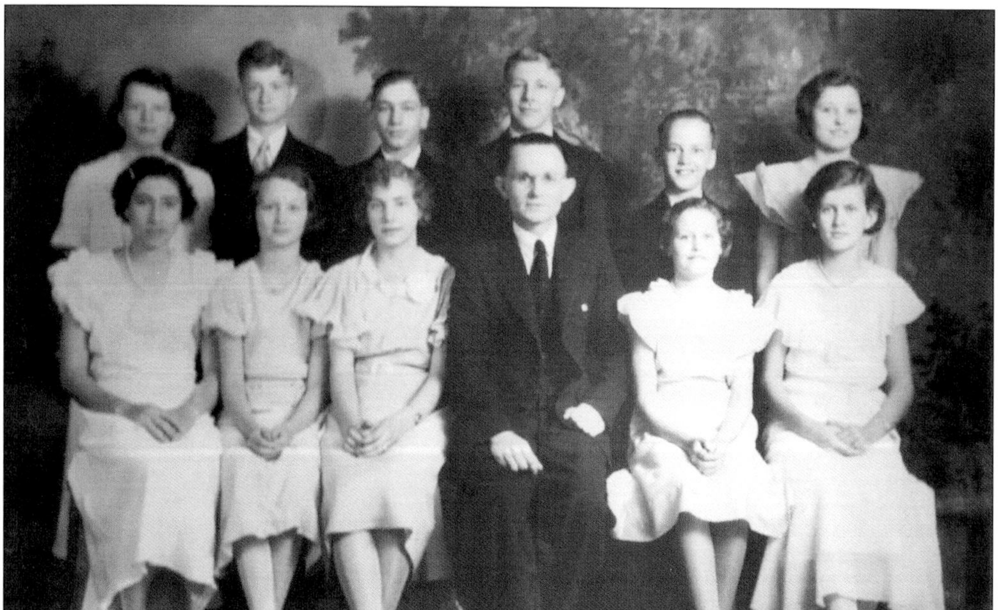

This picture portrays the 1934 confirmation class from the Zion Evangelical Church of Wakarusa. From left to right, the members are pictured as follows: (first row) Ruth Zeiger, Lucille Wagner, Vera Weber, Reverend Krueger, Mabel Schweisberger, and Charlotte Beehler; (second row) Ruth Krueger, Eugene Beehler, Victor Klein, Charles Mutti, Herbert Krueger, and Evelyn Schweisberger. (Courtesy of Dennis and Rae Beehler.)

This photograph is of George A. Birk. It was taken on June 20, 1926. George was the trustee for Madison Township, and he also served his country during the Civil War. He came to Madison Township with his brother Jacob in 1860. (Courtesy of Dennis and Rae Beehler.)

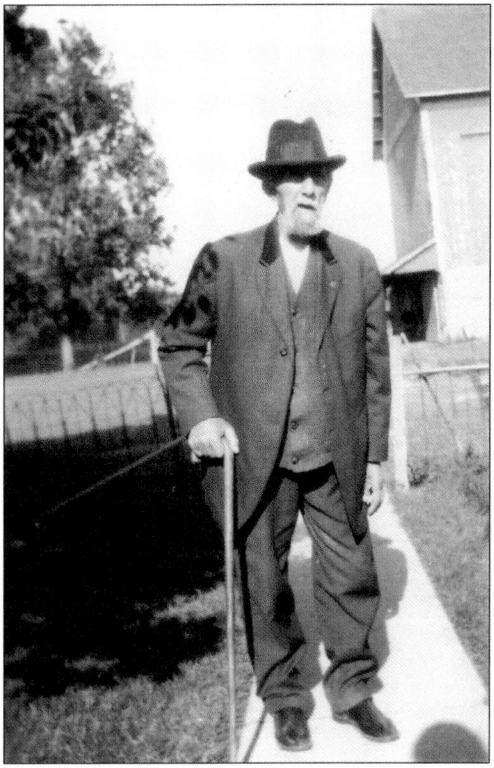

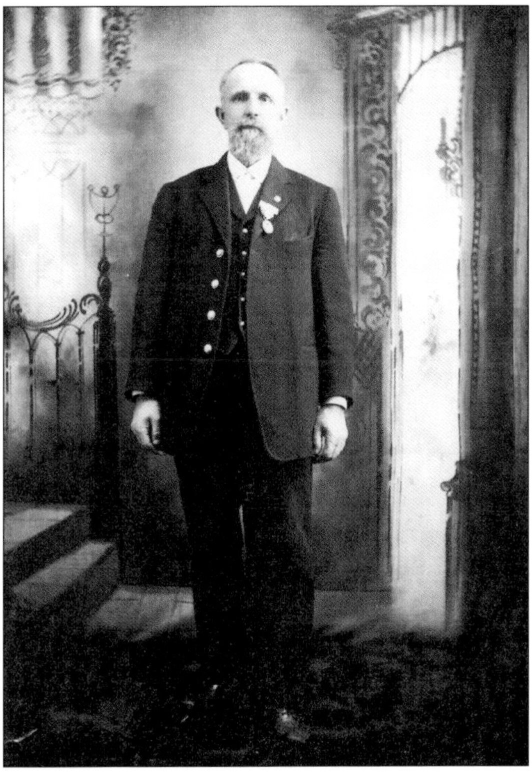

George A. Birk is pictured here with his army medal. In 1863, he was honorably discharged and returned home to build one of the most prominent homesteads in Madison Township. (Courtesy of Dennis and Rae Beehler.)

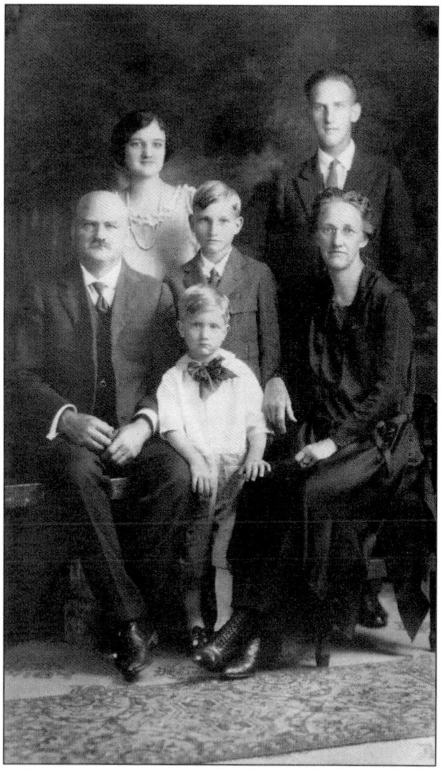

This photograph was taken of the Joseph Beehler family in the 1920s. Pictured from left to right are the following: (first row) Joseph Beehler, Eugene Beehler, Clayton Beehler, and Anna (Birk) Beehler; (second row) Edna Beehler and Clarence Beehler. (Courtesy of Dennis and Rae Beehler.)

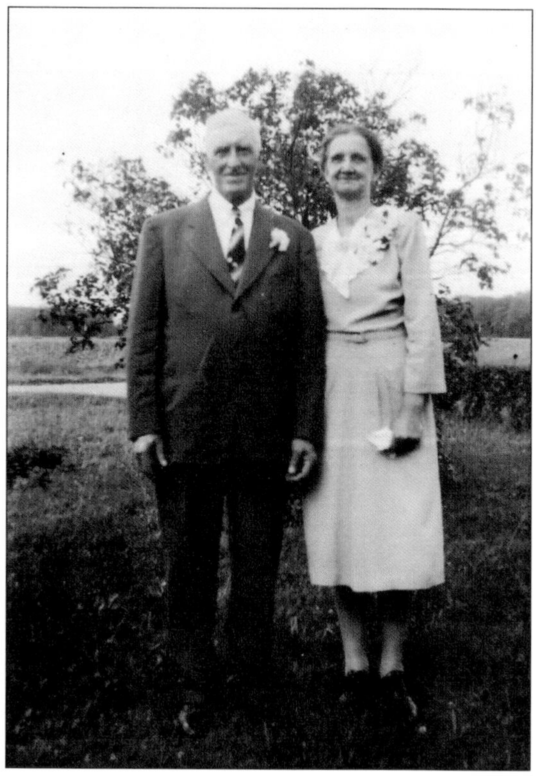

On July 5, 1945, friends and family gathered in Madison Township to celebrate the wedding anniversary of Clara (Birk) Nettrour and Claude Nettrour. (Courtesy of Dennis and Rae Beehler.)

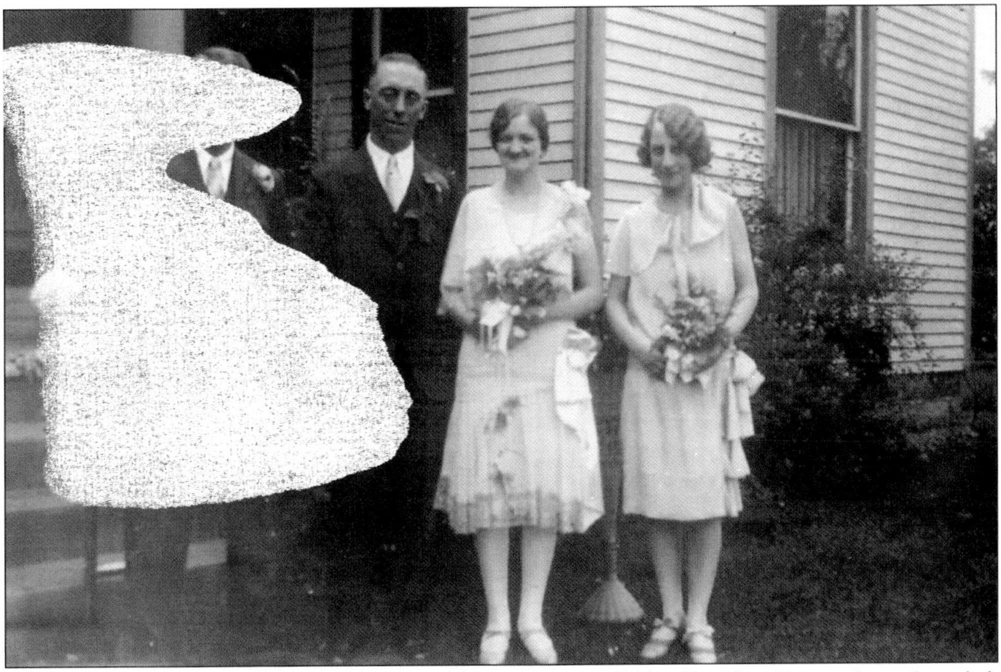

June 20, 1929, was the wedding day of Harold Hartstein and Edna Beehler. Pictured are, from left to right, Clarence Beehler, Harold Hartstein, Edna (Beehler) Hartstein, and Helen ?. (Courtesy of Dennis and Rae Beehler.)

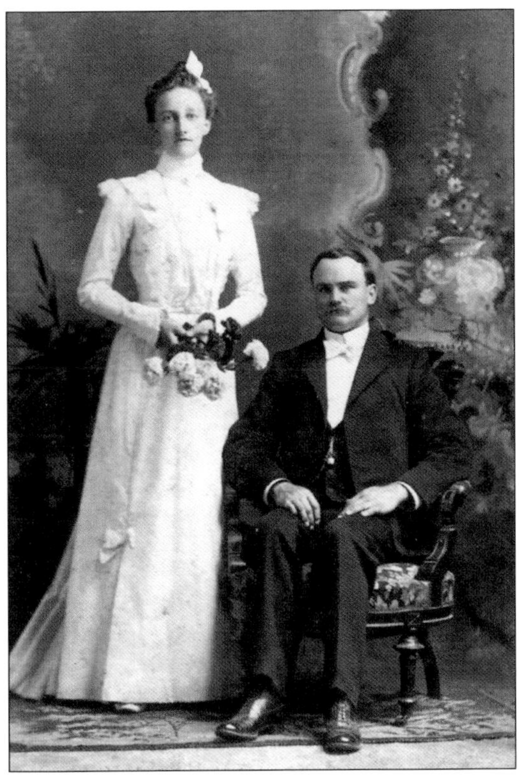

On June 20, 1901, Anna (Birk) Beehler and Joseph Beehler wedded. They built their homestead on Osborne Road between Elm and Dogwood Roads, in Madison Township. (Courtesy of Dennis and Rae Beehler.)

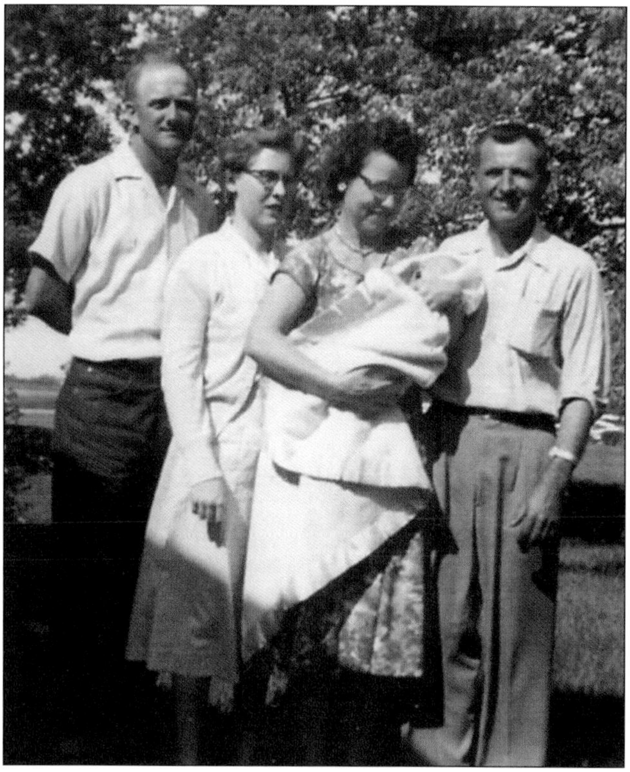

In celebration of the birth of Dennis Beehler in June 1956, this photograph was taken of, from left to right, Eugene Beehler, Alice (Ort) Beehler, Elsie Schweisberger (holding Dennis Beehler), and Kenneth "Short" Schweisberger. (Courtesy of Dennis and Rae Beehler.)

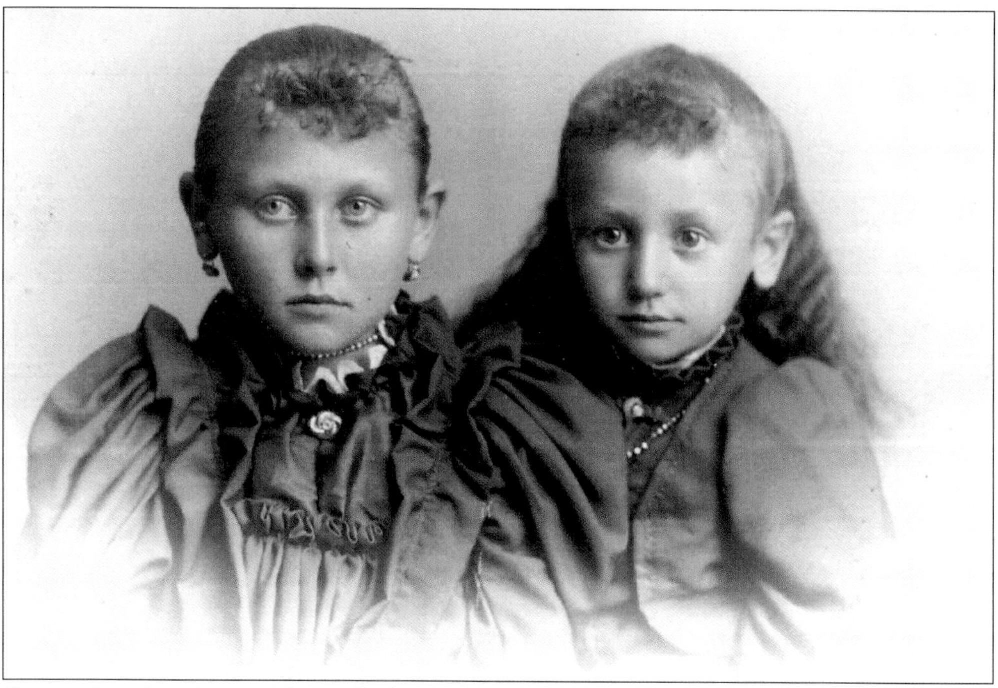

Captured in this photograph are the beautiful young faces of Matilda Catherine Beehler (left) and Carrie Elizabeth Beehler. They are the daughters of Peter and Charlotte Beehler. This photograph was taken around 1890. (Courtesy of the author.)

This photograph is of Philipp Beehler and Anna (Liztenberger) Beehler, the parents of Charlotte, Philip B., Adam, August, Anna E., Peter, Katharina, Karolina, Karl, Peter, Katharina, August, Karl C., Anna, and Jakob K. Beehler. (Courtesy of the author.)

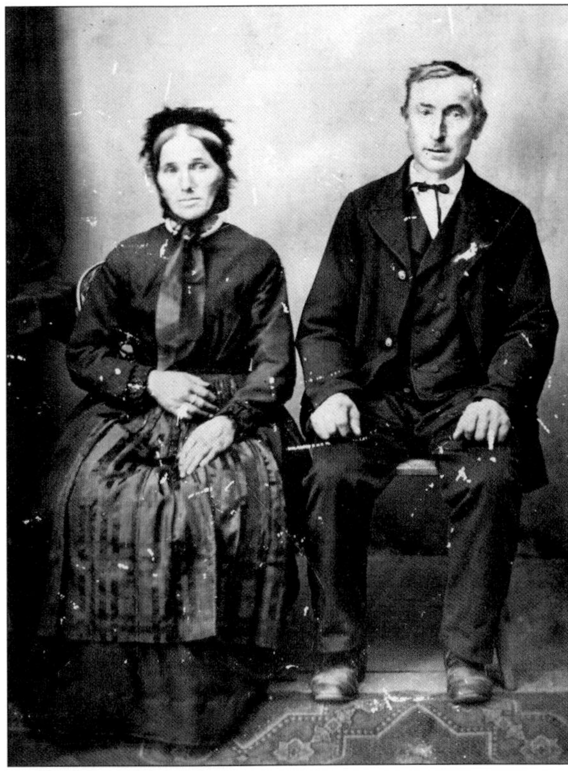

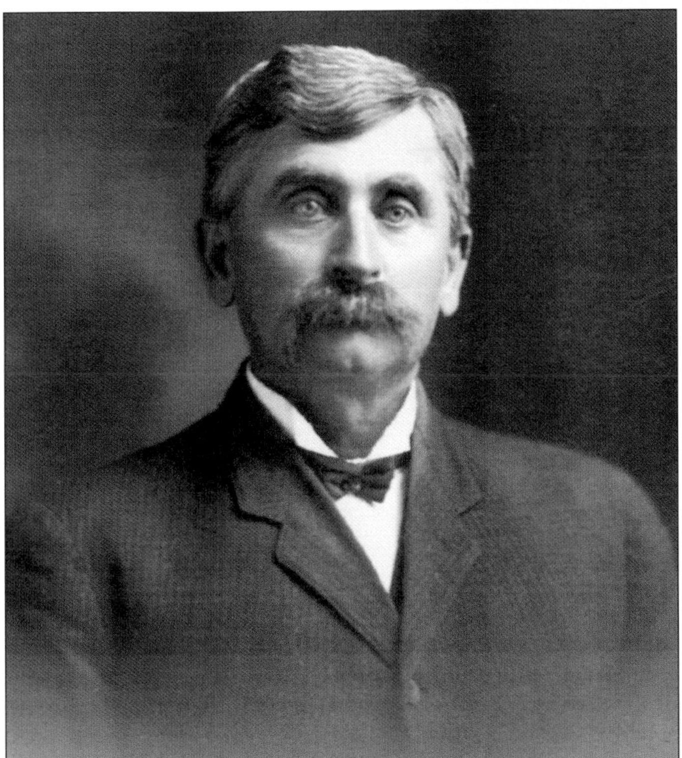

This photograph is of Peter Beehler. He and his father were some of the early settlers in Madison Township. Peter's farm was one of the most prominent in Madison Township. (Courtesy of the author.)

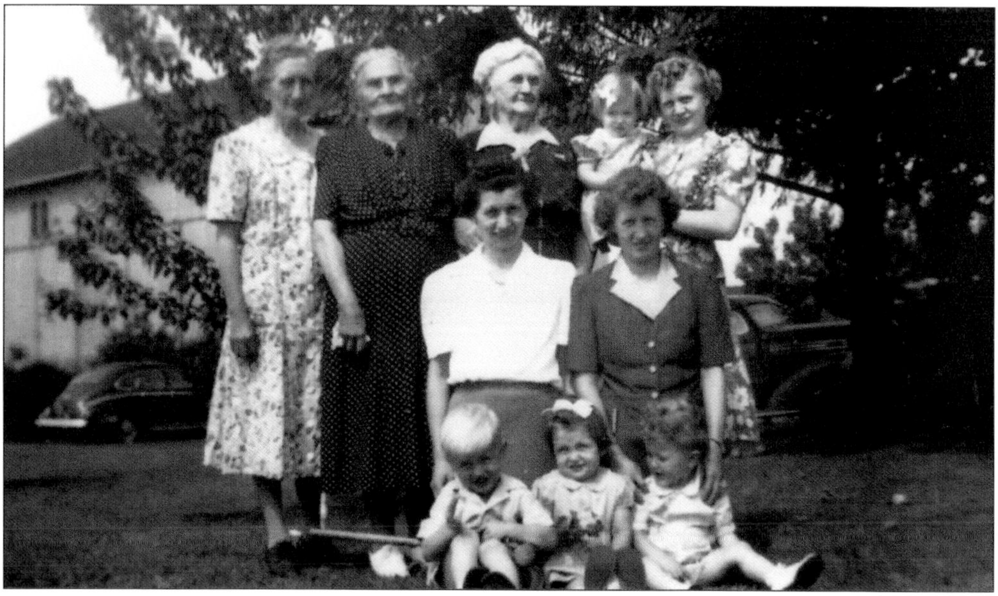

This family photograph was taken on a lovely Sunday afternoon on the front lawn of the homestead of Cora and Millard Battles on Ironwood Road in Penn Township. Pictured are, from left to right, the following: (first row) Terry Crowel, Judith Martin, and Bobby Crowel; (second row) Jeanette (Battles) Martin and Erma (Battles) Crowel; (third row) Cora (Klinkner) Battles, Anna (Kaiser) Battles, Emma (Seifer) Klinkner, and Patricia Beehler, held by her mother Virginia (Battles) Beehler. (Courtesy of the author.)

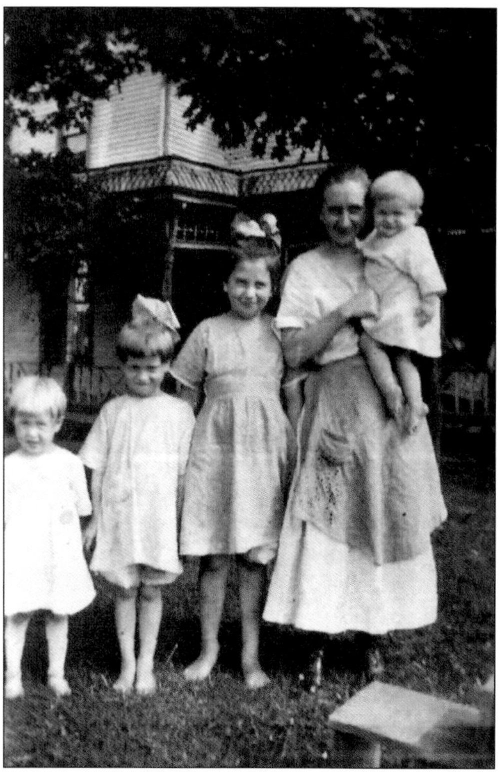

In another photograph taken at the Battles home on Ironwood Road are, from left to right, Erma Battles, Jeanette Battles, Helen Battles, and Cora (Klinkner) Battles (holding Emma "Virginia" Battles). (Courtesy of the author.)

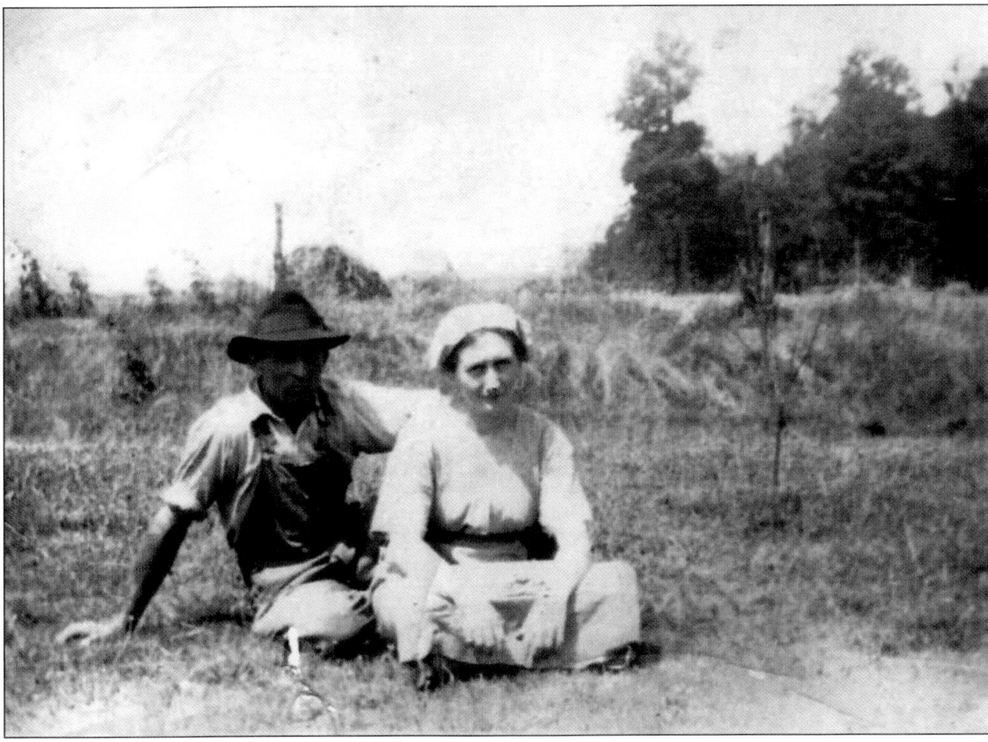

Millard T. Battles and Cora P. (Klinkner) Battles are enjoying a bit of sunshine. They may have decided to take a break from farming and enjoy the day on their property on Ironwood Road in Penn Township. (Courtesy of the author.)

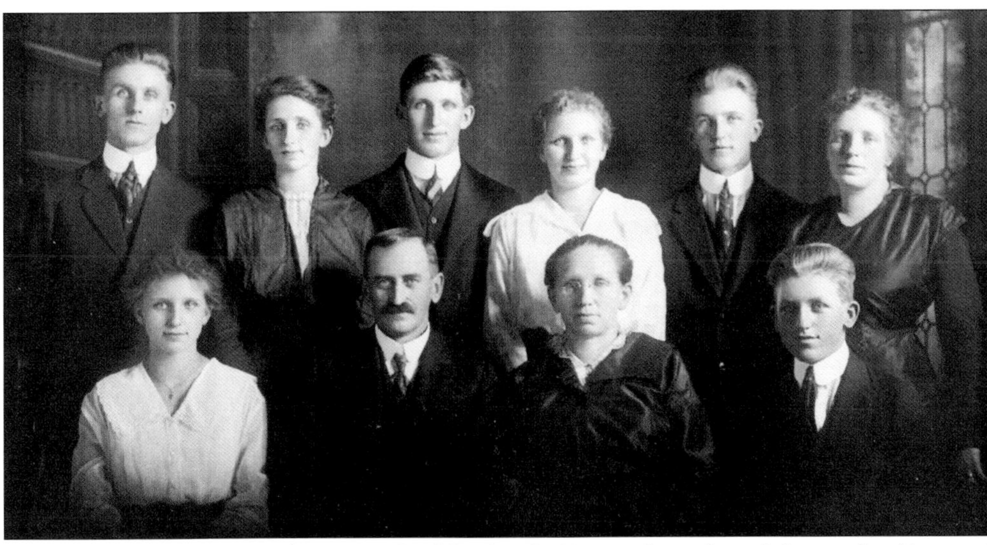

This photograph portrays the Henry Beehler family. Pictured are, from left to right, (first row) Minnie (Beehler) Lisinmier, Henry Beehler, Catherine (Beehler) Klein, and Fred Beehler; (second row) Jay Beehler, Ella (Beehler) Hahn, Charles Beehler, Emma (Beehler) Wylie, Phillipp Beehler, and Clara (Beehler) Crofoot. (Courtesy of Dale and Carol Hahn.)

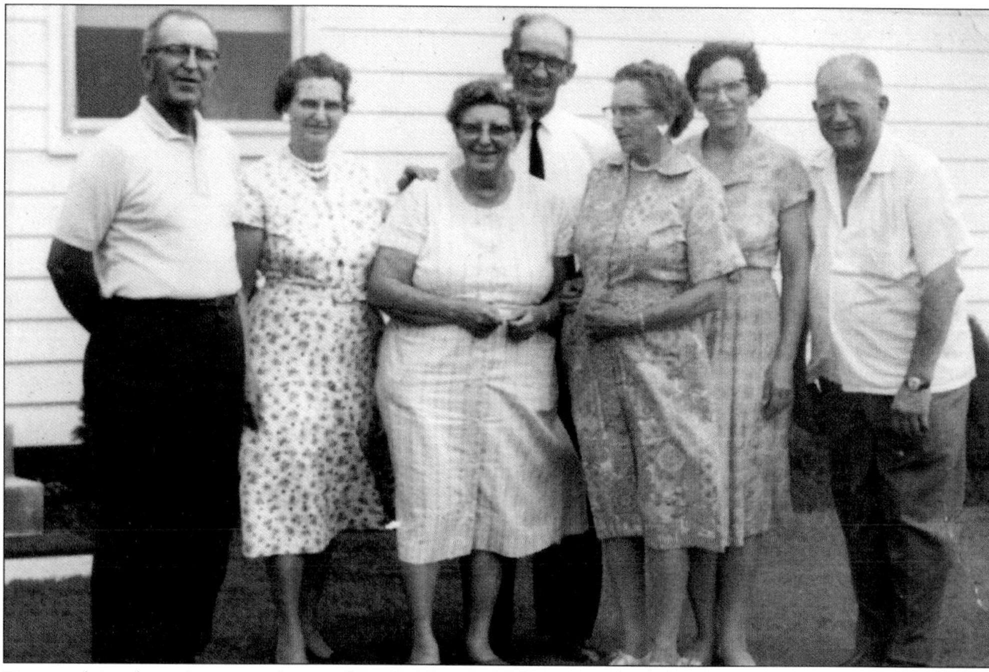

Pictured in this photograph are the children of Henry and Catherine Beehler. They are, from left to right, Phillipp Beehler, Emma (Beehler) Wylie, Clara (Beehler) Crofoot, Charles Beehler, Ella (Beehler) Hahn, Minnie (Beehler) Lisinmier, and Fred Beehler. (Courtesy of Dale and Carol Hahn.)

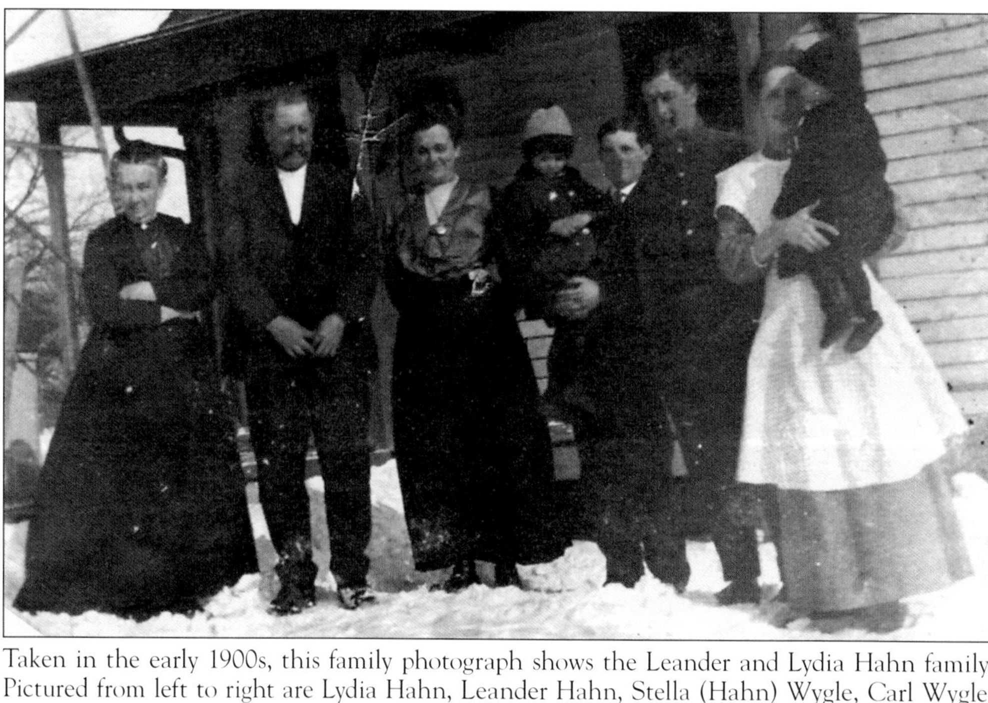

Taken in the early 1900s, this family photograph shows the Leander and Lydia Hahn family. Pictured from left to right are Lydia Hahn, Leander Hahn, Stella (Hahn) Wygle, Carl Wygle, Charles Wygle, George Hahn, and Ella (Beehler) Hahn, who is holding Charles Hahn. (Courtesy of Dale and Carol Hahn.)

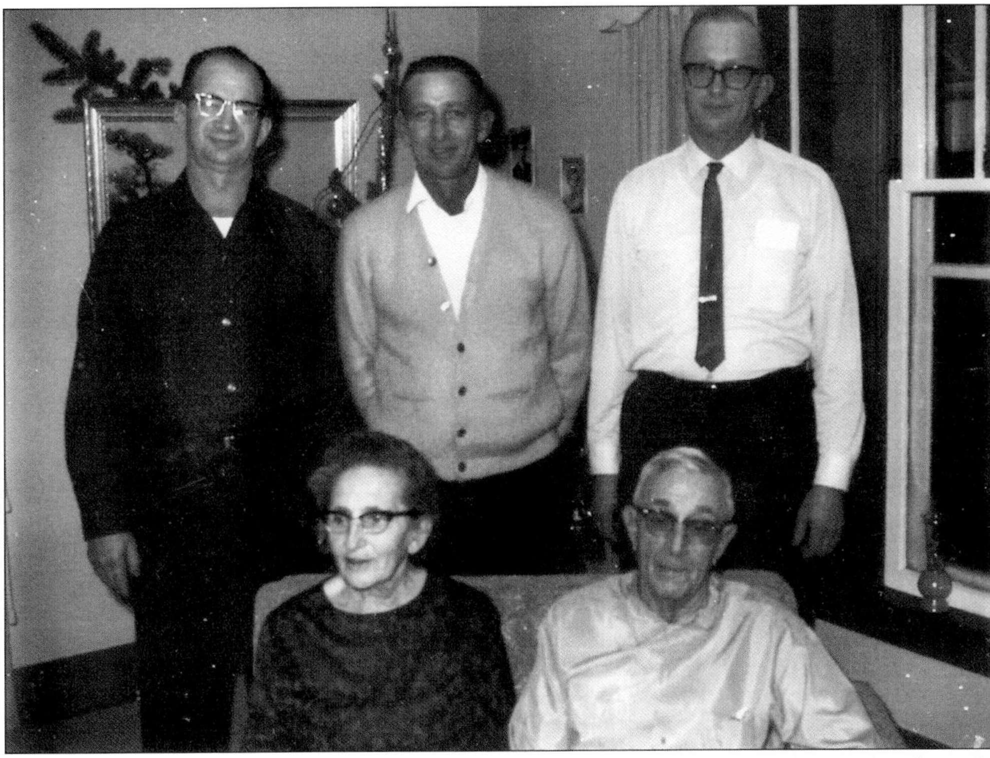

This family photograph shows, from left to right, Charles Hahn, Dale Hahn, Richard "Dick" Hahn, Ella Hahn, and George Hahn. The Hahns made their home on Kelley Road in Penn Township. (Courtesy of Dale and Carol Hahn.)

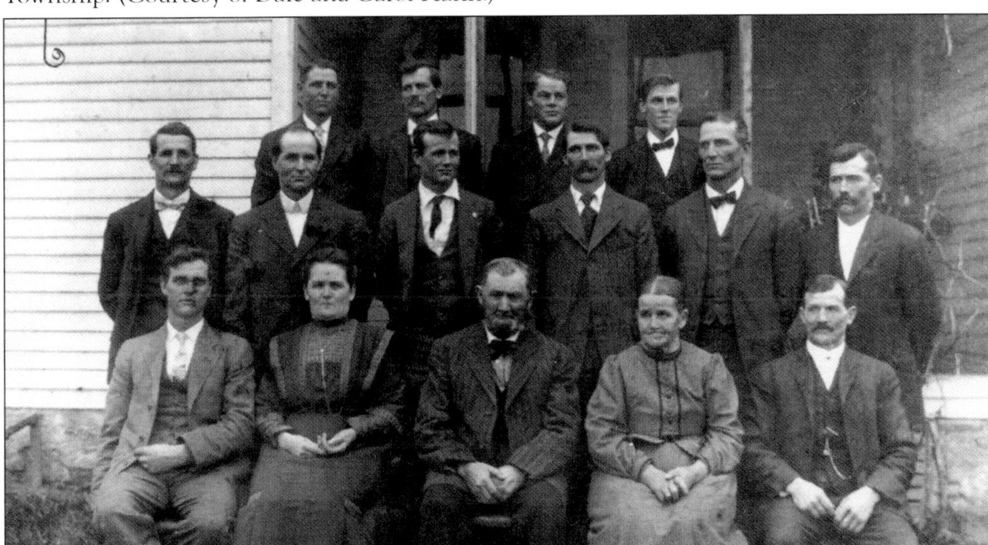

Taken on February 17, 1911, this photograph shows the Jacob Schutz family. Pictured are, from left to right, the following: (first row) Charles Schutz, Elizabeth Schutz, Jacob Schutz, Sophia (Ripple) Schutz, and John Schutz; (second row) William Schutz, Fred Schutz, Peer Schutz, Philip Schutz, Jacob Schutz, and Albert Schutz; (third row) Edward Schutz, David Schutz, George Schutz, and Henry Schutz. (Courtesy of Evelyn [Beehler] Salyer.)

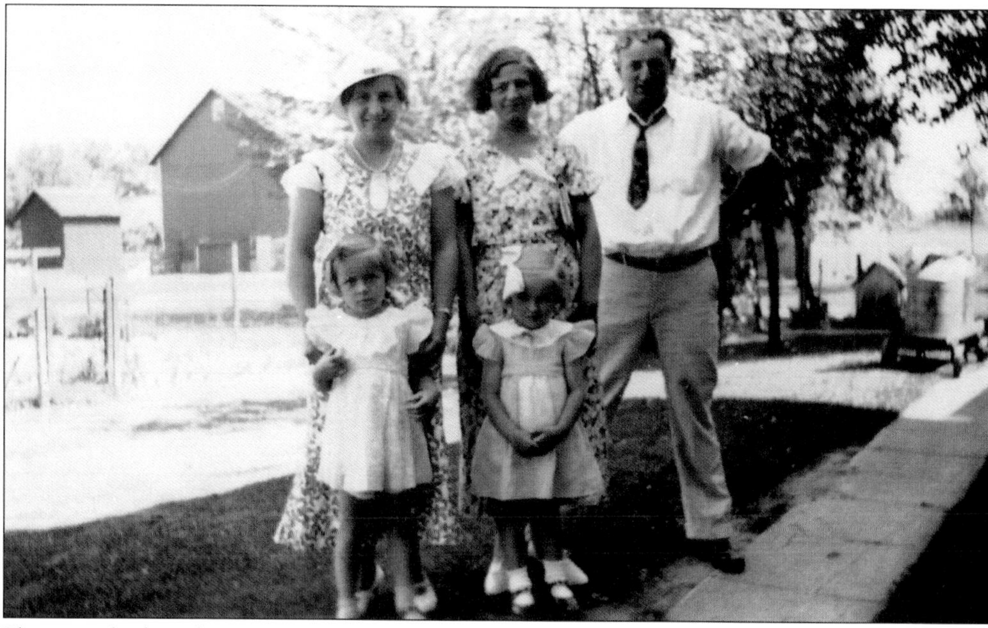

Photographed in this picture, from left to right, are as follows: (first row) Norma Beehler and Evelyn Beehler; (second row) Carrie (Zeiger) Mochel, Myrtle (Mochel) Beehler, and Carl Mochel. (Courtesy of Evelyn [Beehler] Salyer.)

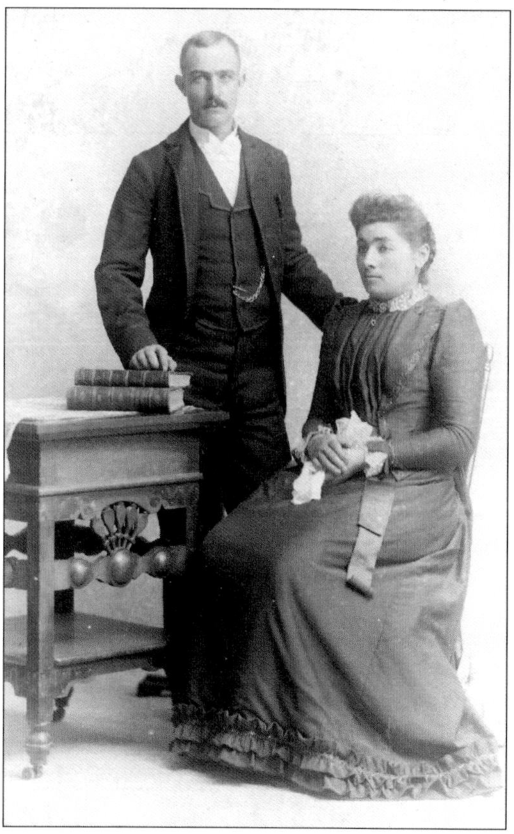

Edward Mochel and Louise (Weiss) Mochel raised their family in Woodland, Indiana. (Courtesy of Evelyn [Beehler] Salyer.)

Pictured here are Leonard Weiss and Christiane Weiss. They were the proud parents of Louise (Weiss) Mochel, who married Edward Mochel. (Courtesy of Evelyn [Beehler] Salyer.)

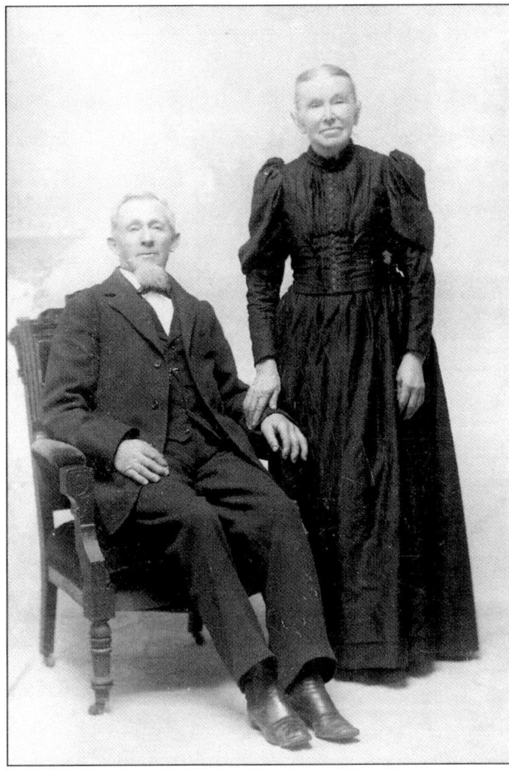

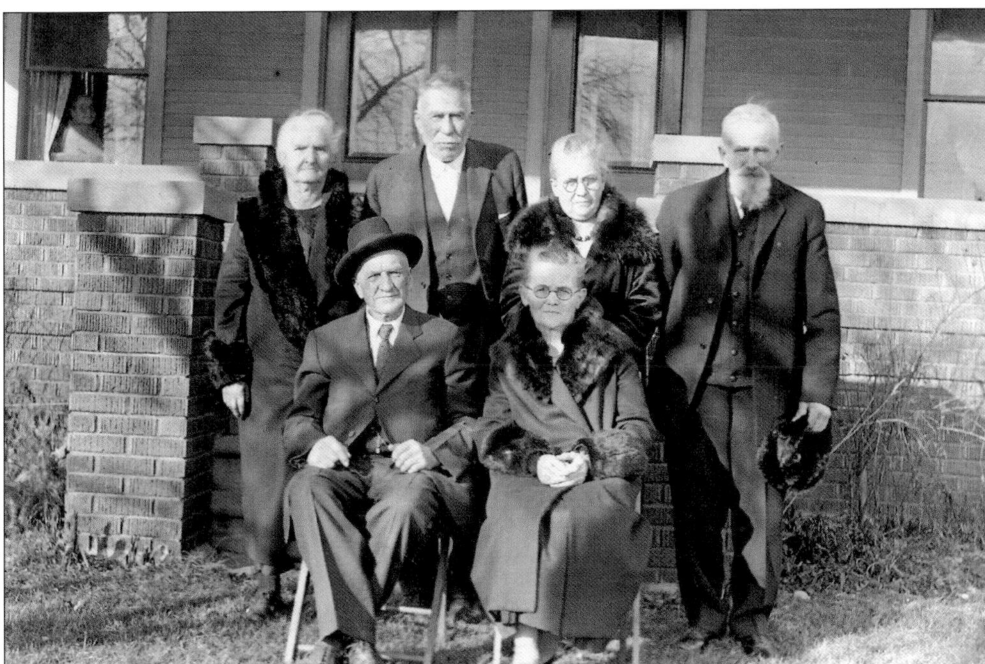

Celebrating the 50th anniversary of Philip and Elizabeth Beehler at their home on New Road are Joseph Maier, unidentified, Louis Bollenbacher, Katharina Bollenbacher, Philip Beehler, and Elizabeth Beehler. (Courtesy of Evelyn [Beehler] Salyer.)

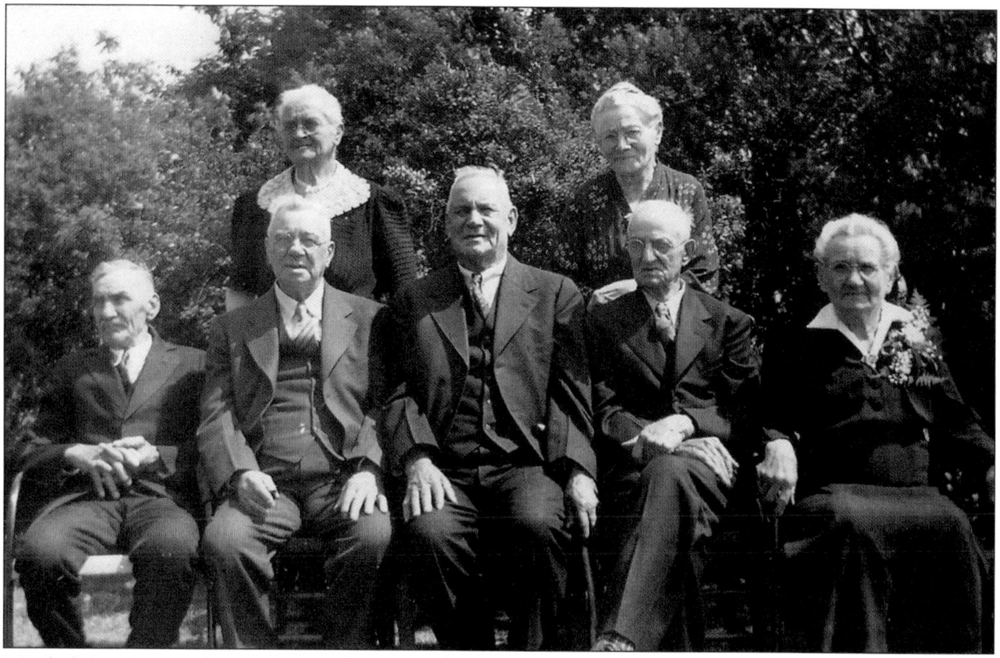

Mochel family members, all over 80 years of age, are pictured here. They are, from left to right, as follows: (first row) John Mochel, Martin Mochel, Ernest Mochel, Edward Mochel, and Kate (Mochel) Marker; (second row) Mary Mochel and Louise Mochel. (Courtesy of Evelyn [Beehler] Salyer.)

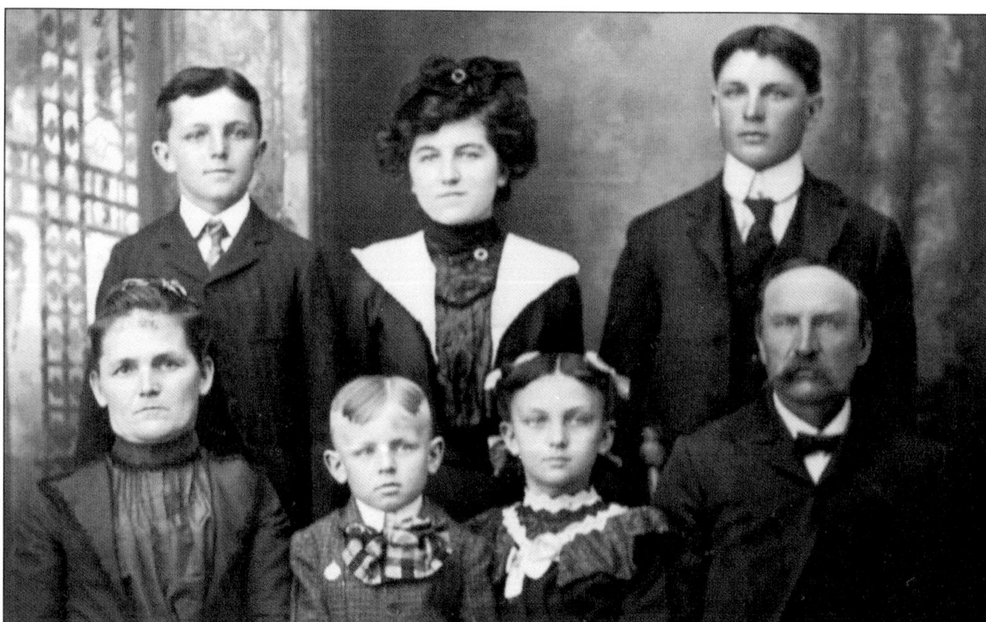

This portrait of the Philip W. Beehler family was taken around 1900. Pictured are, from left to right, the following: (first row) Elizabeth (Schutz) Beehler, Richard Beehler, Hattie Beehler, and Philip W. Beehler; (second row) William Beehler, Laura Beehler, and Albert Beehler. (Courtesy of Evelyn [Beehler] Salyer.)

Frederick Feitz came to Madison from Switzerland in 1883. (Courtesy of Helen [Rader] Marker.)

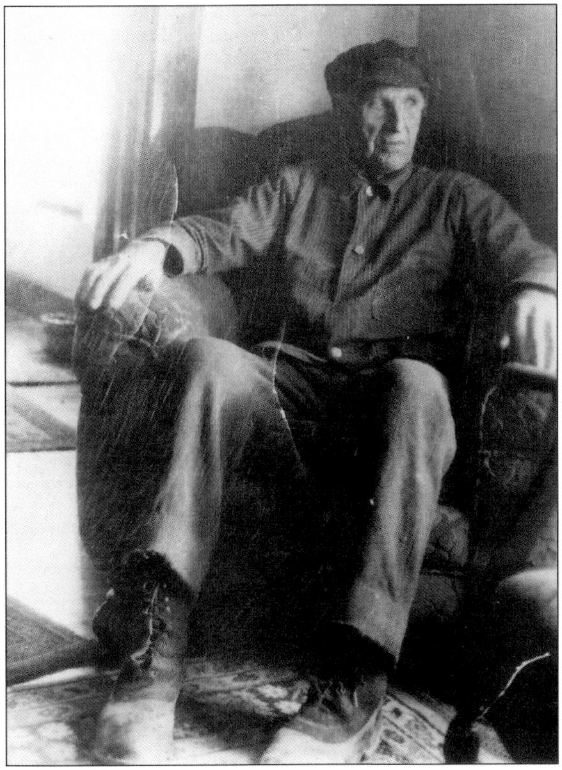

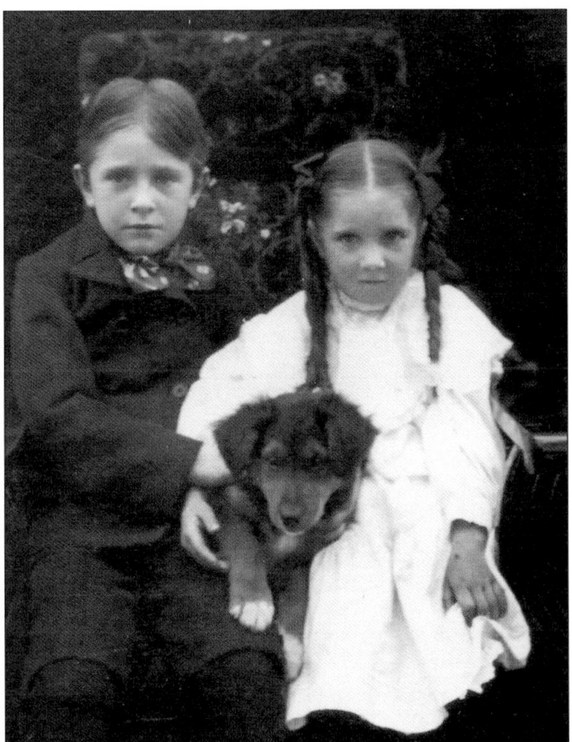

Pictured here in 1907, Clarence Rader and Leoneda Rader were born in a home on Patterson Road, one mile east of Wyatt. (Courtesy of Helen [Rader] Marker.)

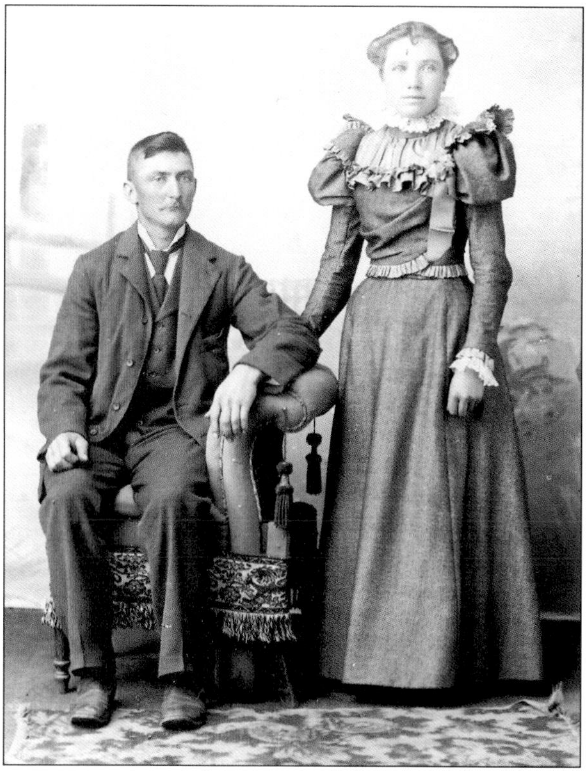

In 1899, John Rader and Marianne Sterchi were married. They made their home on Patterson Road in Madison Township, just east of Wyatt, Indiana. (Courtesy of Helen [Rader] Marker.)

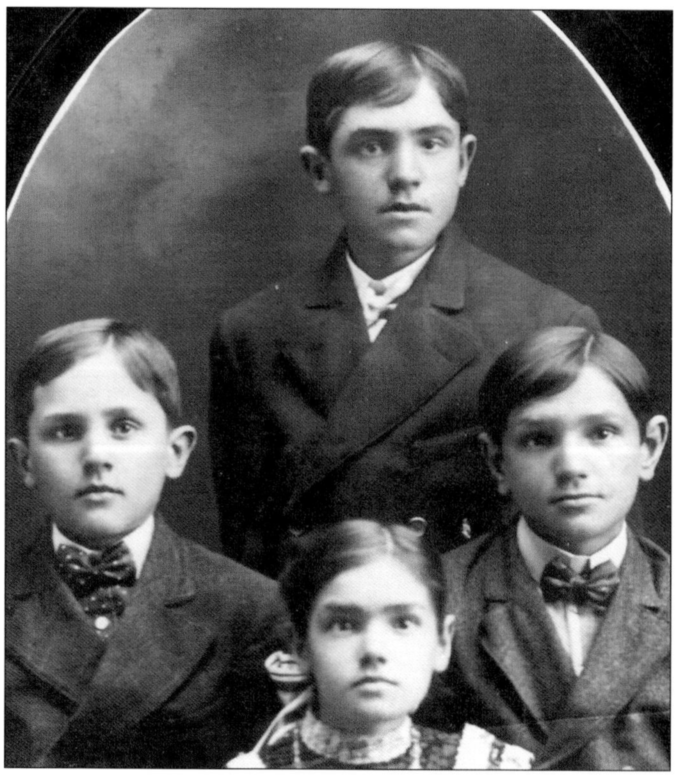

The proud parents of these children were Jacob Marker and Katherine (Mochel) Marker. The children pictured are (first row) Ruth Marker, (second row) Sam Marker (left) and Reuben Marker, and (third row) Clint Marker. (Courtesy of Helen [Rader] Marker.)

Photographed here, from left to right, are Henry Rader, Elizabeth Rader, and Pauline Rader of Madison Township. (Courtesy of Helen [Rader] Marker.)

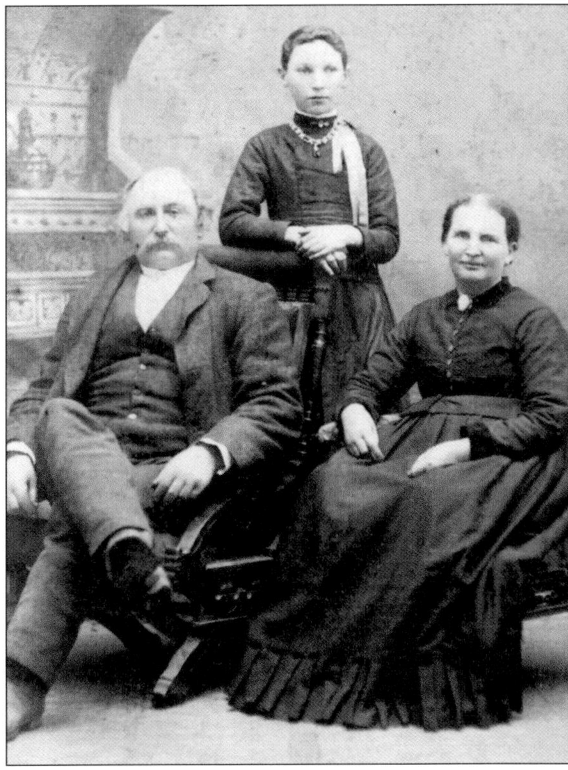

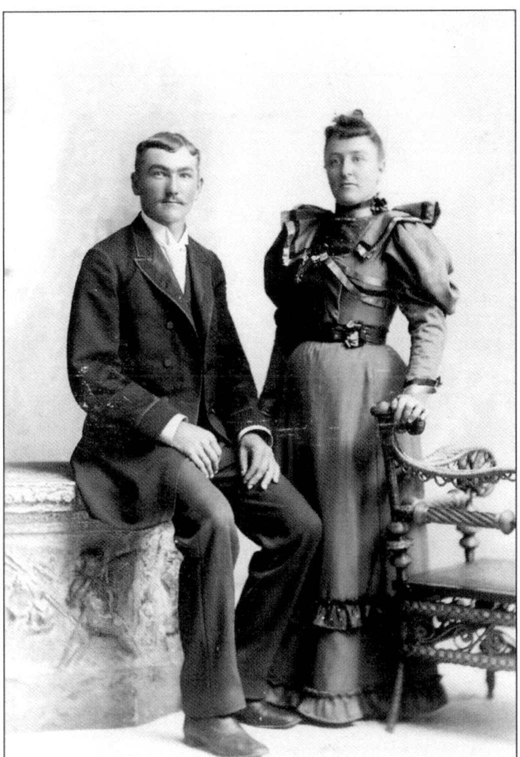

This happy couple is Albert Boss and Margaretha (Rader) Boss. (Courtesy of Helen [Rader] Marker.)

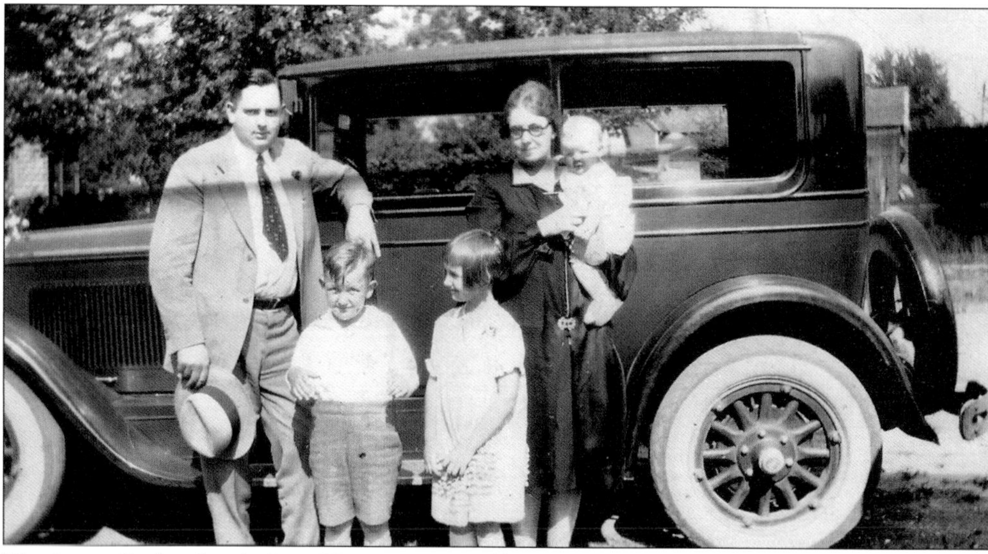

The Louis Gerber family from Wyatt is pictured here. They are, from left to right, Louis Gerber, Robert Gerber, Deloris Gerber, Marie Gerber, and Verdene Gerber. Louis owned the Farmers State Bank of Wyatt for several years. (Courtesy of Verdene [Gerber] Hunke.)

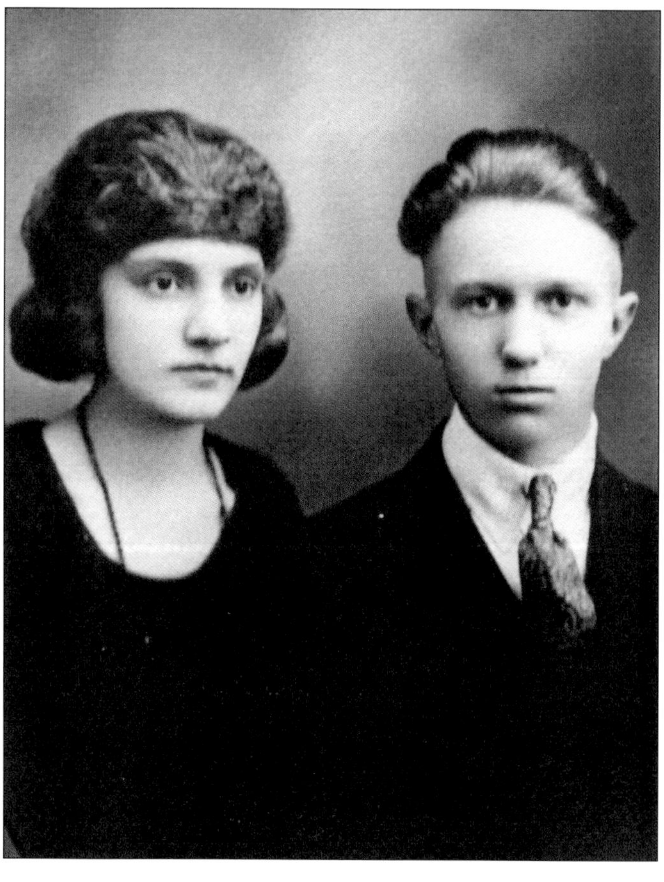

In 1922, in Madison Township, Dora M. Schalliol and Herbert G. Fredericks were united in marriage. (Courtesy of Dora M. [Schalliol] Fredericks.)

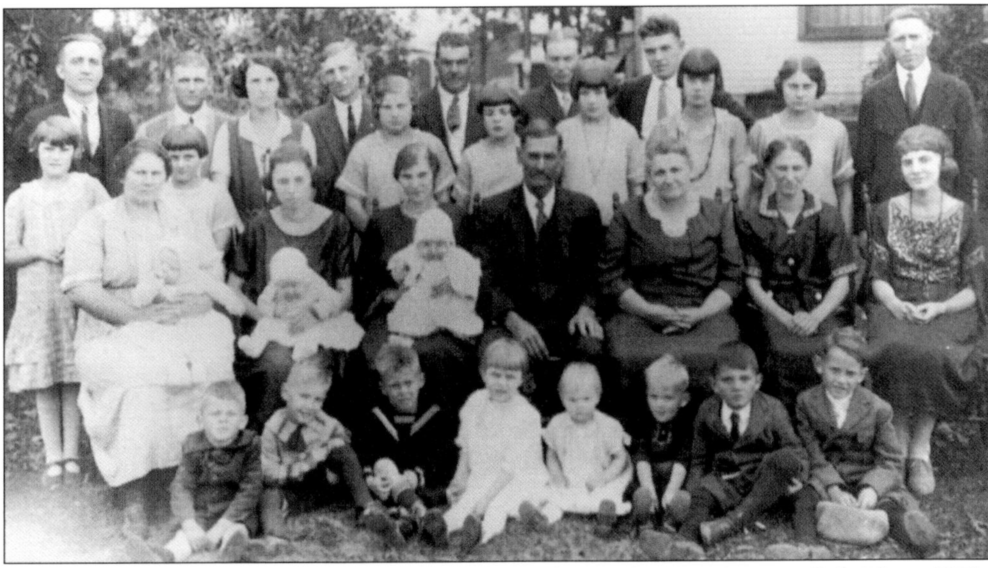

Pictured here are, from left to right, the following: (first row) Irvin Hygema, Dale Ehret, Willis Schalliol, Margaret Hunsberger, Lois Hunsberger, Carl Ehret, Donald Hygema, and Winfred Schalliol; (second row) Cora (Schalliol) Hygema (holding a baby), Irene (Schalliol) Ehret (holding a baby), Maude (Schalliol) Hunsberger (holding a baby), Julius Schalliol, Matilda (Harter) Schalliol, Alva (Schalliol) Hoover, and Dora (Schalliol) Fredericks; (third row) Esther Schalliol, Fern Fitz, Grace Hoover, Erma Hygema, Treva Hygema, Mabel Hygema, Dora Hoover, and Herbert Fredericks; (fourth row) Russell Ehret, Jesse Schalliol, LaVerge Schalliol, Harvey Schalliol, Irvin Hygema, Amos Hoover, and Vernon Schalliol. (Courtesy of Dora [Schalliol] Fredericks.)

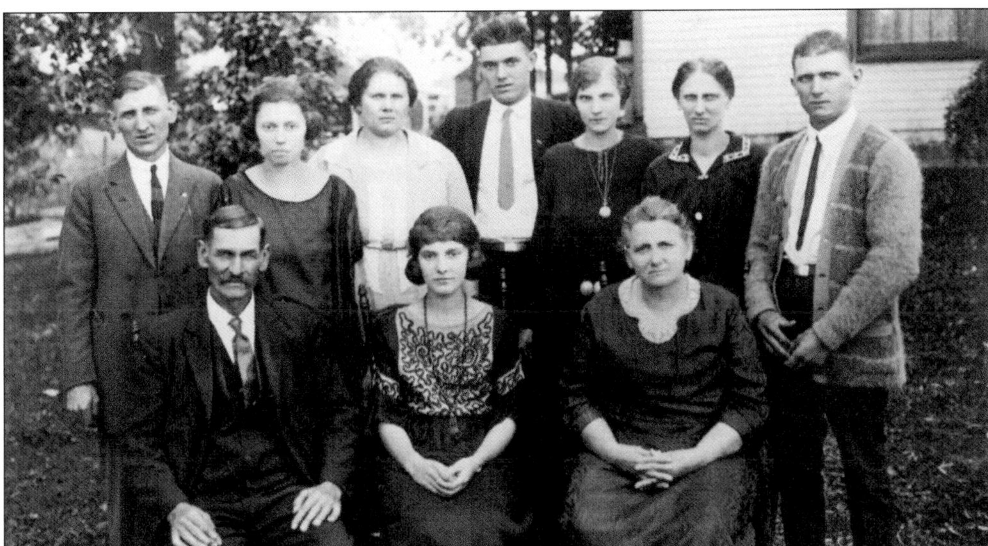

The portrait captures the Julius Schalliol family. Pictured are, from left to right, as follows: (first row) Julius Schalliol, Dora (Schalliol) Fredericks, and Matilda (Harter) Schalliol; (second row) Harvey Schalliol, Irene (Schalliol) Ehret, Cora (Schalliol) Hygema, Vernon Schalliol, Maude (Schalliol) Hunsberger, Alva (Schalliol) Hoover, and Jesse Schalliol. (Courtesy of Dora [Schalliol] Fredericks.)

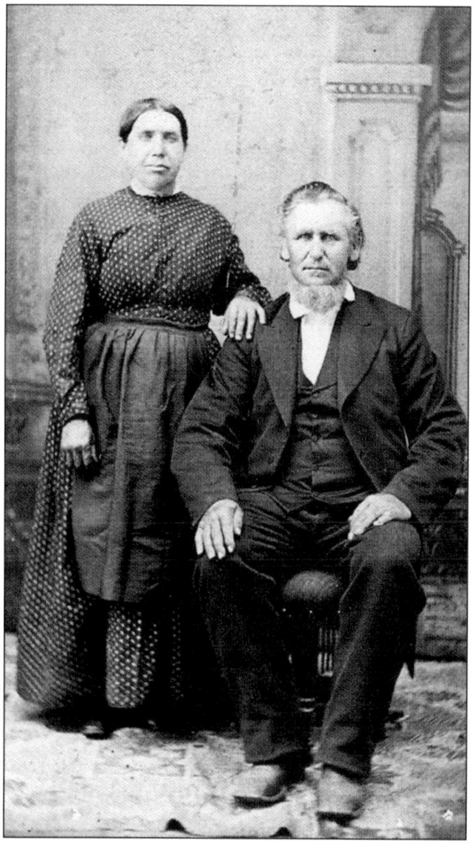

This portrait shows Mary Barbara (Weible) Beehler and George Peter Beehler. They were the parents of Jacob, Joseph, Frederick, Adam, Sarah, Charles, Philip, and Peter Beehler. (Courtesy of the author.)

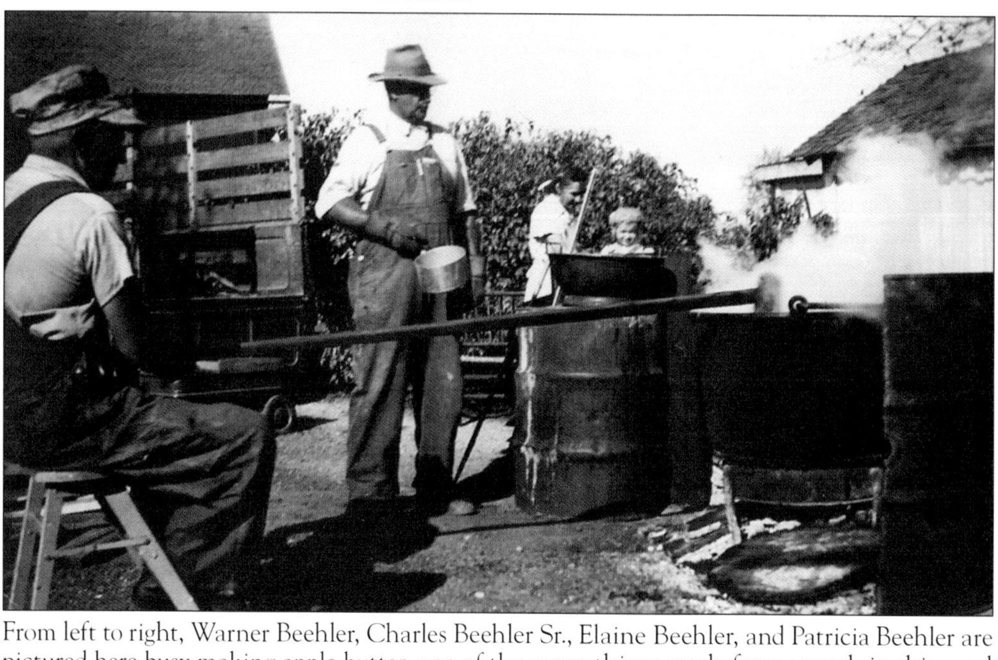

From left to right, Warner Beehler, Charles Beehler Sr., Elaine Beehler, and Patricia Beehler are pictured here busy making apple butter, one of the many things made from scratch in this rural area. (Courtesy of the author.)

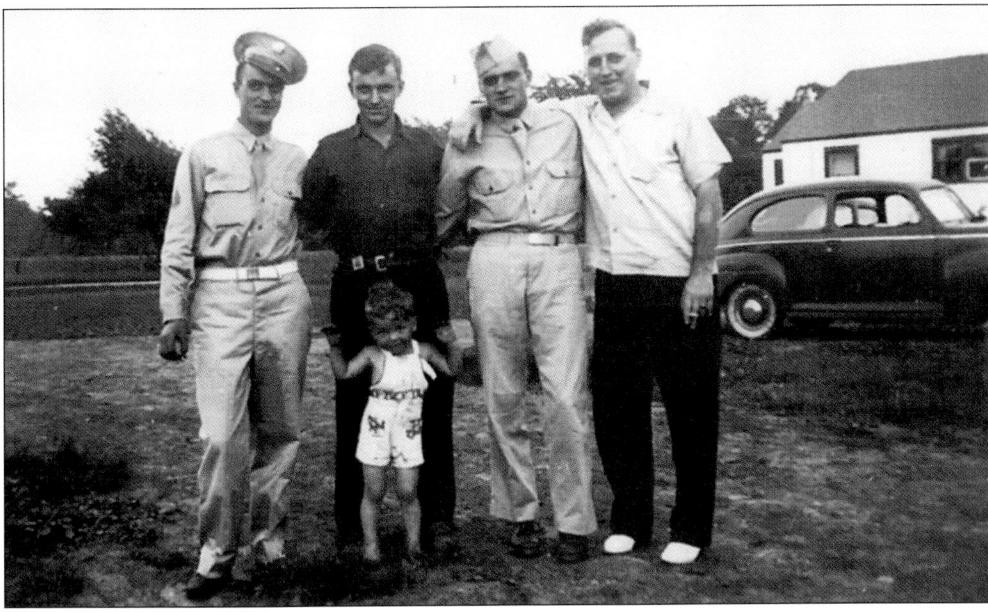

In 1941, during World War II, two residents of Madison Township were getting ready to leave for the army. From left to right, Wilbur Reum and Warren Reum joined Carl R. Lubahn, Lester Lubahn, and Michael Reum (in front), who were also getting ready to leave. (Courtesy of Charles and Dorothy [Reum] Neer.)

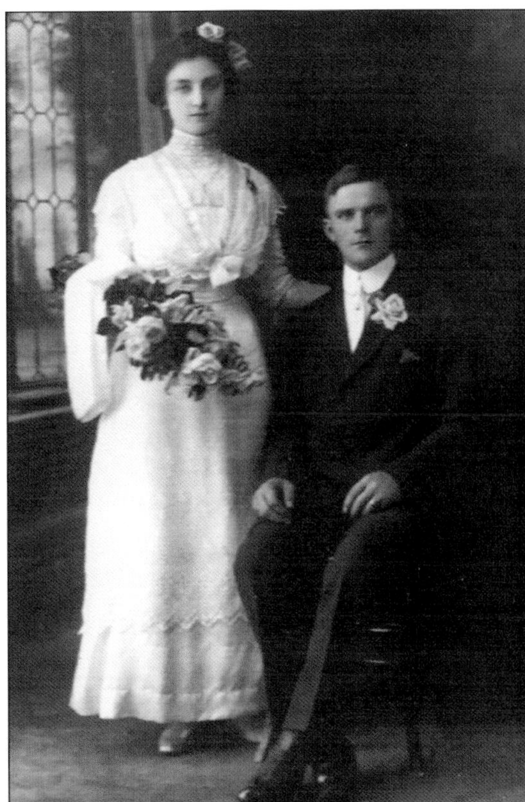

On April 16, 1914, Hattie Elizabeth Beehler and John Arthur Reum were united in marriage in Madison Township, where they made their home. (Courtesy of Charles and Dorothy [Reum] Neer.)

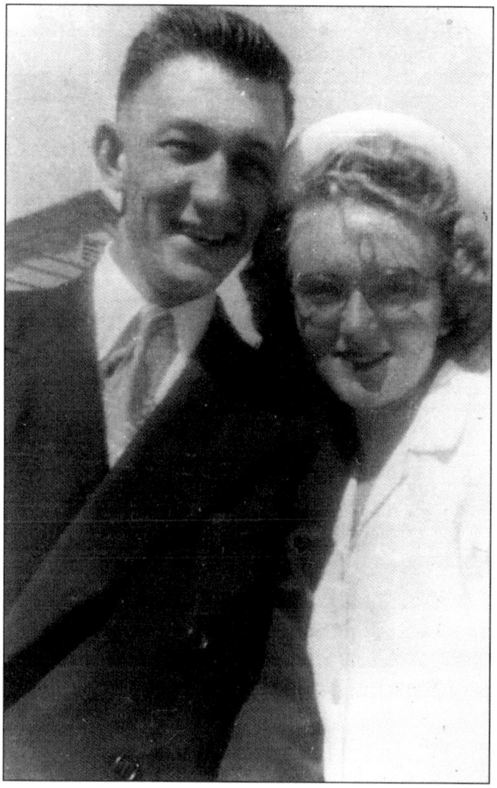

This portrait of Dorothy (Reum) Neer and Charles Neer Sr. was taken in 1948. (Courtesy of Charles and Dorothy [Reum] Neer.)

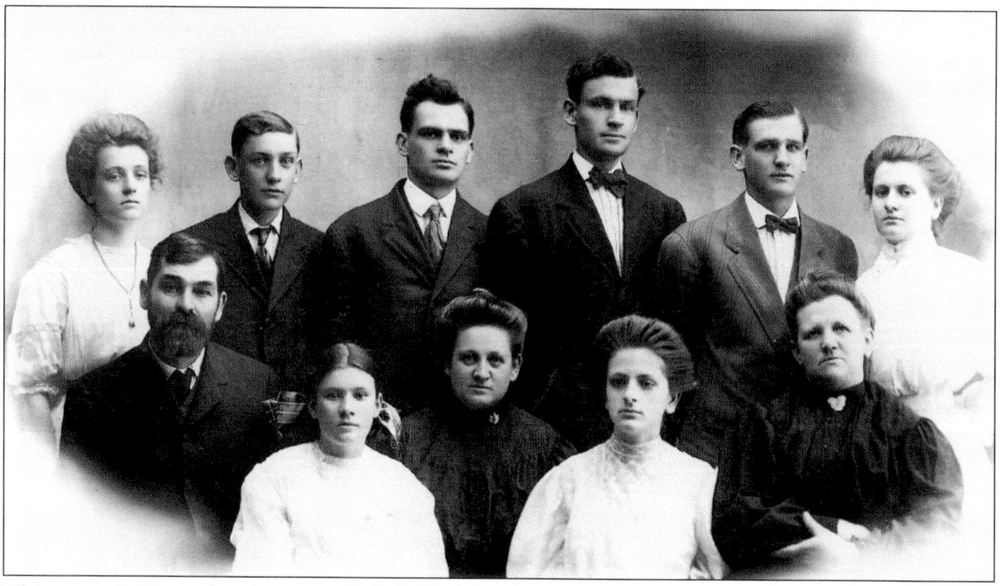

This portrait shows the Augustus G. Schalliol family. Pictured are, from left to right, the following: (first row) Augustus Schalliol, Elsie Schalliol, Ida Schalliol, Minnie Schalliol, and Dorothea S. W. (Bollenbacher) Schalliol; (second row) Amelia Schalliol, Grover Schalliol, Walter Schalliol, Victor Schalliol, Thaddeus Schalliol, and Nora Schalliol. The Schalliols owned and operated the Klondike Exchange, the first telephone service in the area, on Beech Road. They also had their own family band. (Courtesy of the author.)

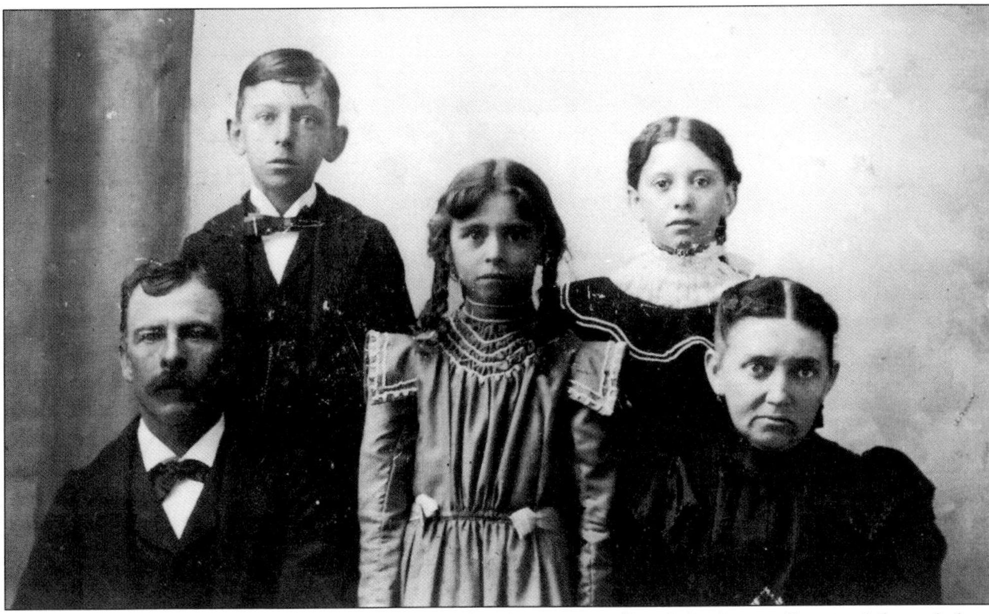

The Kettrings were known as a prominent family in Woodland, Indiana. Pictured from left to right are as follows: (first row) Jacob Kettring, Jennie Kettring, and Catherine Kettring; (second row) Walter Kettring and Loda Kettring. (Courtesy of John and Judy Marker.)

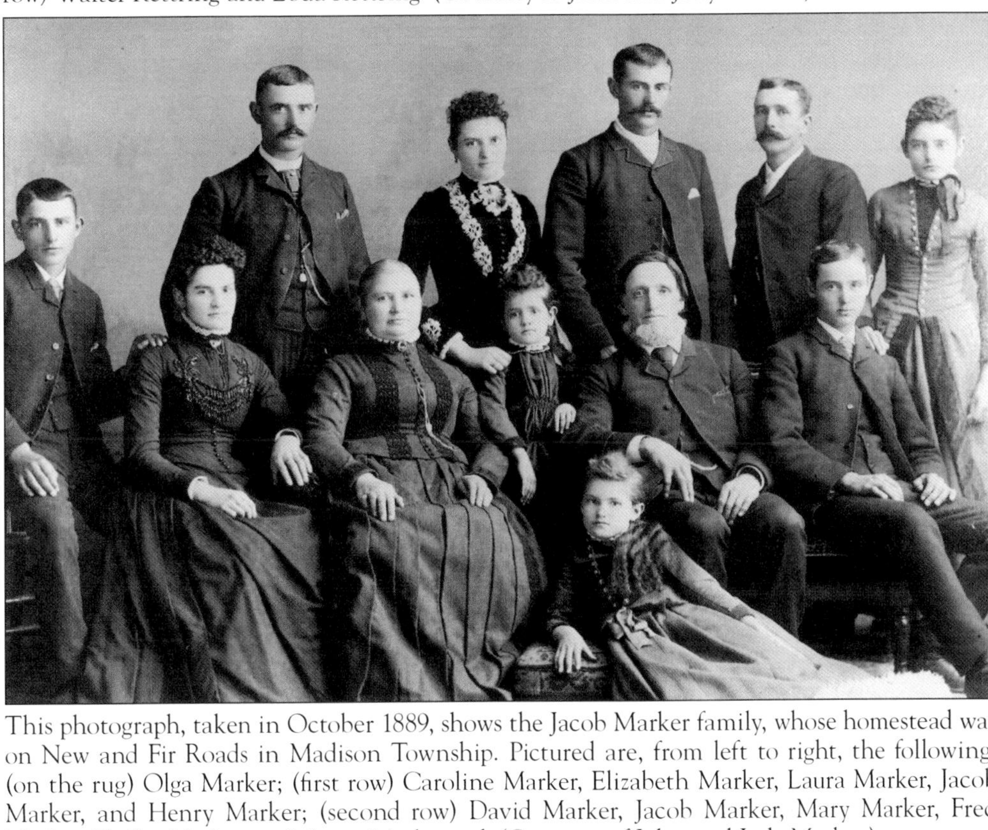

This photograph, taken in October 1889, shows the Jacob Marker family, whose homestead was on New and Fir Roads in Madison Township. Pictured are, from left to right, the following: (on the rug) Olga Marker; (first row) Caroline Marker, Elizabeth Marker, Laura Marker, Jacob Marker, and Henry Marker; (second row) David Marker, Jacob Marker, Mary Marker, Fred Marker, Phillip Marker, and Anna Markerand. (Courtesy of John and Judy Marker.)

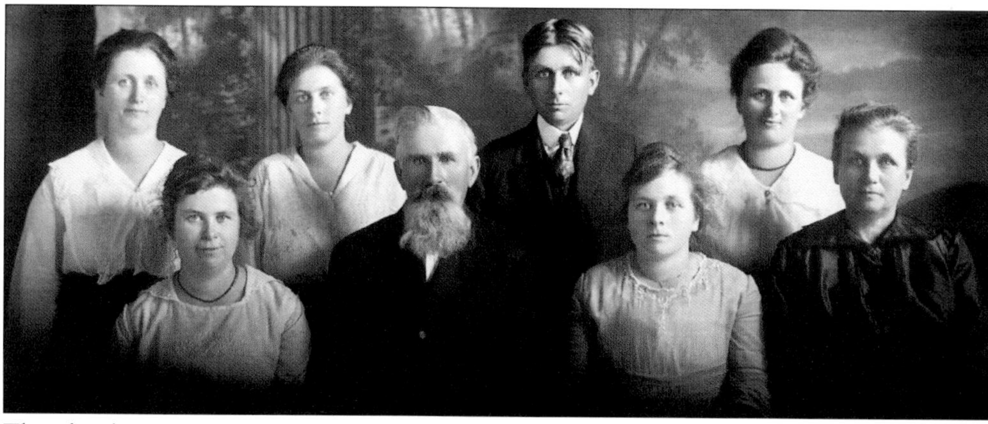

This family picture shows, from left to right, the following: (first row) Anna Fox, Louis Bollenbacher, Nellie Birk, and Catherine (Hesch) Bollenbacher; (second row) Nora Martin, Edna Martin, Jacob Bollenbacher, and Hattie Beehler. (Courtesy of Jeanette [Battles] Martin.)

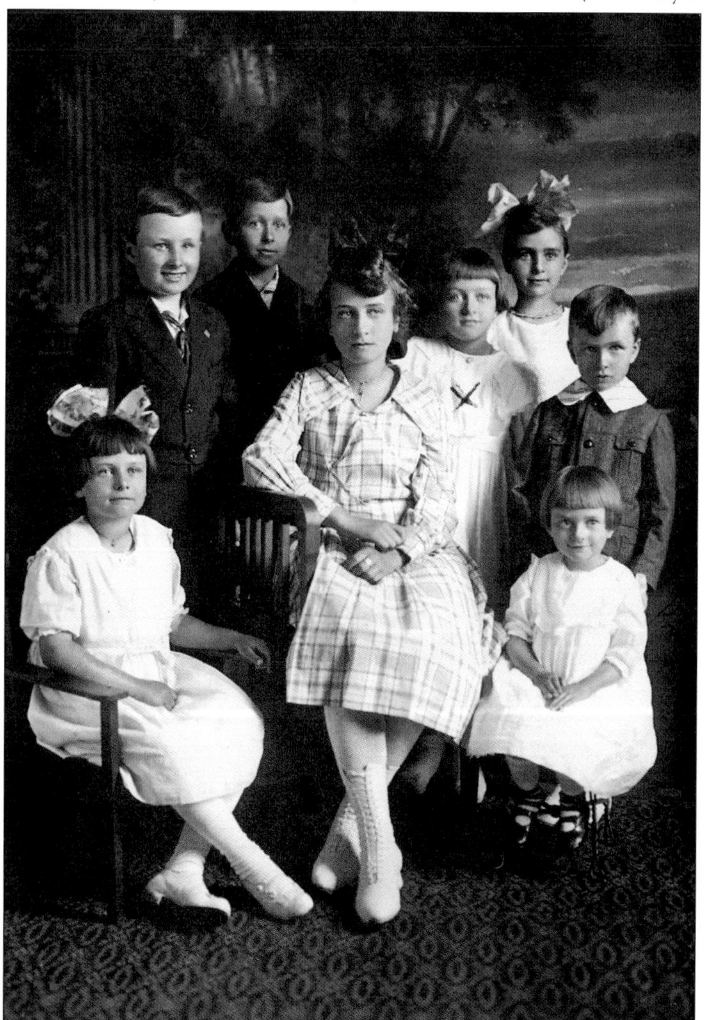

Pictured here are, from left to right, Estella Oberly (sitting), Ted Beehler, Carl Martin, Violet Fox (sitting), Maria Schultz, Ruth Martin, Loyal Beehler, and Mary Martin. (Courtesy of Jeanette [Battles] Martin.)

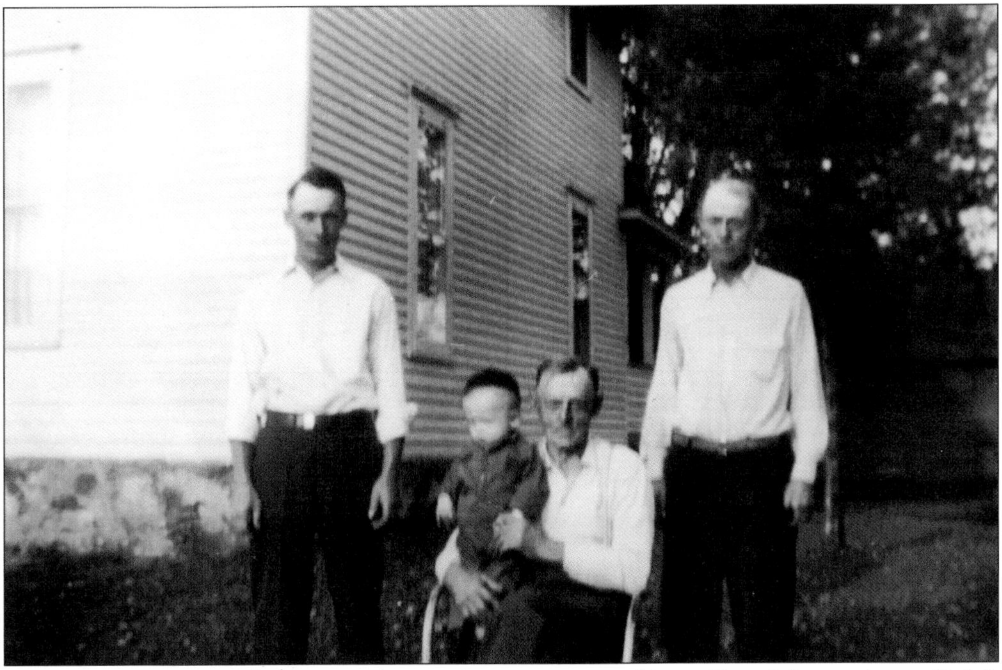

Four generations of Madison Township residents are pictured here. From left to right are Ralph Roeder, Leroy Roeder, Charles Roeder, and Harold Roeder. (Courtesy of Susie [Roeder] Pogue.)

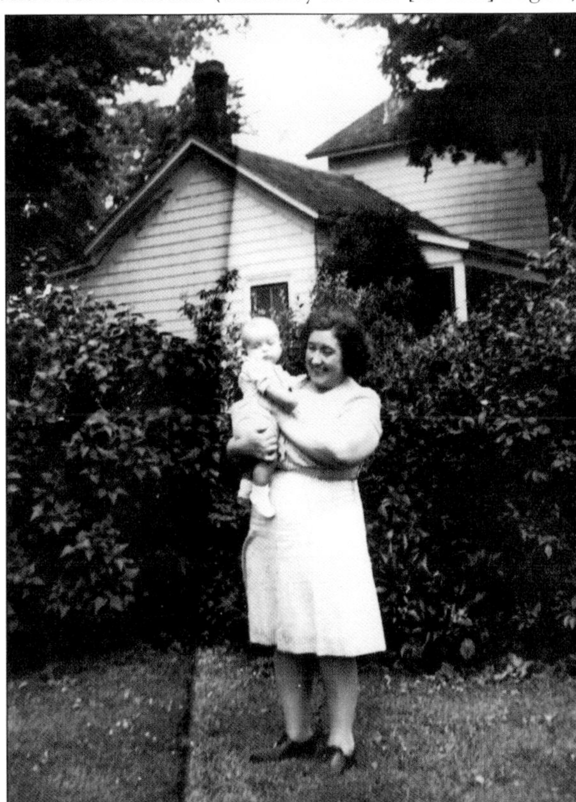

What a happy occasion for Eva Roeder! She is pictured here holding her first grandchild, Leroy Roeder. (Courtesy of Susie [Roeder] Pogue.)

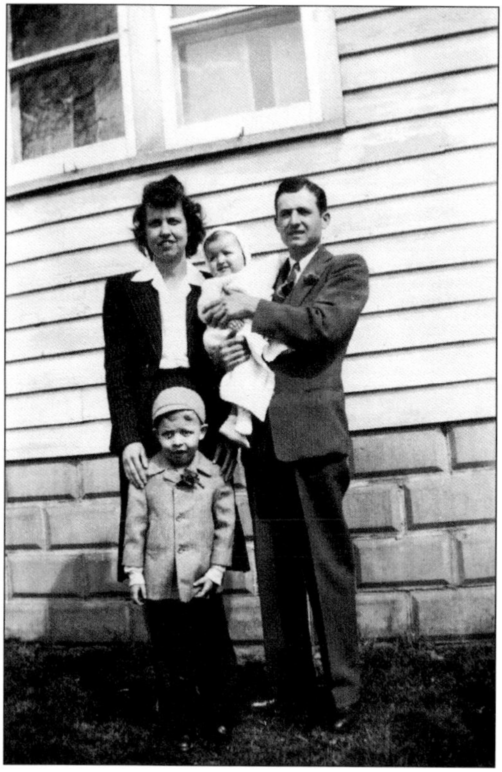

The Schweisberger family lived on Osborne Road in Madison Township. Pictured from left to right are Elsie M. (Riggs) Schweisberger, Ruthann Schweisberger, Kenneth Schweisberger, and Robert Schweisberger (in front). (Courtesy of Craig Lechlitner.)

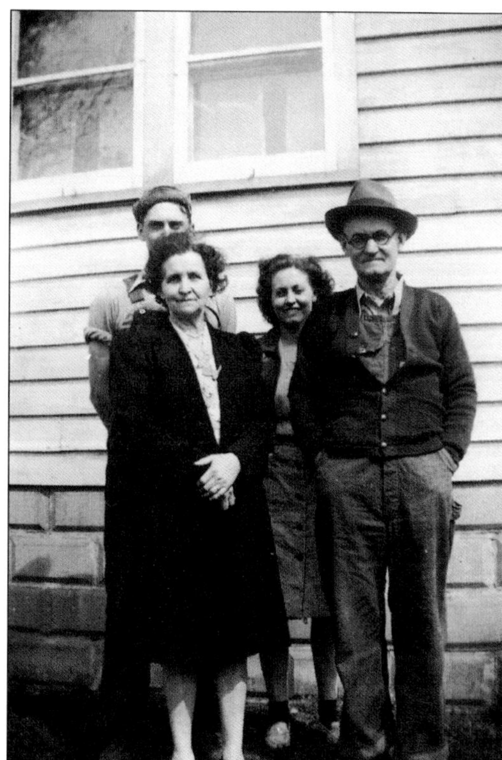

Several generations of Schweisbergers lived together on the Osborne Road homestead. Pictured from left to right are Ida E. (Beehler) Schweisberger, Elmer Lechlitner, Mabel "Toot" (Schweisberger) Lechlitner, and Alex Schweisberger. (Courtesy of Craig Lechlitner.)

Elmer and Mabel "Toot" (Schweisberger) Lechlitner founded their own family homestead on Cedar Road in Madison Township. (Courtesy of Craig Lechlitner.)

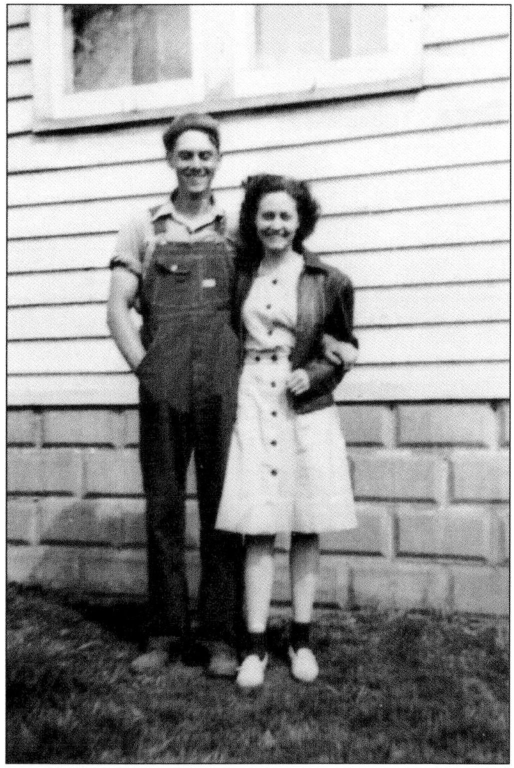

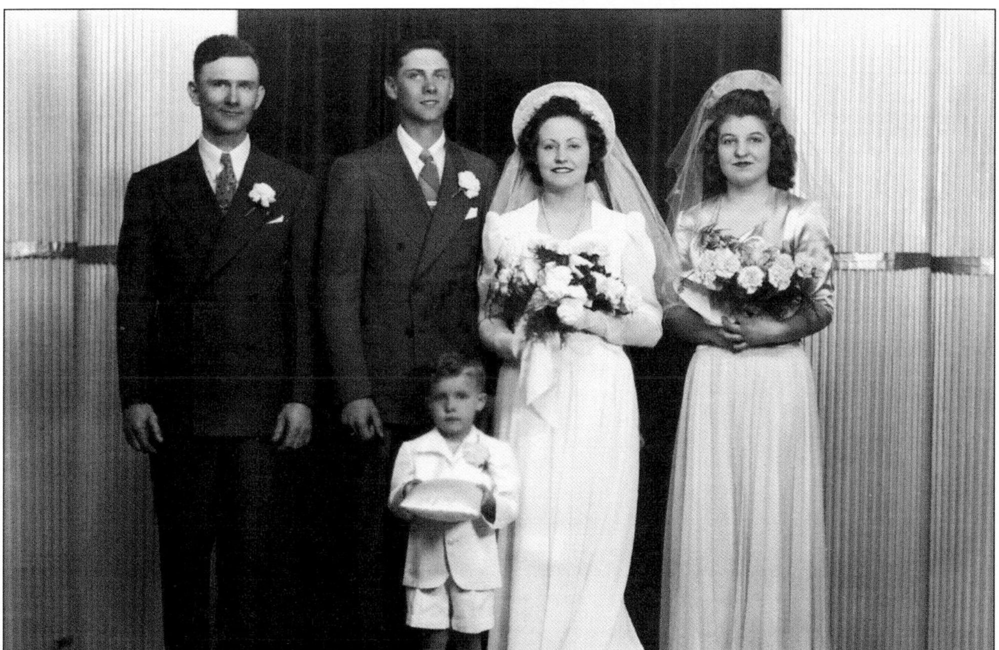

Pictured on the wedding day of Elmer Lechlitner and Mabel "Toot" (Schweisberger) Lechlitner are, from left to right, Alvin Lechlitner, Elmer, Mabel, Delores (Schweisberger) Cook, and Robert Schweisberger. (Courtesy of Craig Lechlitner.)

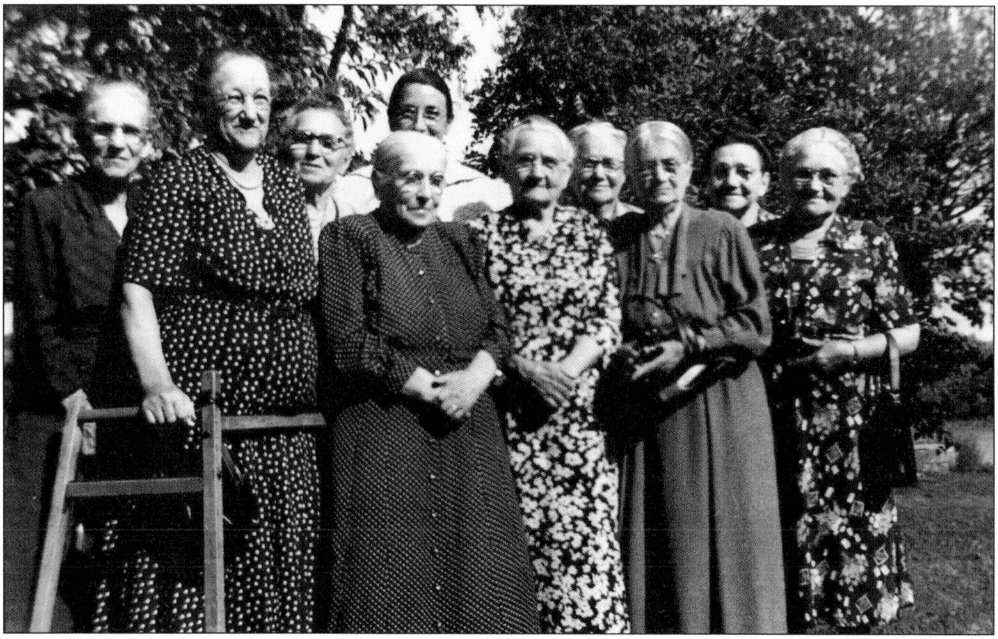

The following women attended a gathering at an Absent Indida class in 1953. From left to right are Minnie Marker, Anna Beehler, Lena Zeiger, Blanche Coonfare, Emma Birk, Catherine Marker, Mabel Schmeltz, Catherine Bollenbacher, Libby Hesch, and Yetta Keil. (Courtesy of the author.)

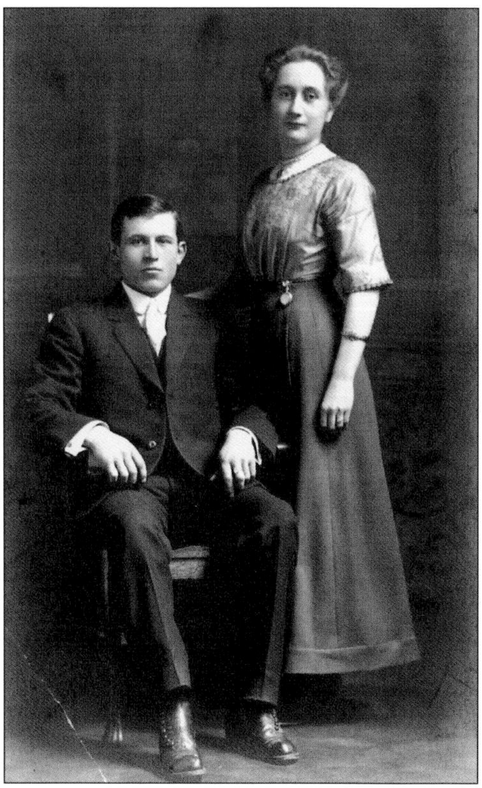

Millard T. Battles and Cora P. (Klinkner) Battles are pictured here. They had six daughters and one son. They made their home on Ironwood Road in Penn Township. (Courtesy of the author.)

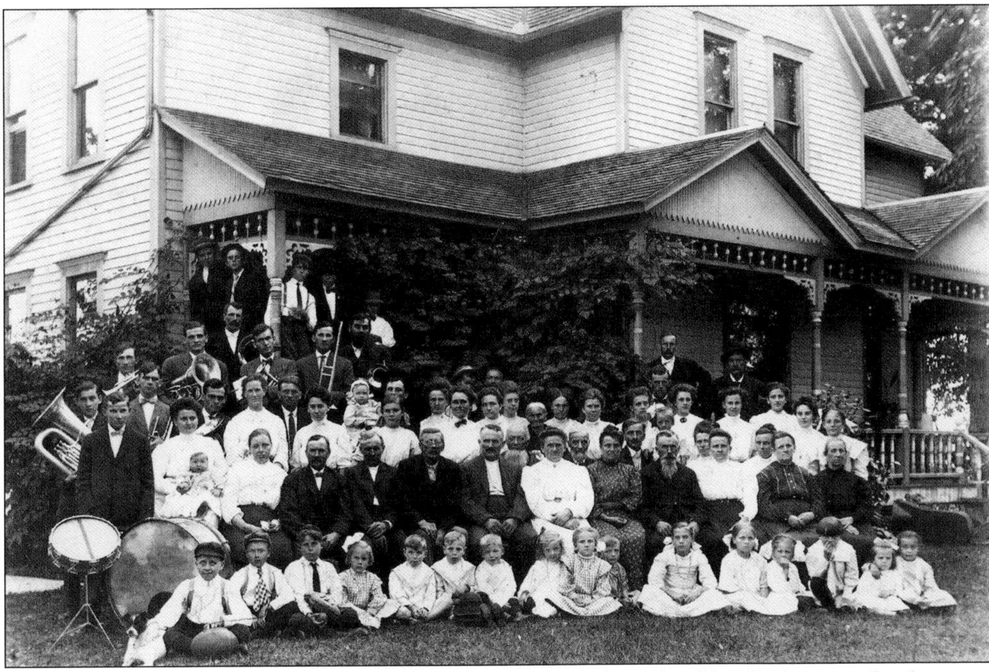

This Schalliol reunion took place on Beech Road at the Klondike Exchange, the home of Augustus Schalliol and family. During the reunion, Augustus and his children played music for all their guests. (Courtesy of the author.)

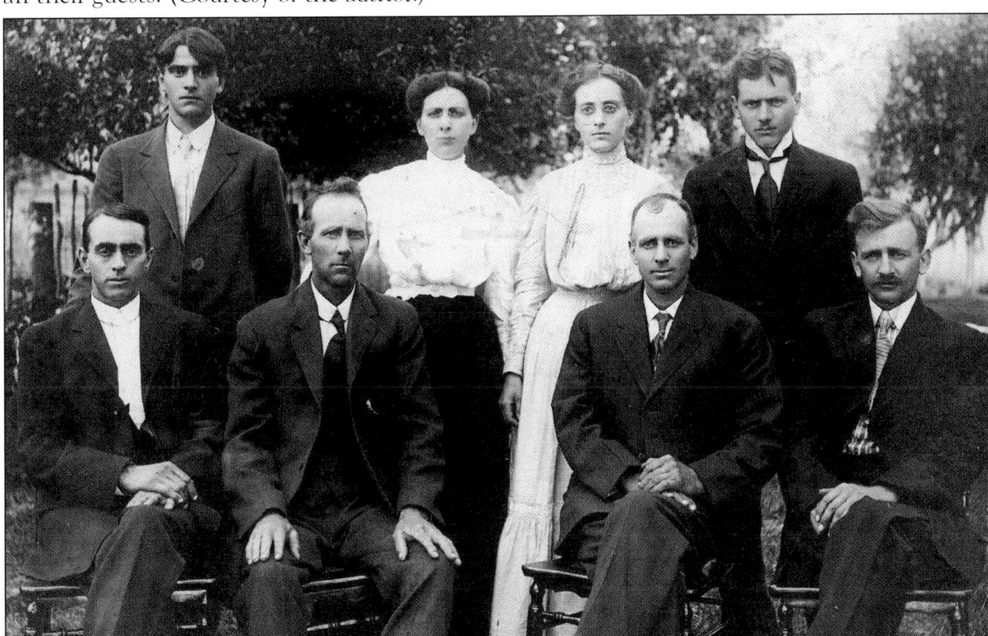

The Weaver Martin family lived in Madison Township. Pictured from left to right are the following: (first row) Jonas Martin, Sam Martin, Henry Martin, and Weaver Martin; (second row) Minno Martin, Rebecca Martin, Catherine Martin, and Noah Martin. (Courtesy of Jeanette [Battles] Martin.)

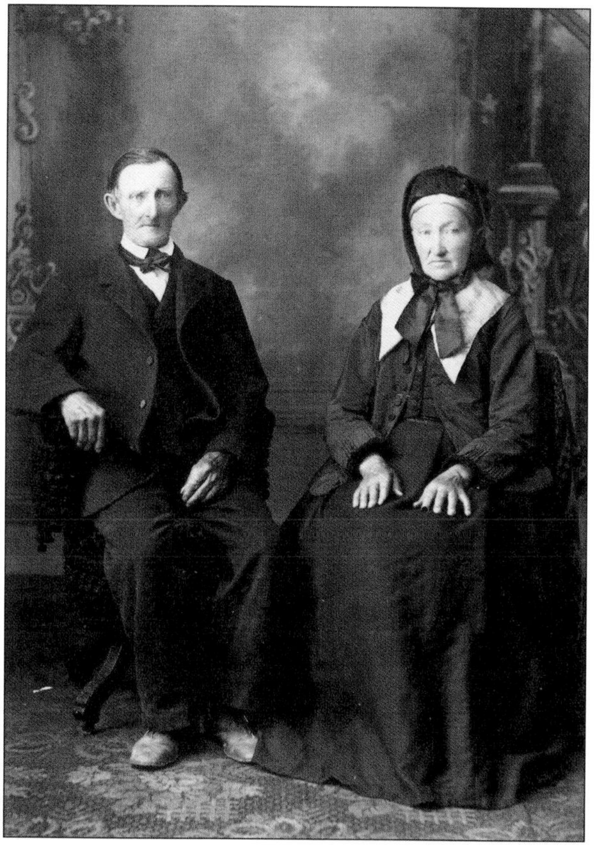

This photograph shows John Berger and Rosina (Haueter) Berger. They were born in Switzerland and came to Madison Township to raise their family. They lived on Beech Road. (Courtesy of Vicki Berger.)

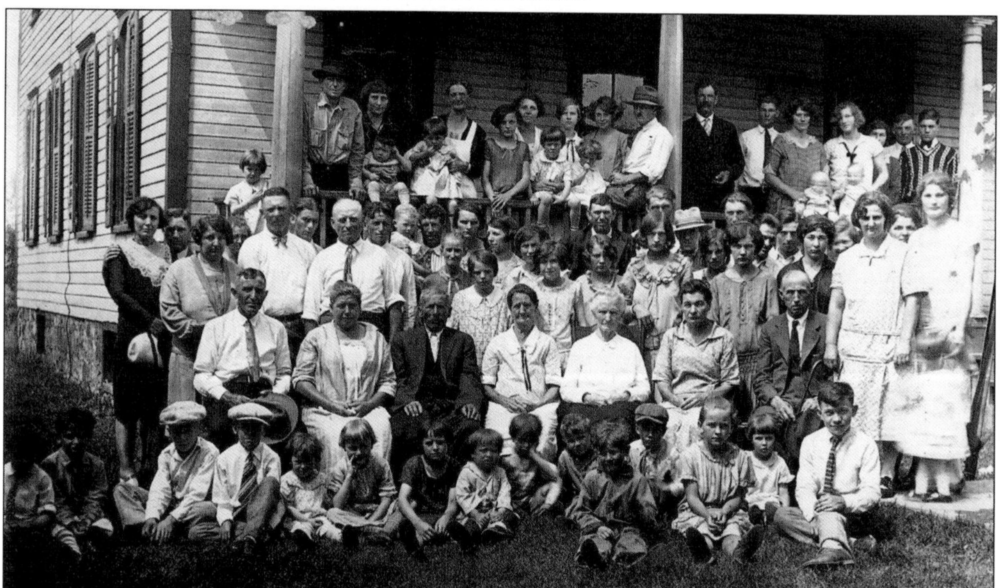

Depicted here is a Shaffer-Berger reunion that took place on July 1, 1928. The home was built by John and Margarita Shaffer on a long lane off of Madison Road, between Beech and Cedar Roads in Madison Township. (Courtesy of Vicki Berger.)

This family photograph shows, from left to right, Gustav Nebtor Contat, Antoine Contat (father), Louis Contat, and Lena Contat. They came from France in 1905 to stay in the home of John and Louise Berger, on Layton Road in Penn Township. (Courtesy of Rosemary [Contat] Dixon.)

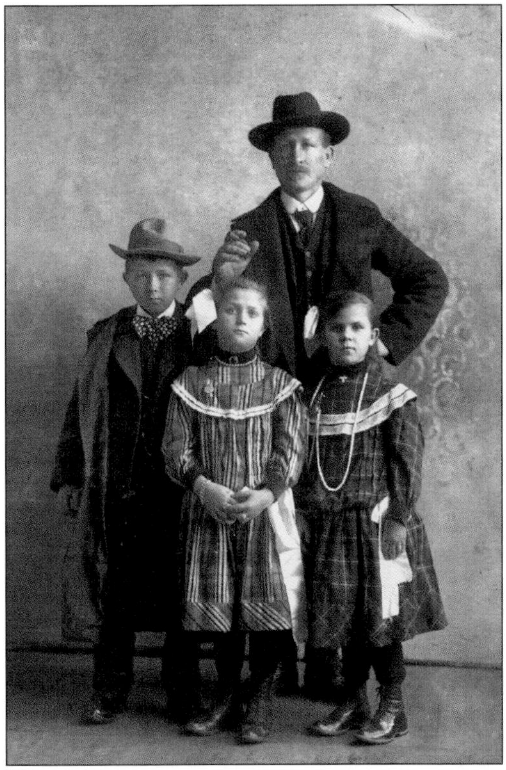

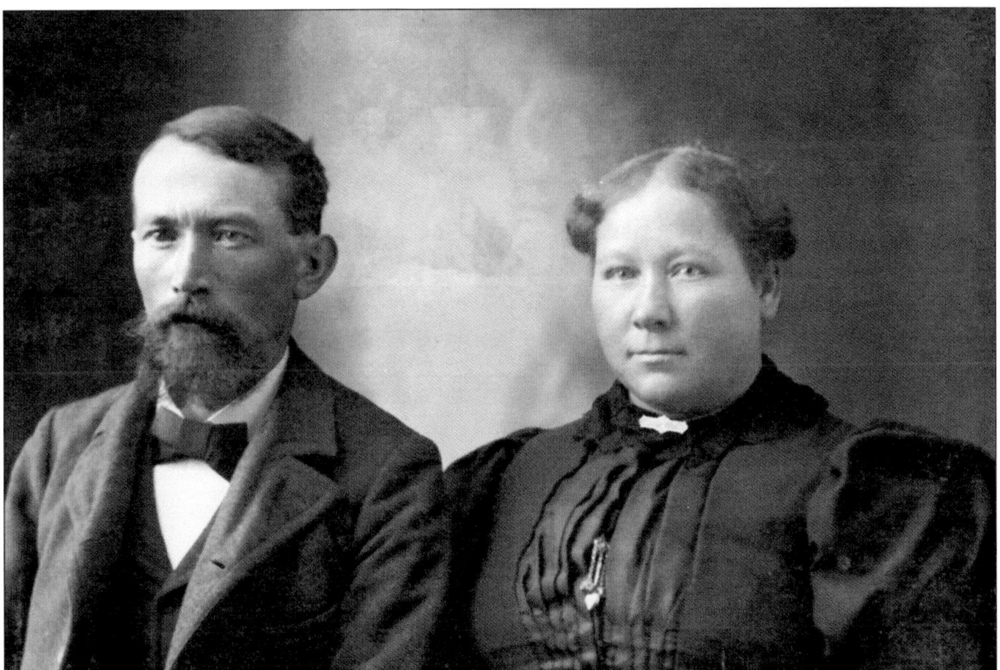

Pictured here are John Berger and Louise (Contat) Berger. They made their home on Layton Road between Elm Road and Bremen Highway, in Penn Township. (Courtesy of Rosemary [Contat] Dixon.)

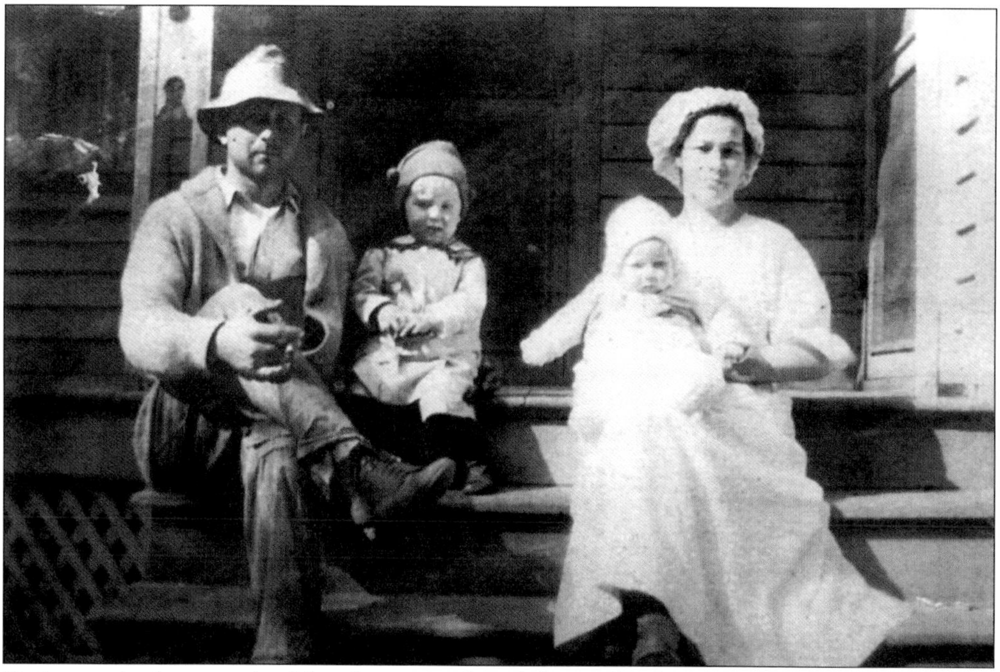

Sitting on the front porch of their home are, from left to right, Gustave Contat, Charles Contat, Michael Contat, and Anna (Bachman) Contat. Their home was located on the west side of Elm Road, just north of New Road. (Courtesy of Rosemary [Contat] Dixon.)

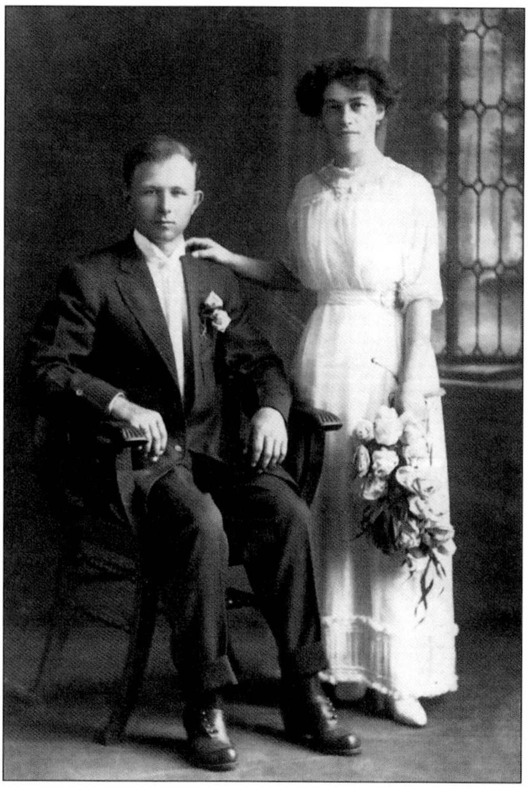

On August 9, 1913, Gustave Contat was united in marriage to Anna Bachman. They made their home in Madison Township. (Courtesy of Rosemary [Contat] Dixon.)

Sitting on the back of the family vehicle are Charles Contat and his lovely wife, Mildred (Matz) Contat. (Courtesy of Rosemary [Contat] Dixon.)

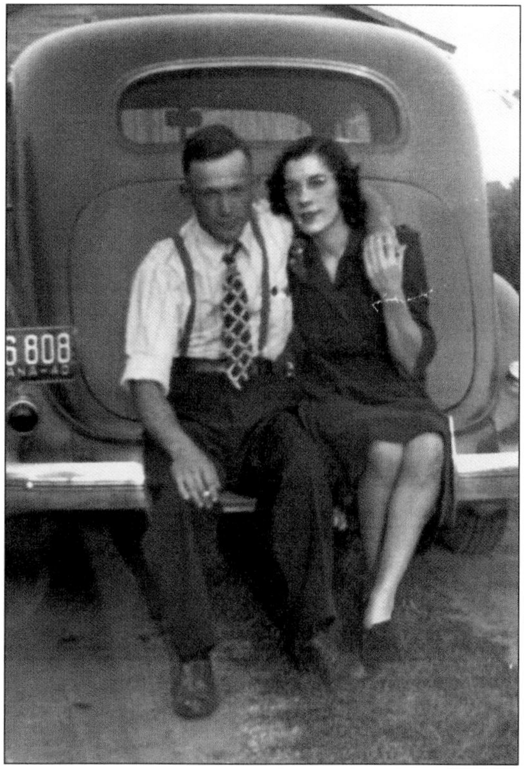

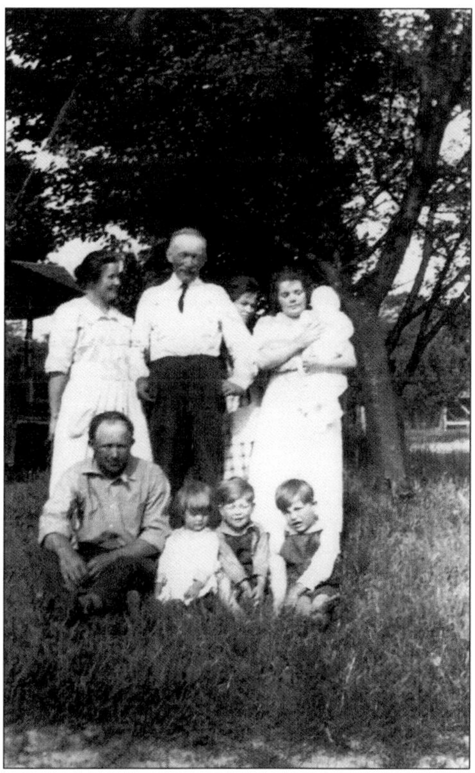

This family photograph was taken at the home of John and Lora Berger. Pictured are, from left to right, the following: (first row) Gustave Contat, Ruth Contat, Charles Contat, and Michael Contat; (second row) Lora (Mutti) Berger, John Berger, Anna (Bachman) Contat, and Flora (Guerne) Schroeder, holding Laura Contat. (Courtesy of Rosemary [Contat] Dixon.)

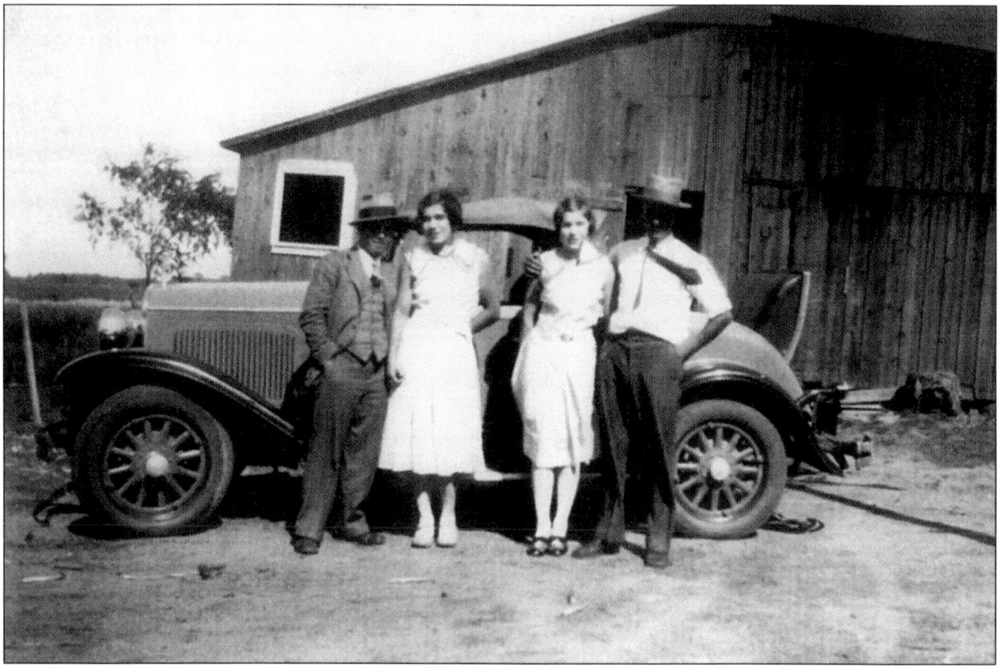

This photograph was taken in 1930 on Harrison and Blackberry Roads, in Penn Township. Pictured here from left to right are Charles G. Contat, Mildred (Matz) Contat, Martha Matz, and Emil Lauffer. (Courtesy of Rosemary [Contat] Dixon.)

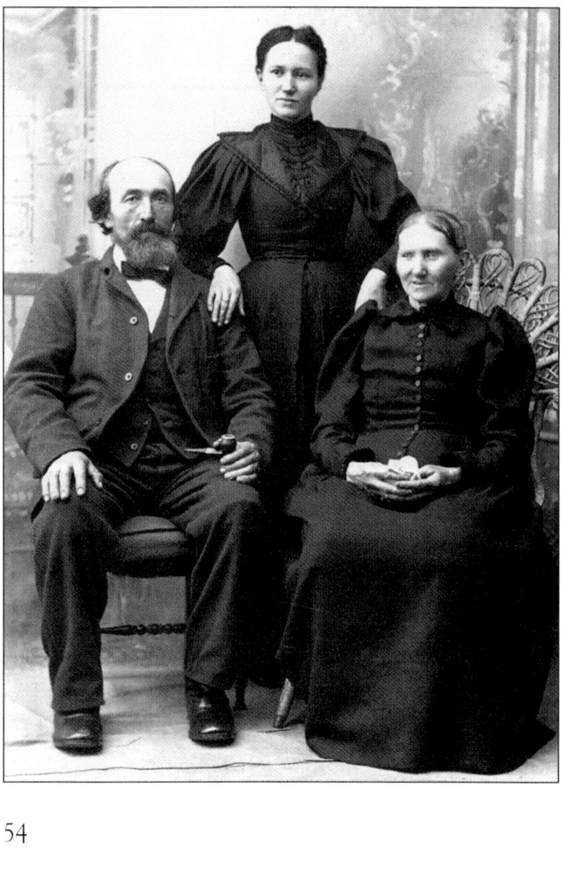

From left to right, Samuel Berger, Rosena Berger, and Magdalena (Kohler) Berger made their home on Dogwood Road between Patterson and Riley Roads. (Courtesy of Vicki Berger.)

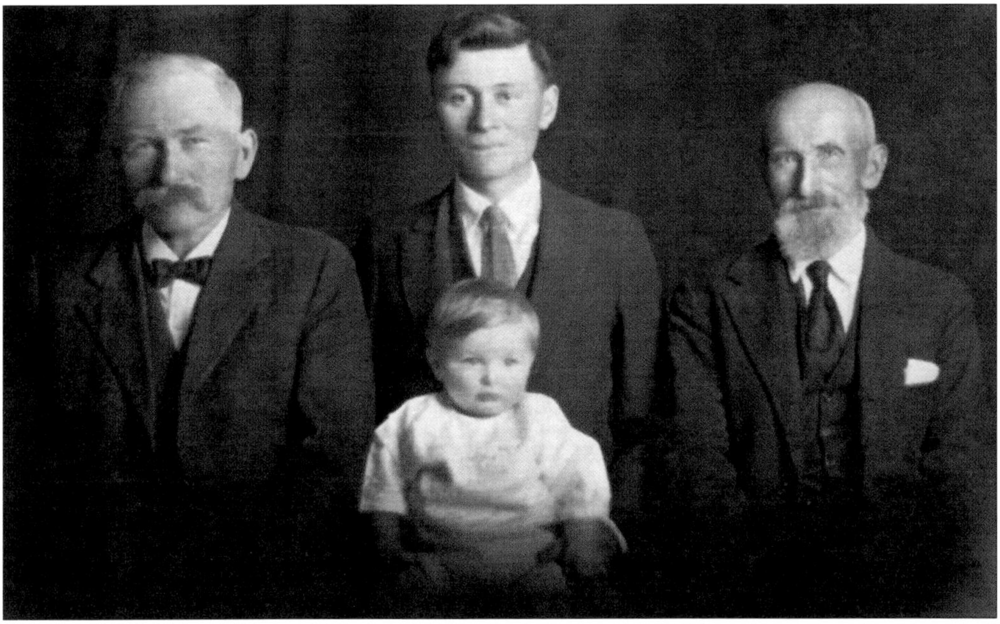

This four-generation photograph was taken in 1926 on Layton Road in Penn Township. Pictured are (front) Lester Devon Berger and, from left to right, Emil S. Berger, Victor Emanuel Berger, and Samuel Berger. (Courtesy of Vicki Berger.)

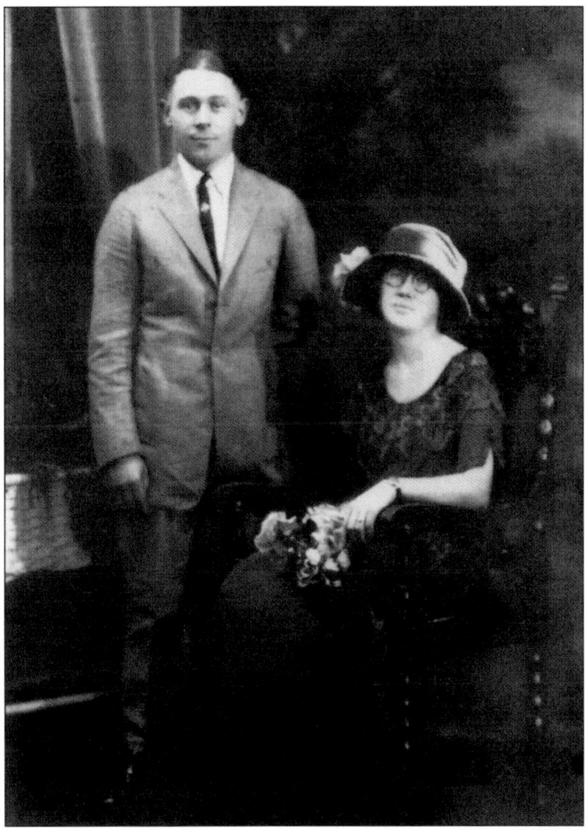

Louis Von Gruiengen and Matilda Berger made their home on Quarrels Road in Madison Township. (Courtesy of Vicki Berger.)

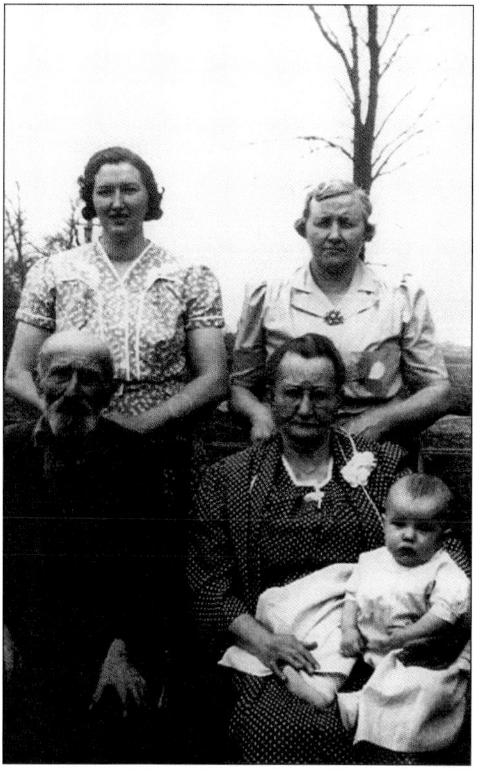

This is a five-generation photograph. Pictured are, from left to right, as follows: (first row) Samuel Berger, Roseanna (Berger) (Sahli) Berger, and Dewaine Dale King; (second row) Alberta (Berger) King, and Rose (Sahli) Berger. (Courtesy of Vicki Berger.)

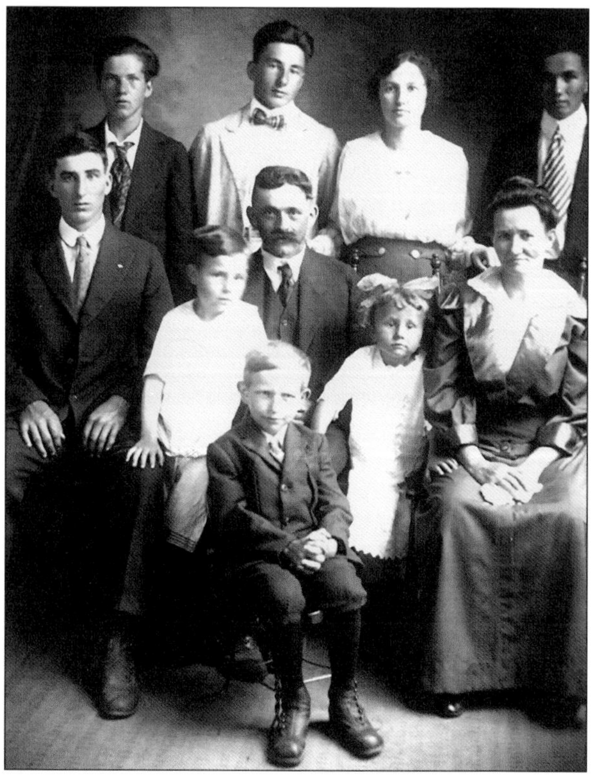

This family photograph was taken in 1918. Pictured are, from left to right, the following: (first row) Ellsworth Berger, Arthur Berger, and Evelyn J. Berger; (second row) Frederick E. Sahli, Jacob F. Berger, and Rosena (Berger) (Sahli) Berger; (third row) Bertold A. Sahli, Walter Sahli, Rosemary Sahli, and Jacob Sahli. (Courtesy of Vicki Berger.)

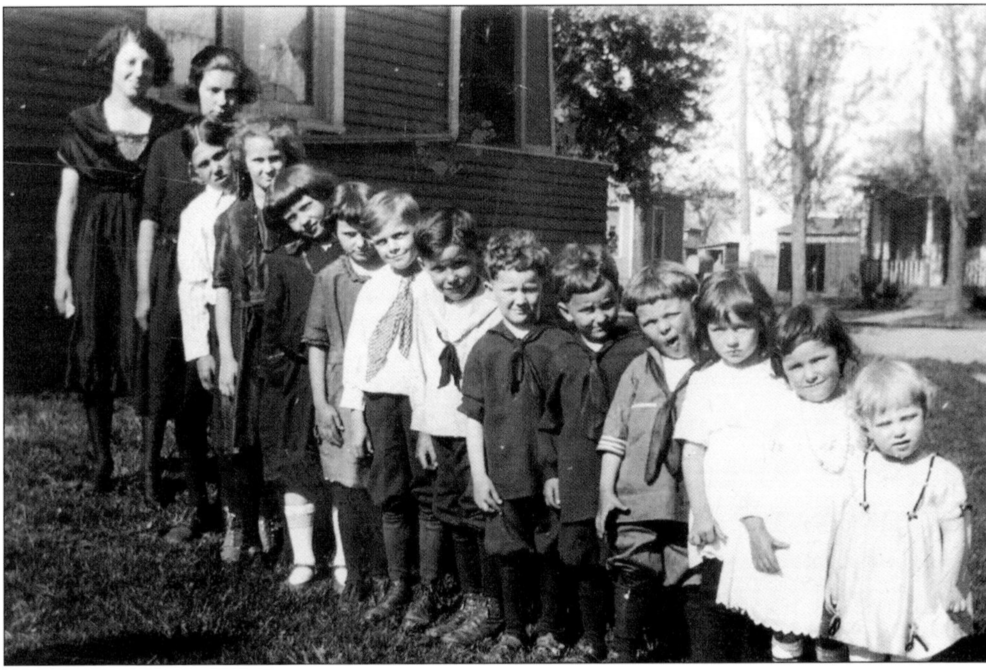

This photograph shows the grandchildren of Joseph Bendit and Sophia (Juillerat) Bendit. The following people are shown from left to right: Minnie Berger, Edna Berger, Harry Berger, Evelyn Bendit, Aline Berger, Donna Bendit, Eldon Bendit, George Berger, Otho Bendit, Cleo Bendit, Norris Bendit, Lucille Bendit, Marie Berger, and Kathryn Bendit. (Courtesy of Vicki Berger.)

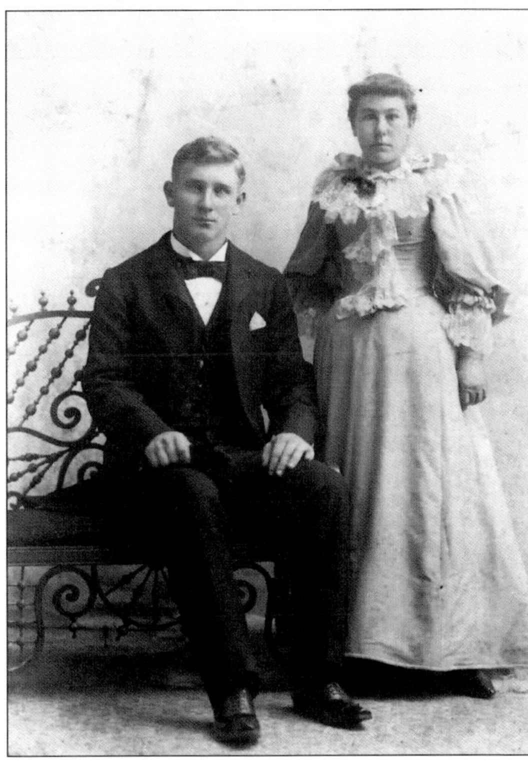

Christian Ferdinand Berger and Maria Anna Mutti were united in marriage on August 10, 1876. They made their home on Beech Road in Madison Township. (Courtesy of Vicki Berger.)

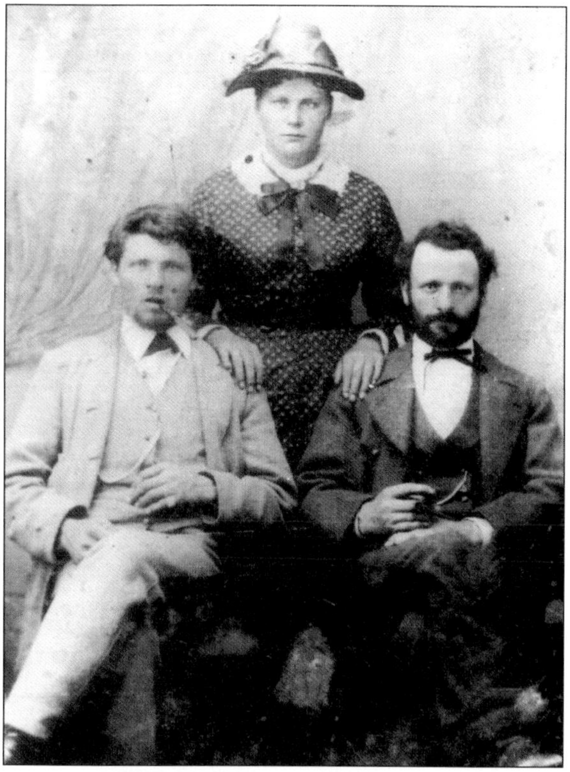

This photograph shows, from left to right, Gottlieb Mutti, Bertha (Mutti) Scheidegger, and Christian Mutti. (Courtesy of Vicki Berger.)

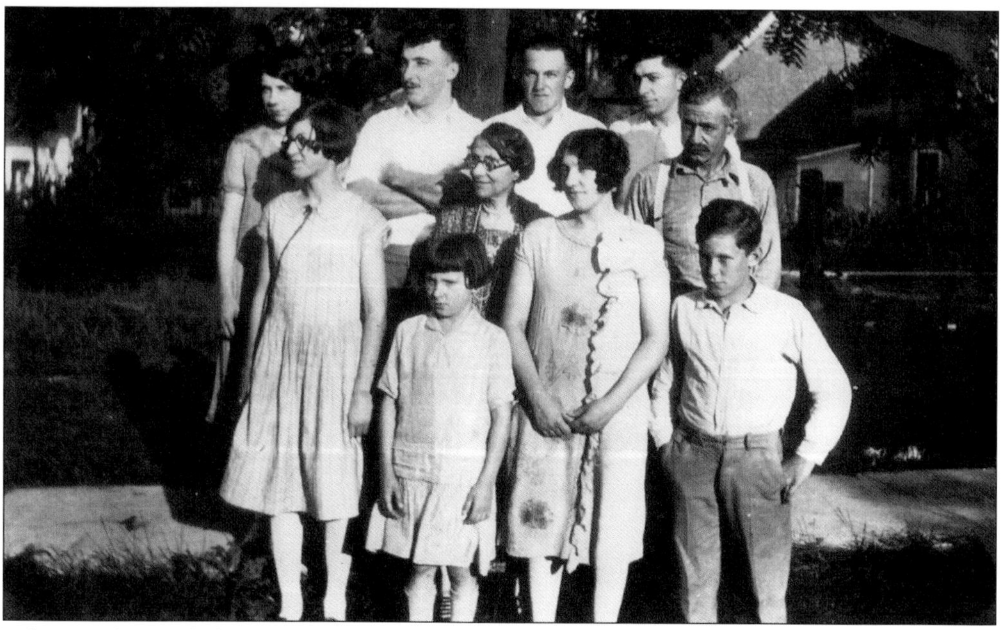

Taken in front of their home in Wyatt, Indiana, this photograph shows the Berger family. Pictured are, from left to right, the following: (first row) Maria Claudia Berger, Minnie Amelia Berger, and George Christian Berger; (second row) Aline Marion Berger, Edith Cecile (Bendit) Berger, and Emile Edward Berger; (third row) Edna Mae Berger, Paul Samuel Berger, Harry Joseph Berger, and Albert Lewis Berger. (Courtesy of Vicki Berger.)

This four-generation photograph shows Minnie (Berger) Hardy (left), Sophia (Juillerat) Bendit, and Edith (Bendit) Berger, who is holding Doris Hardy. (Courtesy of Vicki Berger.)

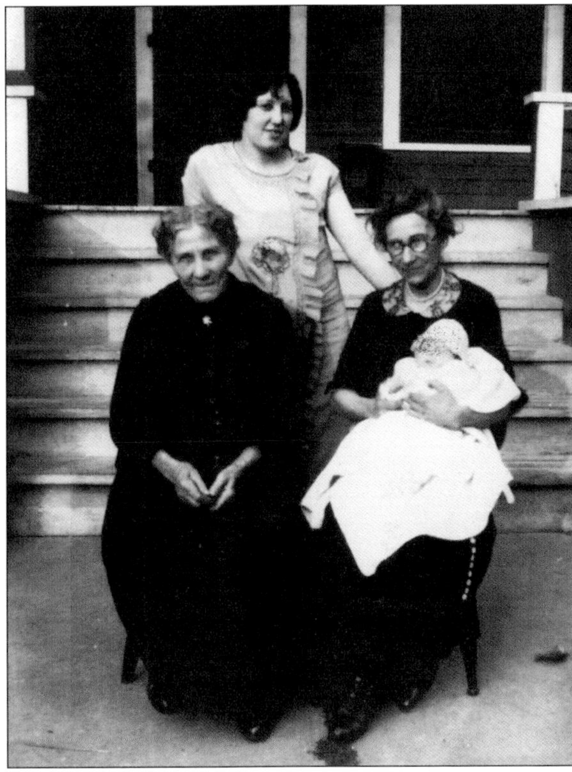

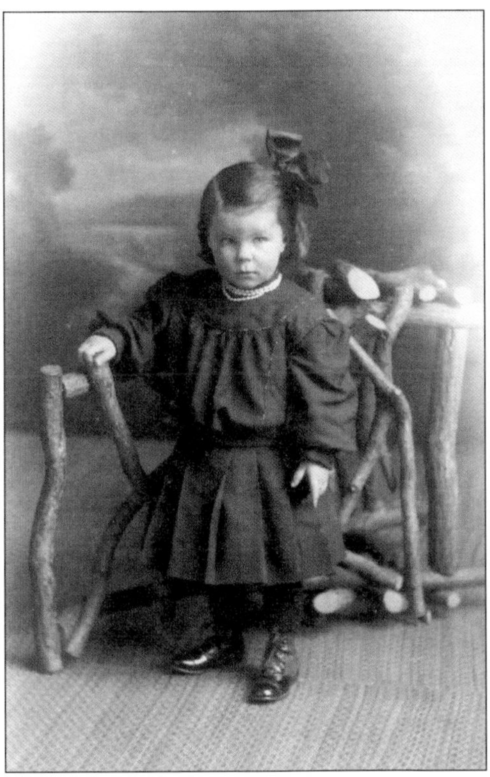

This adorable little girl is Edna Mae Berger. The photograph was taken in 1911 when she was three years old. (Courtesy of Vicki Berger.)

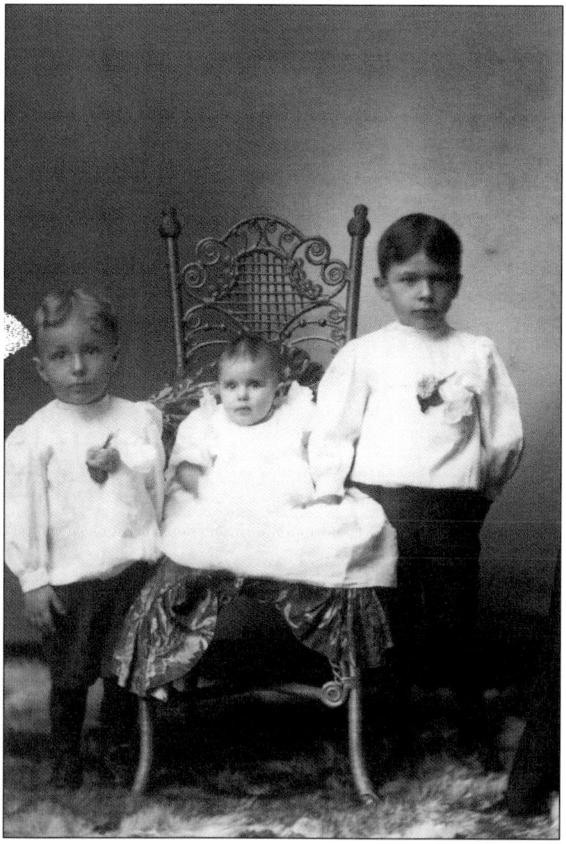

These three beautiful children are, from left to right, Paul Berger, Minnie Berger, and Albert Berger. This photograph was taken in 1905. (Courtesy of Vicki Berger.)

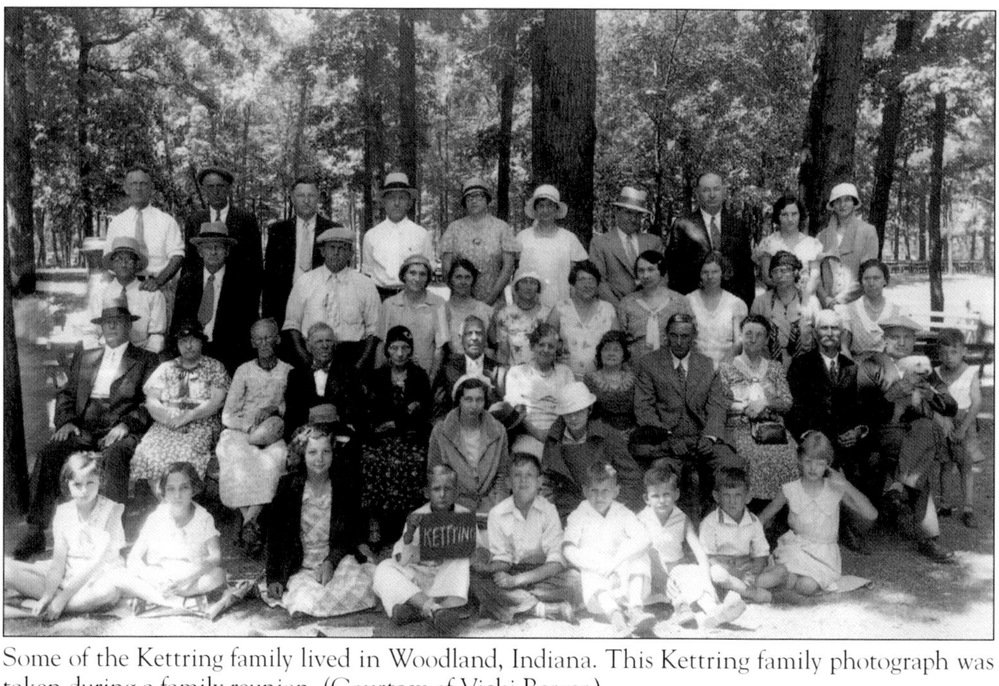

Some of the Kettring family lived in Woodland, Indiana. This Kettring family photograph was taken during a family reunion. (Courtesy of Vicki Berger.)

This Matz family portrait was taken in 1902. Pictured are, from left to right, as follows: (first row) Estella Matz, and George Matz; (second row) Oscar Matz, Charlotte (Schneider) Matz, Laura Matz, and Phillip Matz. (Courtesy of Rosemary [Contat] Dixon.)

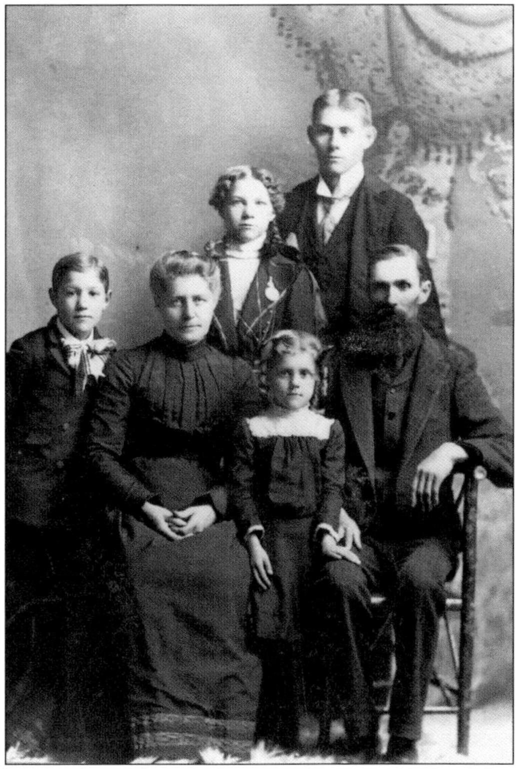

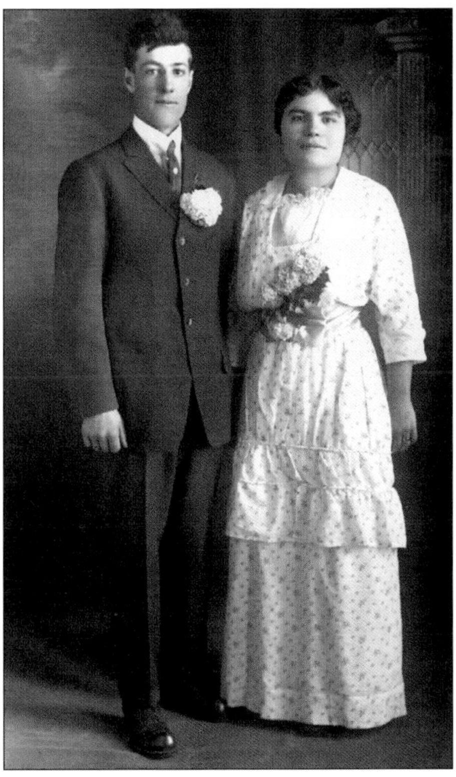

Oscar George Matz and Thelma (Bickell) Matz were united in marriage on May 12, 1914. (Courtesy of Rosemary [Contat] Dixon.)

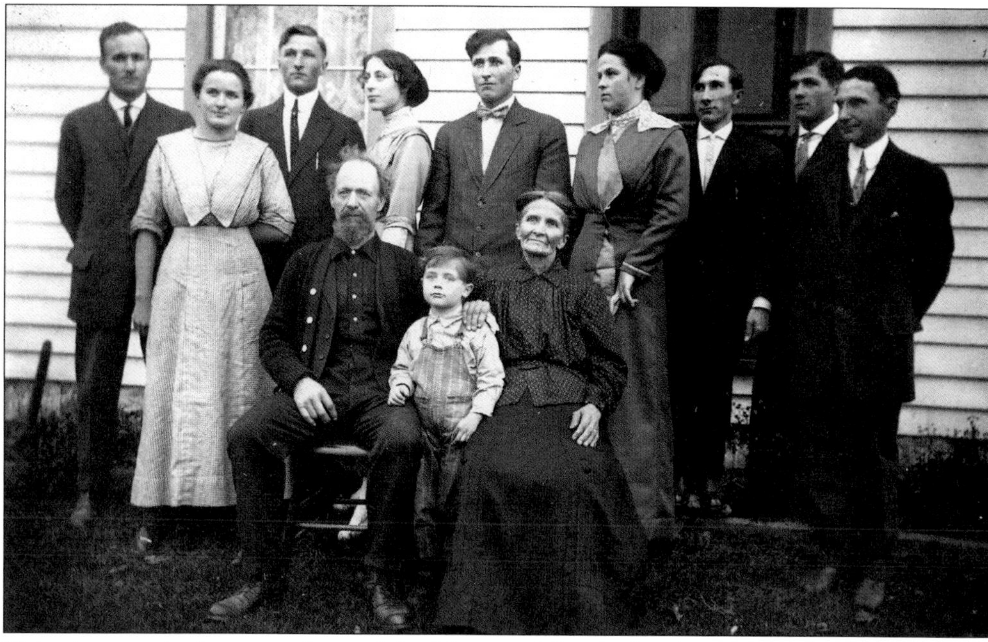

This photograph shows members of the Mutti and Bendit families. Pictured are, from left to right, the following: (sitting) Christian Mutti, Henrietta Helene (Juillerat) Mutti, and Charlie Kaufman; (first row) Lora (Mutti) Berger, Ida (Beron) Bendit, Elsie (Beron) Bendit, and Amos Bendit; (second row) Charles Mutti, Joseph Mutti, Berton Mutti, Lewis Bendit, and Arnold Mutti. (Courtesy of Vicki Berger.)

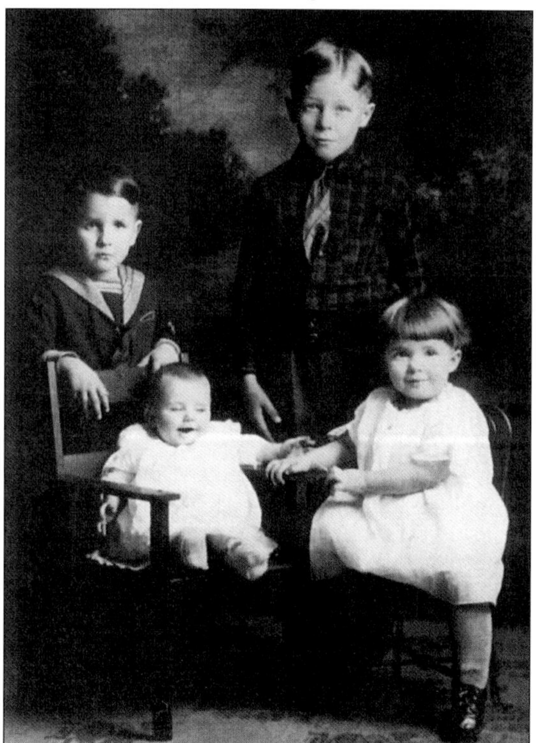

From left to right, this photograph shows (first row) Alice Mutti and Helen Mutti and (second row) Harold Mutti, Charles Mutti, the children of Arnold Mutti and Margaret (Shafer) Mutti. The Muttis made their home on Dogwood Road in Madison Township. (Courtesy of Rosemary [Contat] Dixon.)

The Jacob and Rosina Scheidegger family was photographed here in 1893. Pictured are, from left to right, as follows: Ida Scheidegger, in front; (first row) Jacob Scheidegger, Herman Scheidegger, and Rosina Scheidegger; (second row) Louise Scheidegger, Minnie Scheidegger, and Hermina Scheidegger. This family lived in the Wyatt area. (Courtesy of Vicki Berger.)

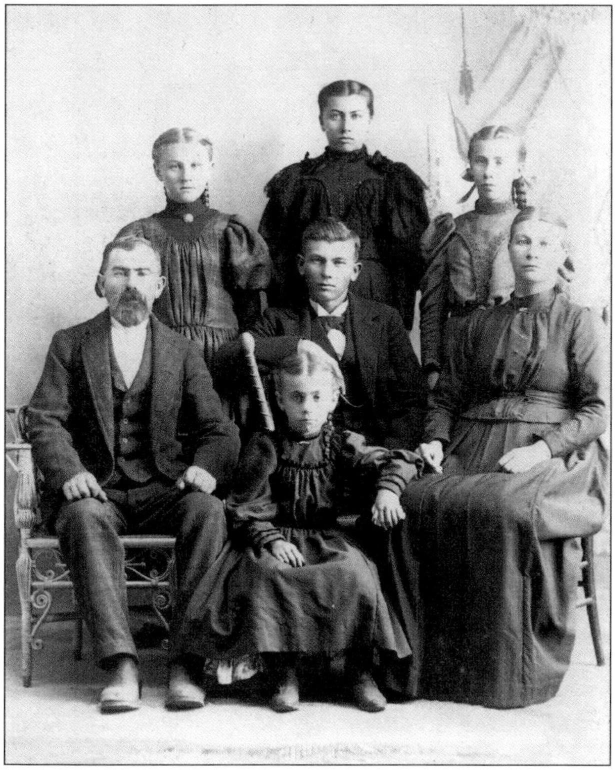

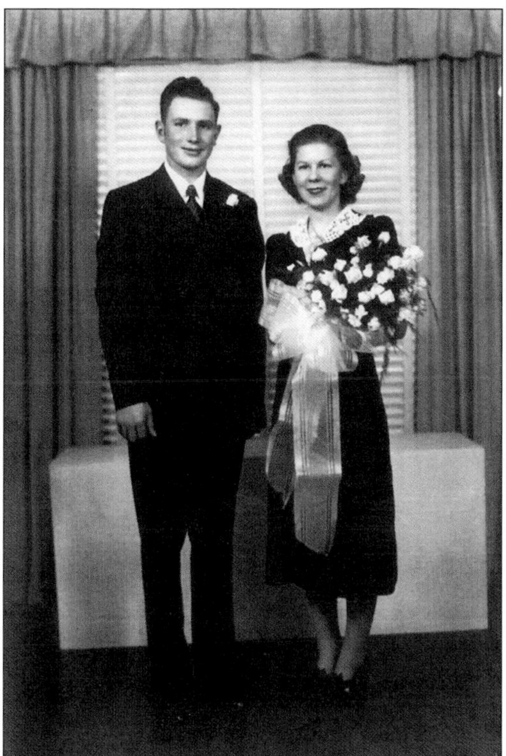

Henry "Hank" Verhaeghe and Bertha (Weber) Verhaeghe united in marriage on December 30, 1939. They lived all their lives on Dogwood Road in Madison Township. (Courtesy of Vicki Berger.)

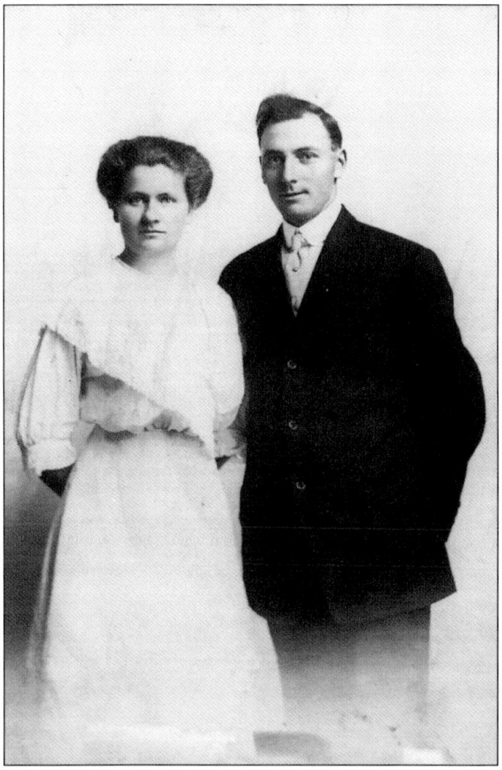

Emma (Scheidegger) Balmer and Charles Balmer were united in marriage on October 5, 1912. (Courtesy of Vicki Berger.)

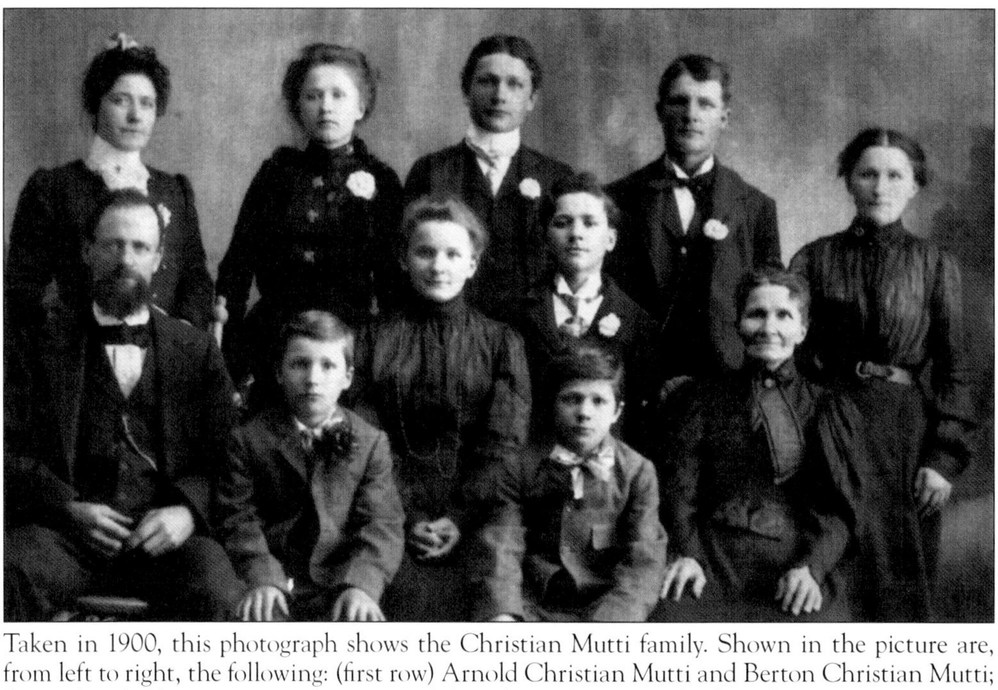

Taken in 1900, this photograph shows the Christian Mutti family. Shown in the picture are, from left to right, the following: (first row) Arnold Christian Mutti and Berton Christian Mutti; (second row) Christian Mutti, Laura Magdalena (Mutti) Berger, Charles Albert Mutti, Henrietta Helene (Juillerat) Mutti; (third row) Elizabeth (Mutti) Kaufman, Lena (Mutti) Birk, Paul Mutti, Ernest Emile Mutti, and Celesta (Mutti) Avery. (Courtesy of Rosemary [Contat] Dixon.)

Emil Frederick Berger and Rosa Anna (Rosti) Berger were united in marriage on September 9, 1905. (Courtesy of Vicki Berger.)

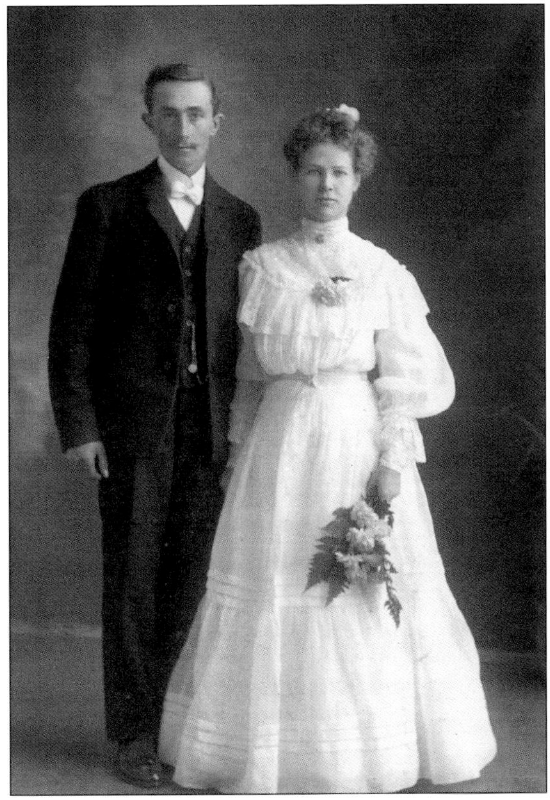

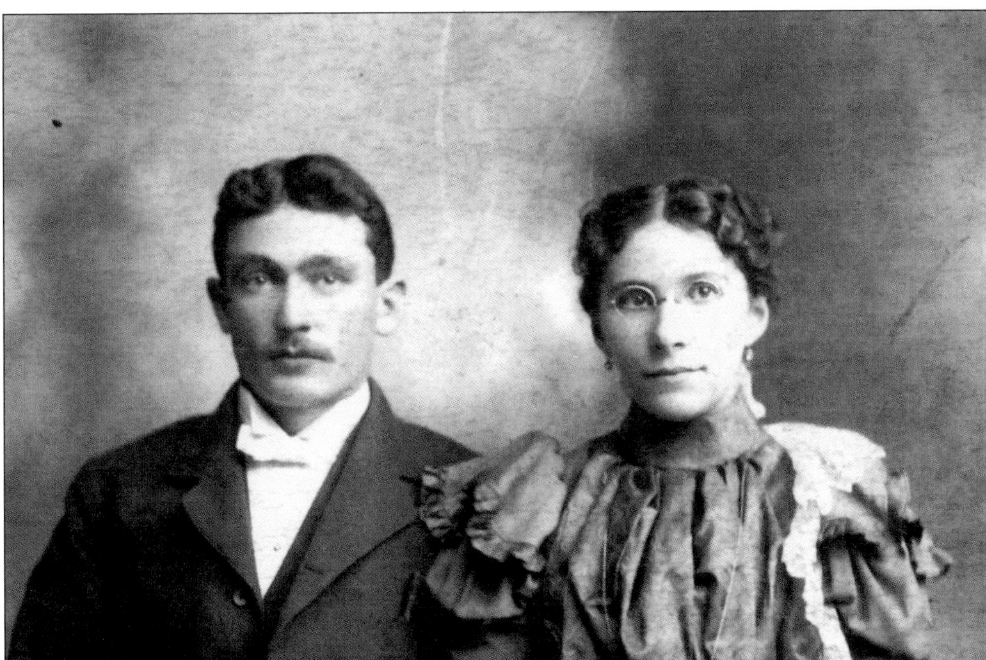

Emile Edward Berger and Edith Cecile (Bendit) Berger became husband and wife on October 26, 1898. (Courtesy of Vicki Berger.)

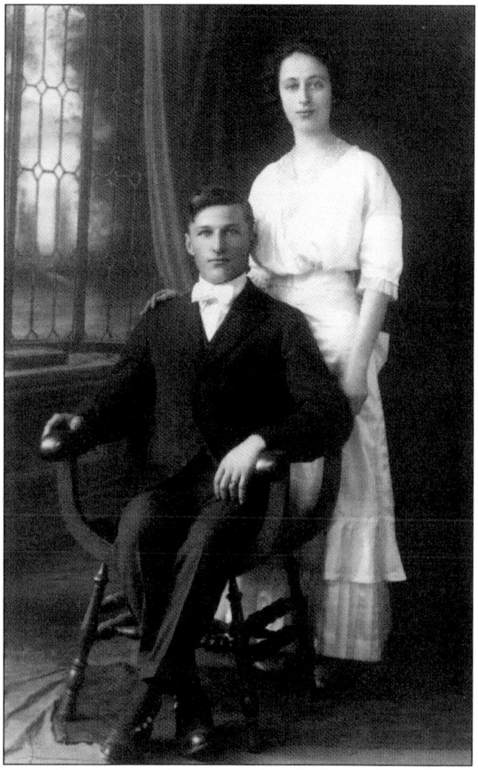

On November 4, 1914, in Wyatt, Indiana, Joseph Jacob Bendit and Ida T. (Beron) Bendit were married. (Courtesy of Vicki Berger.)

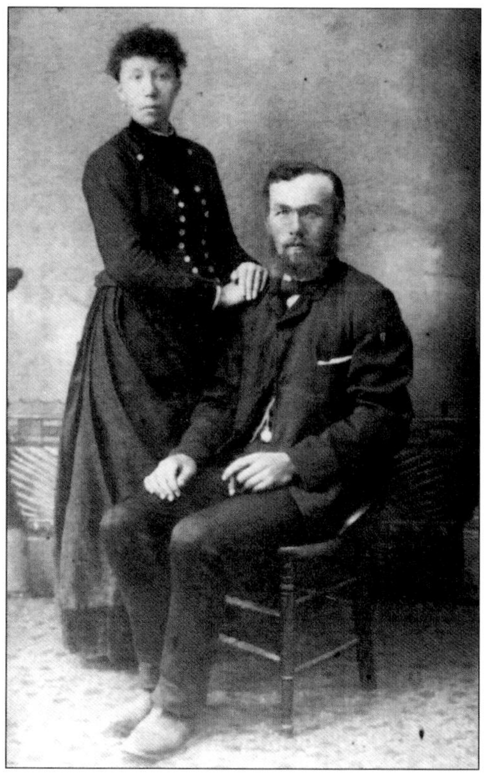

Married in 1887, Jacob Berger and Laurance Louise (Juillerat) Berger made their home in Madison Township. (Courtesy of Vicki Berger.)

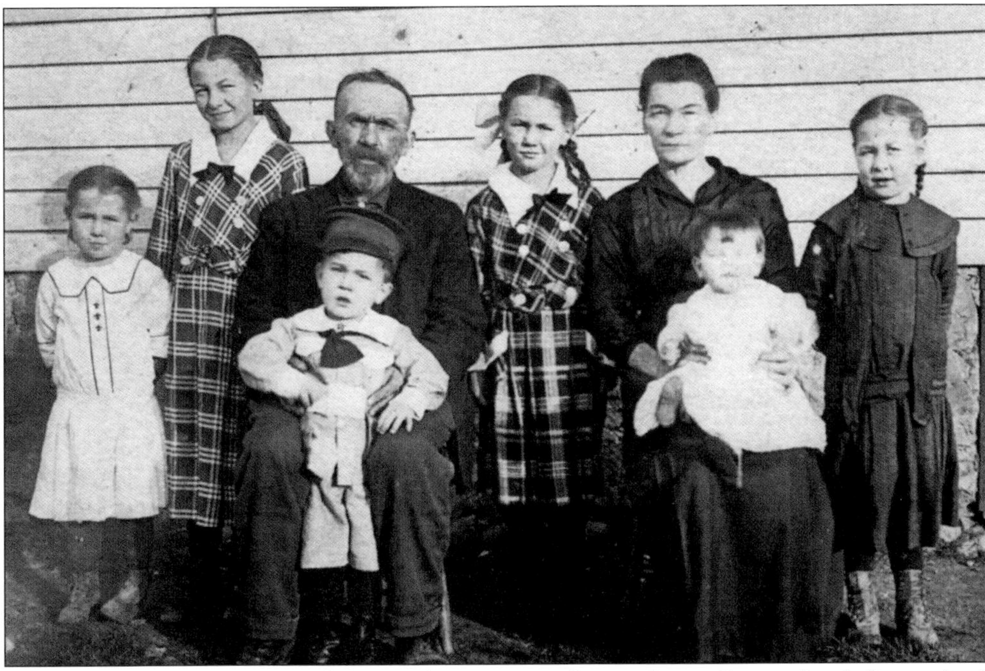

This photograph shows, from left to right, Margaret Berger, Laura Berger, Jacob Berger (with Abraham Berger in front), Anna Berger, Lena (Schutz-Shaffer) Berger (with Katherine Berger on her lap), and Flora Berger. (Courtesy of Ann [Kovach] Fette.)

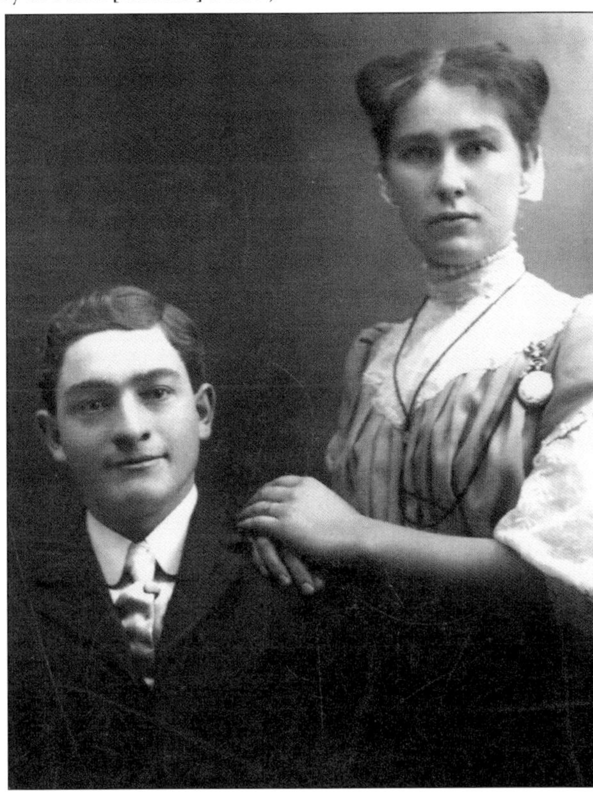

Taken on December 22, 1905, in Madison Township, this photograph depicts Albert Horein and Amelia (Berger) Horein. They were married on this day. (Courtesy of Vicki Berger.)

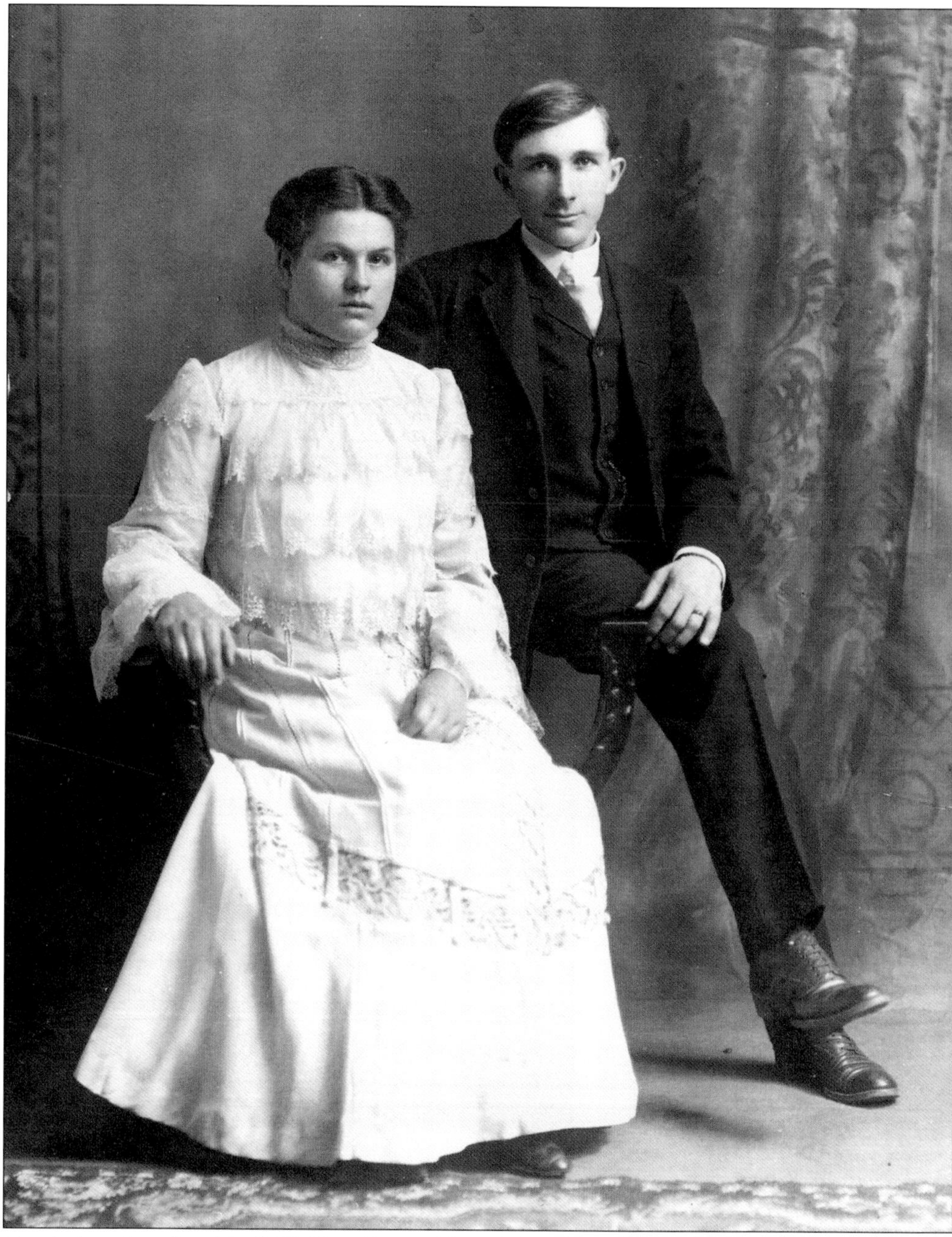

Married on October 12, 1905, Elsie Emma (Beron) Bendit and Lewis Joseph Bendit lived their lives to the fullest in Wyatt, Indiana. Lewis taught school at Madison Township School for 45 years. (Courtesy of Vicki Berger.)

# *Two*

# HOMESTEADS

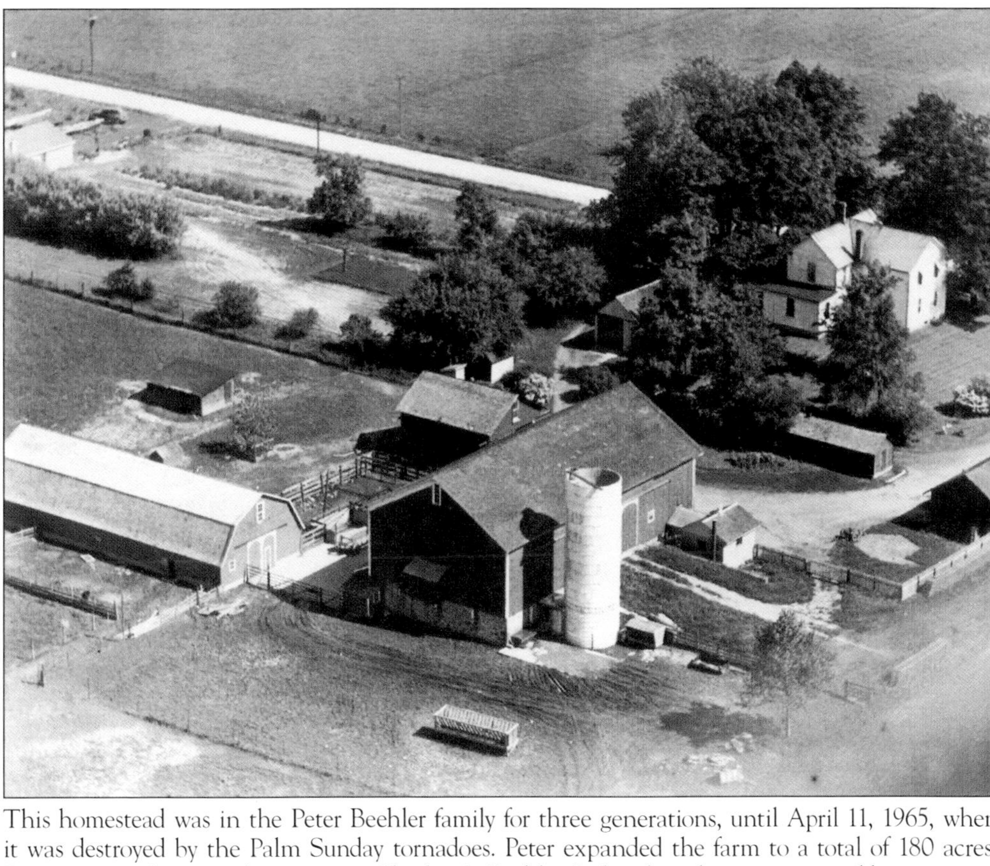

This homestead was in the Peter Beehler family for three generations, until April 11, 1965, when it was destroyed by the Palm Sunday tornadoes. Peter expanded the farm to a total of 180 acres. Representing the second generation, Charles A. Beehler Sr. lived on the property until he remarried and moved to Bluffton, Indiana. Charles A. Beehler Jr. was the third generation to farm the property. This piece of land was one of the most prominent in St. Joseph County. (Courtesy of the author.)

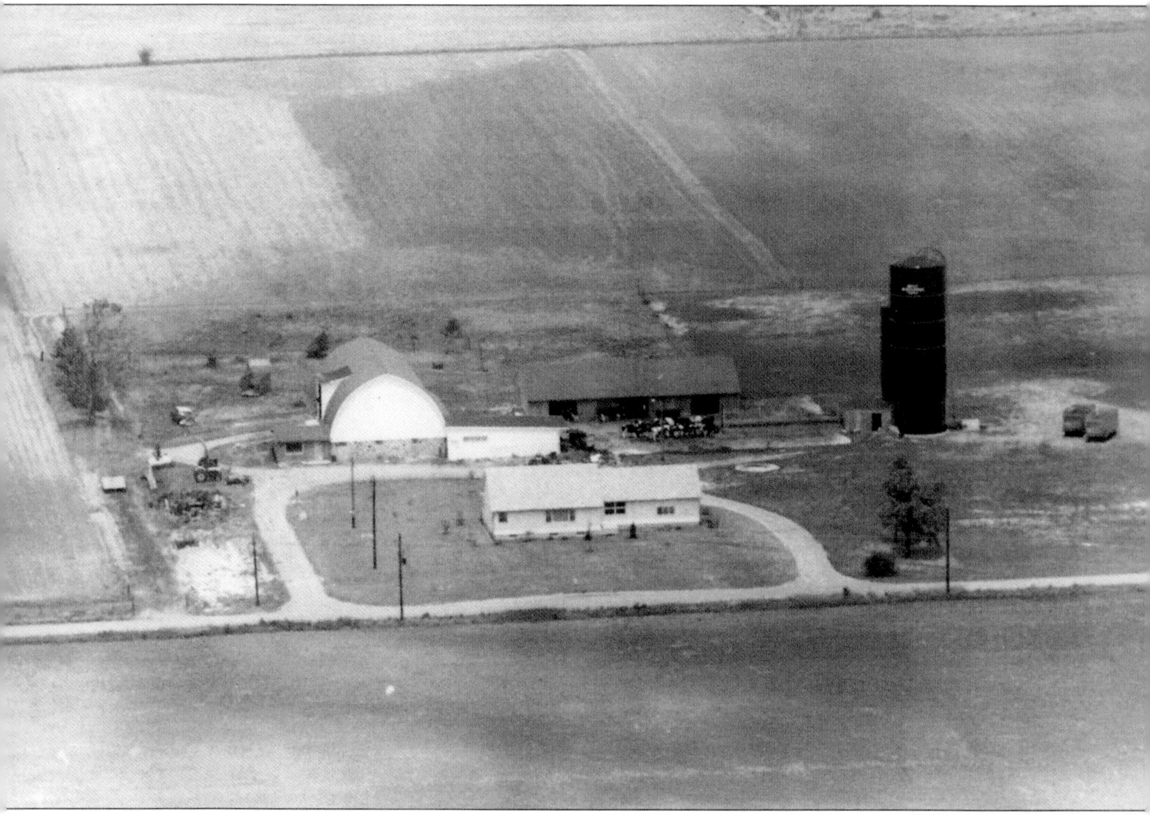

After the Palm Sunday tornadoes, Charles A. Beehler Jr. and Virginia E. Beehler rebuilt their farmhouse and barn, after a total loss that tragic day in April 1965. (Courtesy of the author.)

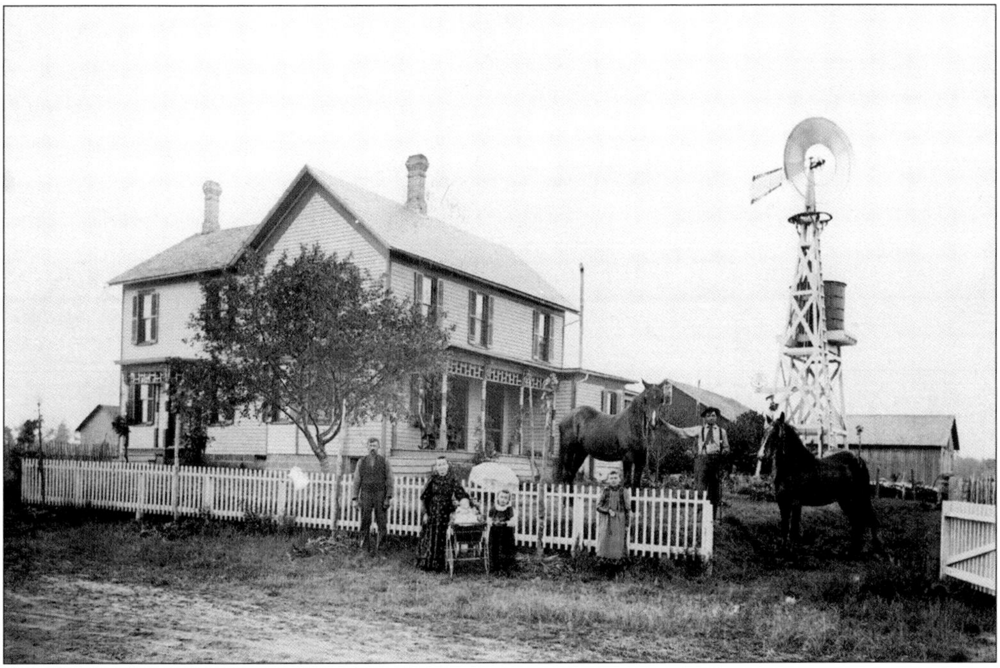

After operating a local sawmill and saving money, Peter Beehler Jr. built this new farmhouse for his family. Pictured are, from left to right, Peter Beehler, Charlotte (Beehler) Beehler, Charles A. Beehler, Carrie Beehler, Matilda Beehler, and a hired man, holding the horses. This photograph was taken around 1896. (Courtesy of the author.)

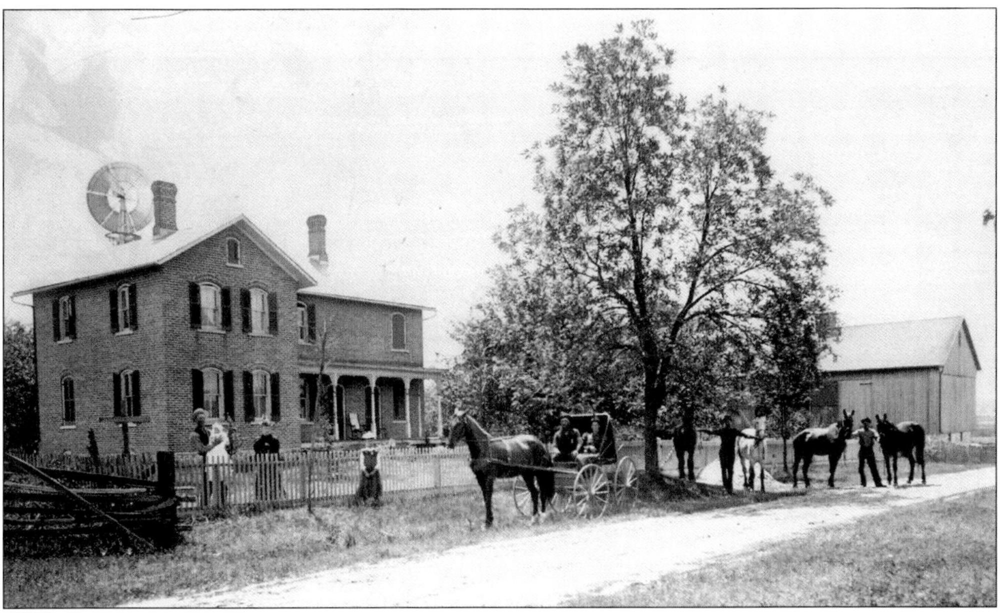

On a summer day in 1895, this photograph was taken on Dogwood Road just north of Pierce Road, in Madison Township. Shown here from left to right are George J. Birk (holding Edgar Birk, born in 1895), Anna Birk (14 years old), Clara Birk (9 years old), George A. and Mary Ann (Kling) Birk (in the buggy), and Frank Birk and Alf Birk, holding the horses. (Courtesy of Fern [Pittman] Beehler.)

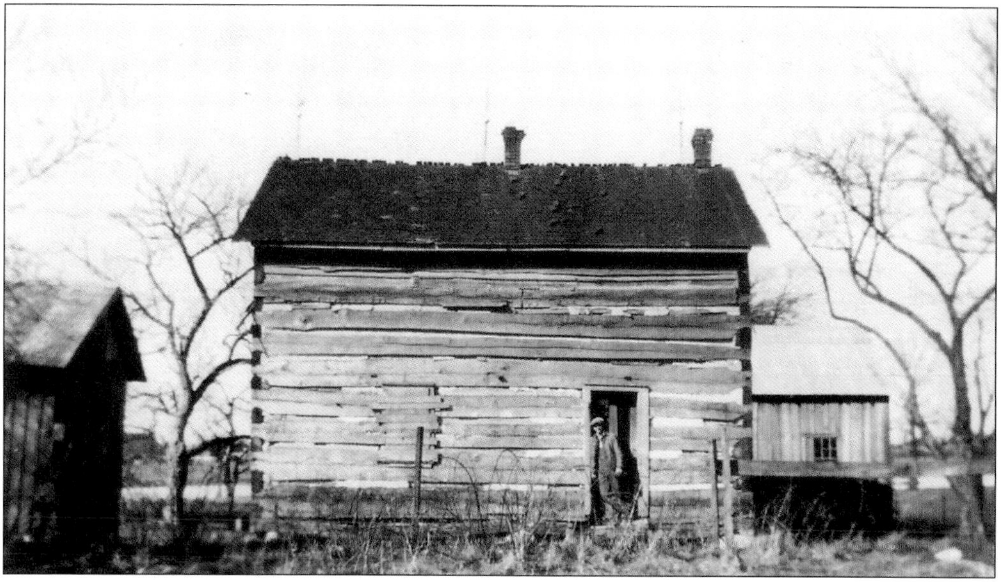

This photograph of the home of Oliver and Eva Pittman was taken on November 6, 1915. The home was located on Beech Road in Madison Township. (Courtesy of Fern [Pittman] Beehler.)

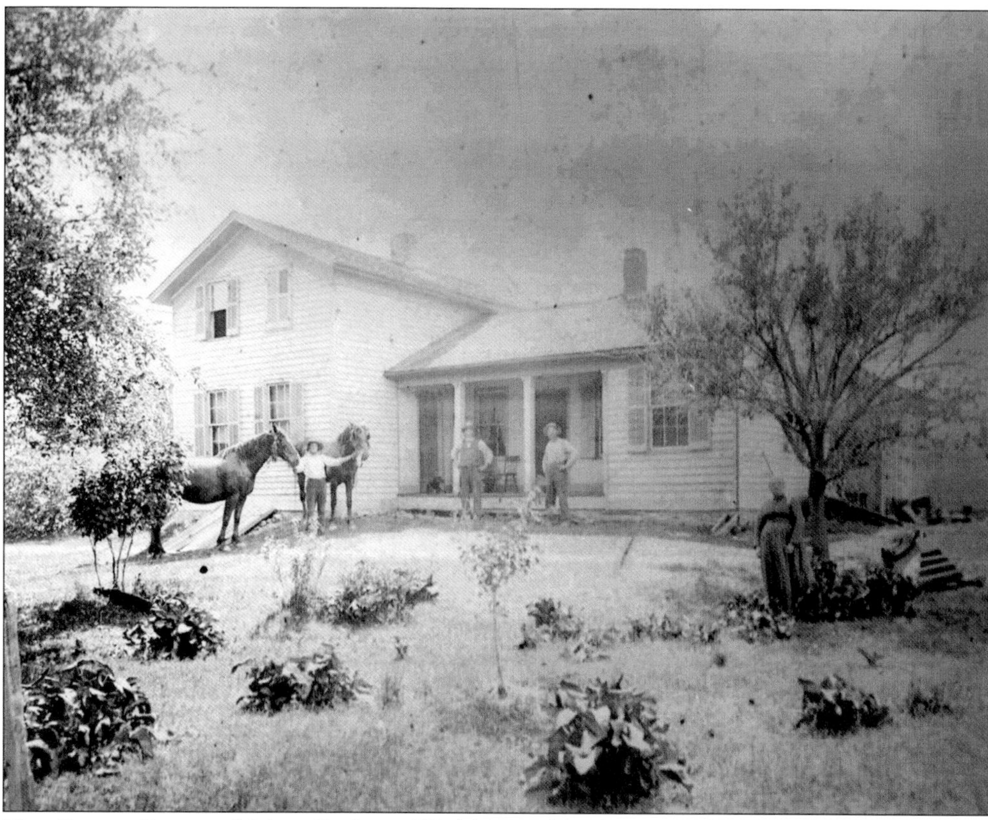

The George Peter and Mary Barbara (Weible) Beehler homestead was located on Dogwood Road, south of New Road. (Courtesy of Dennis and Rae Beehler.)

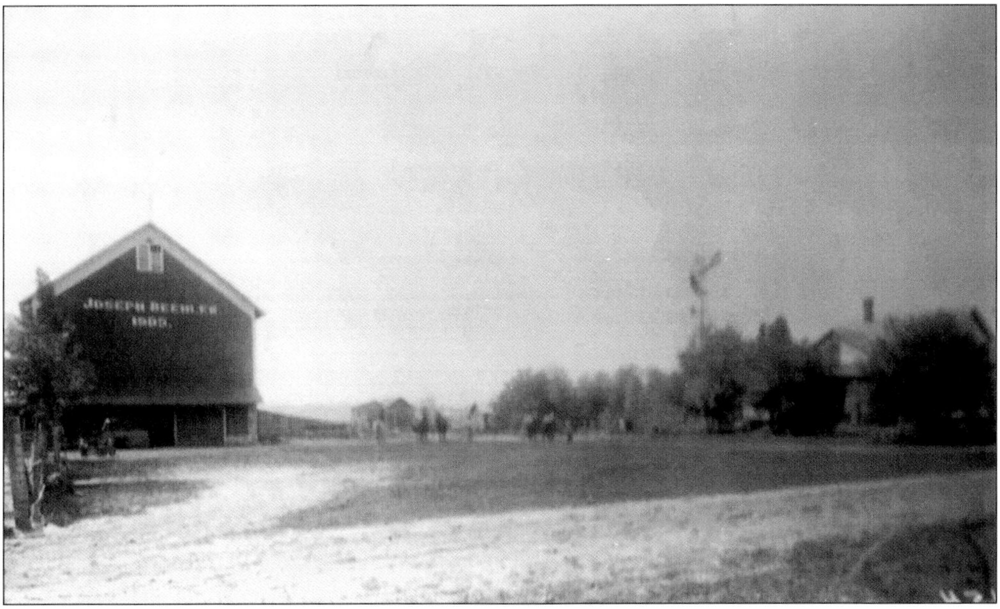

The original homestead of Joseph Beehler was located on Osborne Road between Elm and Dogwood Road. The home is still there today. (Courtesy of Dennis and Rae Beehler.)

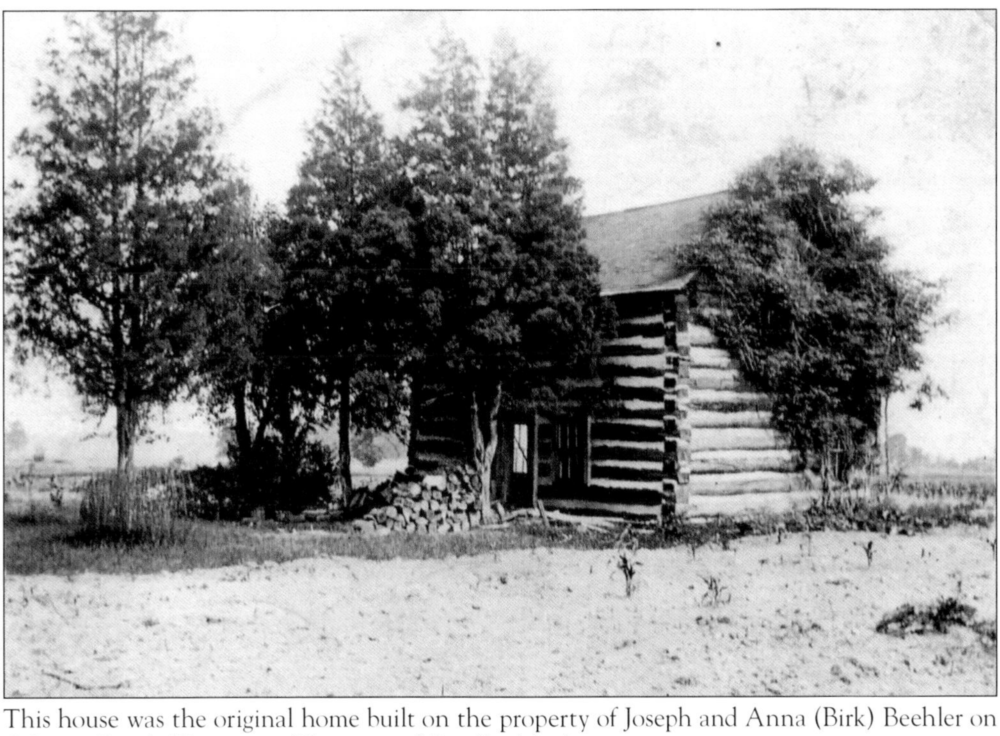

This house was the original home built on the property of Joseph and Anna (Birk) Beehler on Osborne Road. (Courtesy of Dennis and Rae Beehler.)

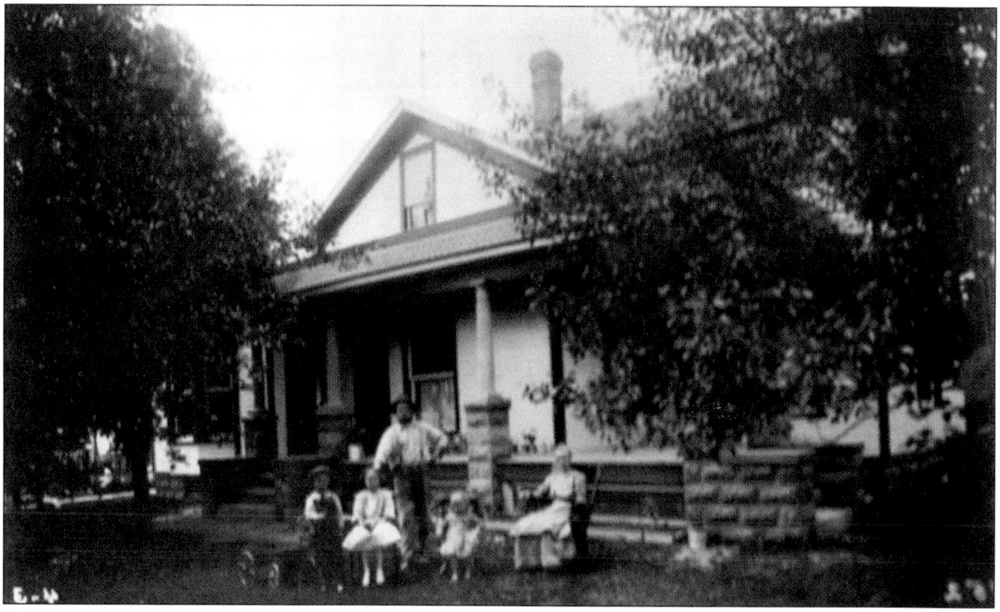

In the summer of 1913, a photograph captured, from left to right, Joseph Beehler, Anna (Birk) Beehler, Clarence Beehler, Edna Beehler, and Clara Beehler at their homestead. (Courtesy of Dennis and Rae Beehler.)

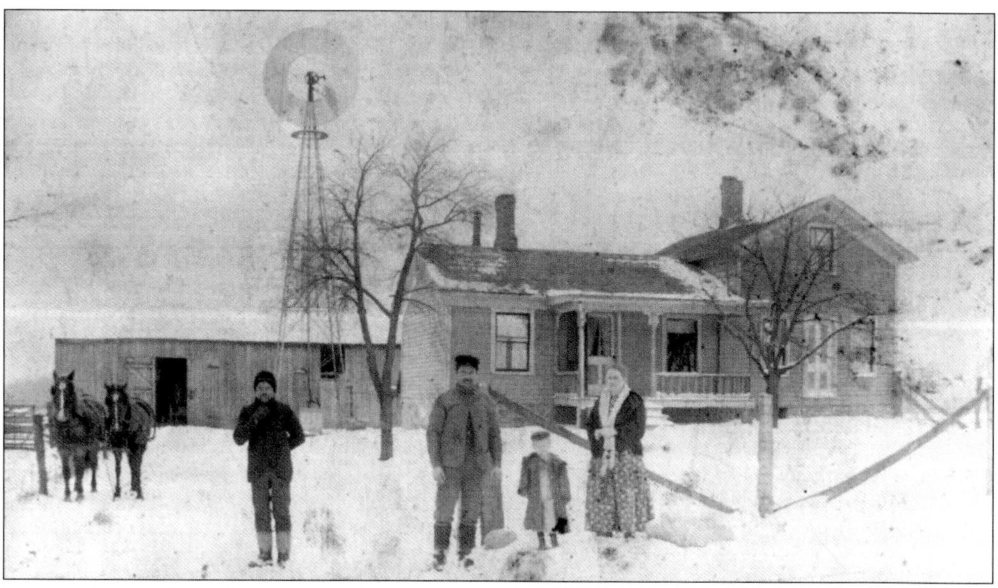

Pictured here with his first wife and first-born son is Joseph Beehler (second from left). Joseph's son is Clement Beehler and his wife is Caroline (Horein) Beehler. (Courtesy of Dennis and Rae Beehler.)

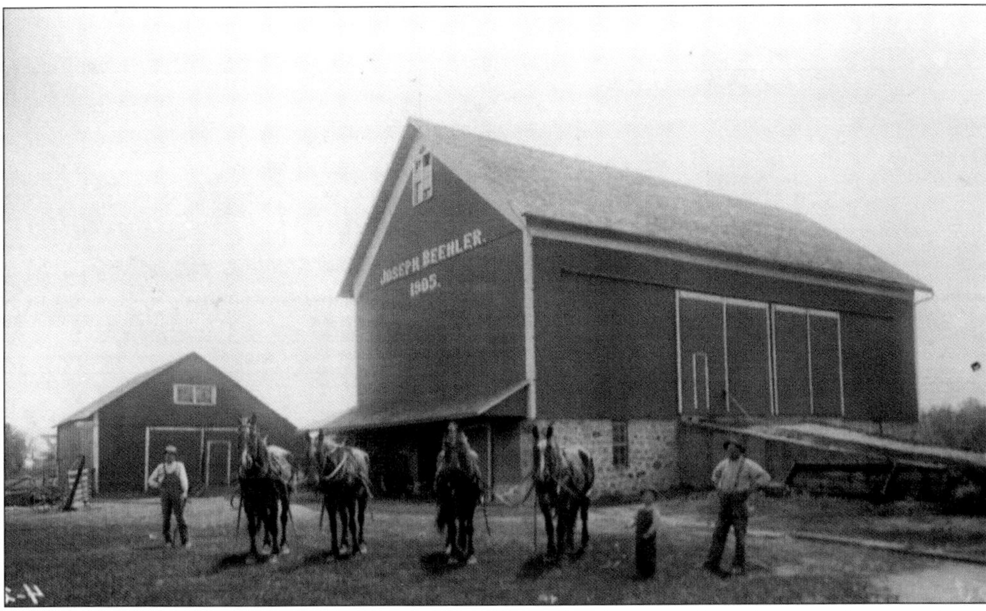


Photographed by the barn as they ready for a day on the farm are, from left to right, Joseph and Clarence Beehler and a hired man. The Beehlers had a total of 180 acres to farm. (Courtesy of Dennis and Rae Beehler.)

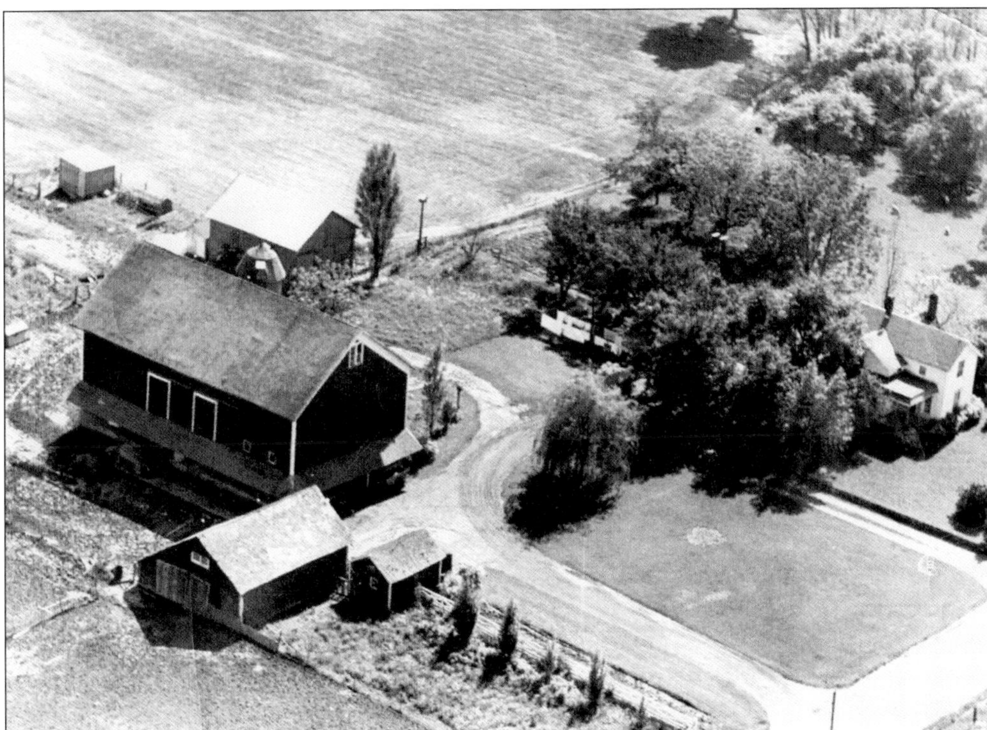

Three generations of Beehlers owned the property on Osborne Road. The first generation was comprised of Joseph and Anna Beehler; the second was Eugene and Alice Beehler; and now Dennis and Rae Beehler live on the site. (Courtesy of Dennis and Rae Beehler.)

The homestead of George and Ella Hahn is located on Kelley Road in Penn Township. (Courtesy of Dale Hahn.)

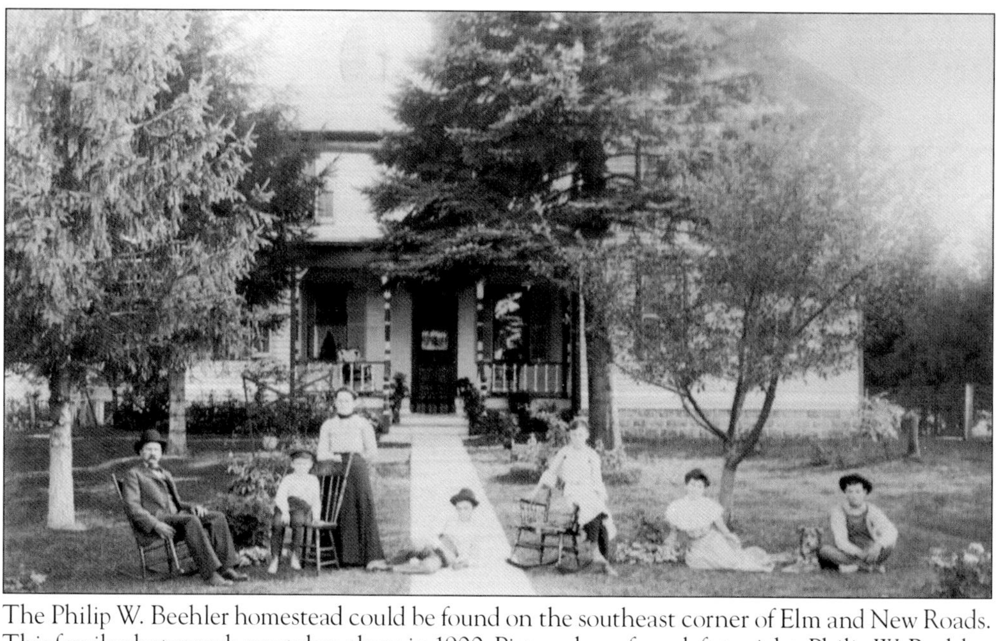

The Philip W. Beehler homestead could be found on the southeast corner of Elm and New Roads. This family photograph was taken there in 1900. Pictured are, from left to right, Philip W. Beehler, Richard Beehler, Elizabeth (Schutz) Beehler, William Beehler, Hattie Reum, Laura Beehler, and Albert Beehler. (Courtesy of Evelyn [Beehler] Salyer.)

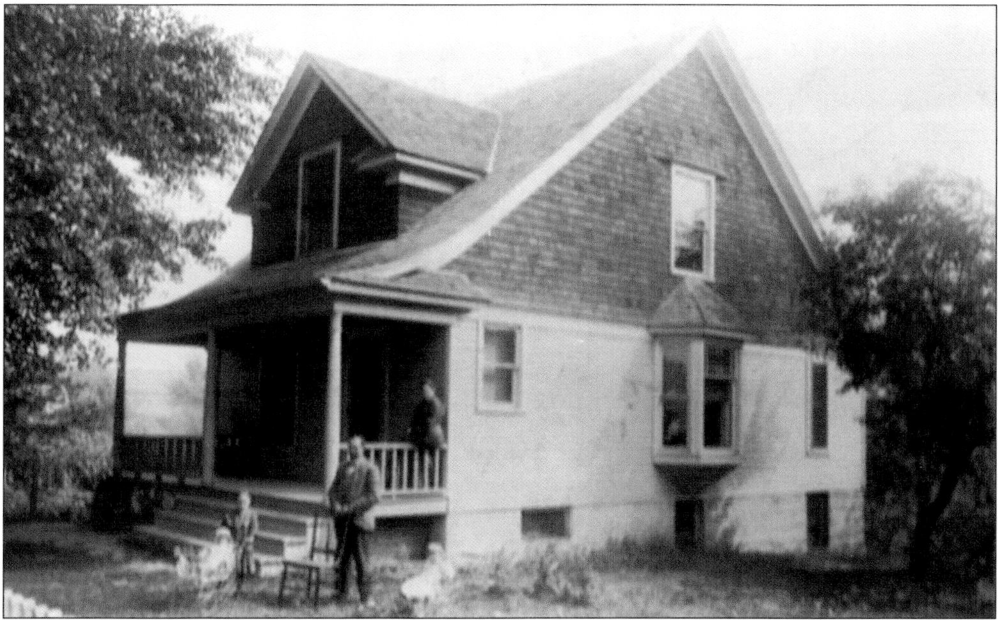

This 1904 photograph was taken in Woodland, Indiana, where the Mochel family made their home. Shown here from left to right are Louise (Weiss) Mochel, Edward Mochel, Marie Mochel, and Myrtle Mochel. (Courtesy of Evelyn [Beehler] Salyer.)

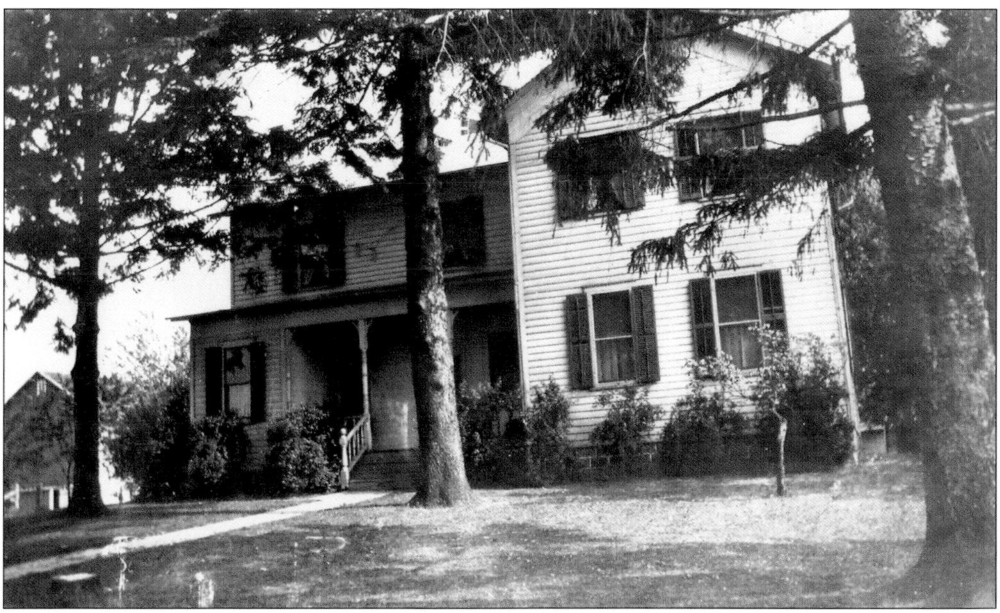

When Richard Beehler had grown to adulthood, he took over the family homestead on New Road in Madison Township. This photograph was taken in 1930. (Courtesy of Evelyn [Beehler] Salyer.)

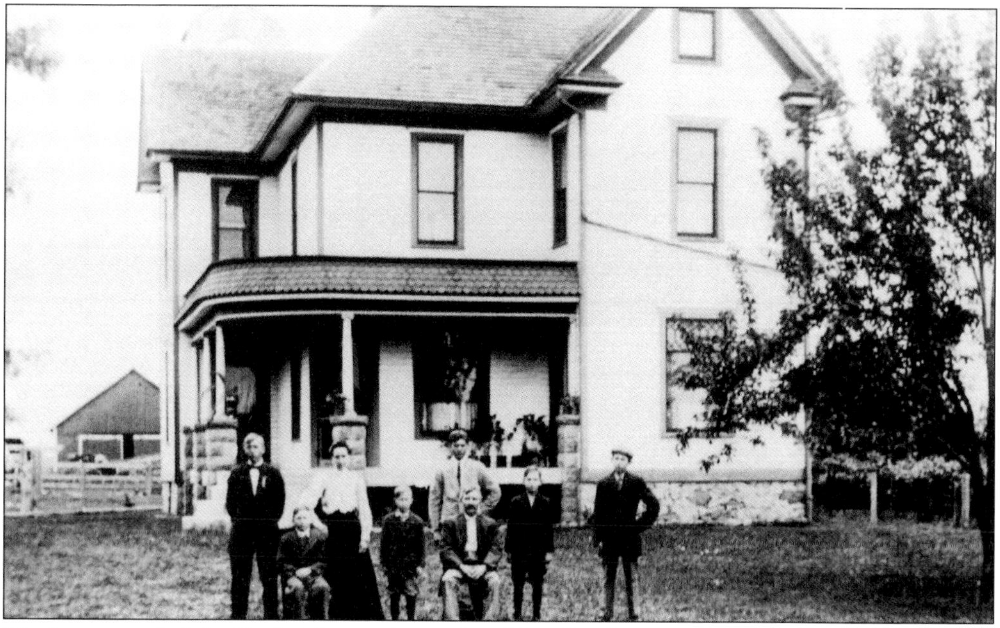

The homestead of the Fredericks was located on New Road just east of Cedar Road, in Madison Township. Pictured here in 1910, from left to right, are Walter Fredericks, Warren Fredericks, Nettie (Anthony) Fredericks, Herbert Fredericks, George Fredericks (sitting), Charles Fredericks, Harry Fredericks, and William Fredericks. The home was destroyed on April 11, 1965, by the Palm Sunday tornadoes. (Courtesy of Dora [Schalliol] Fredericks.)

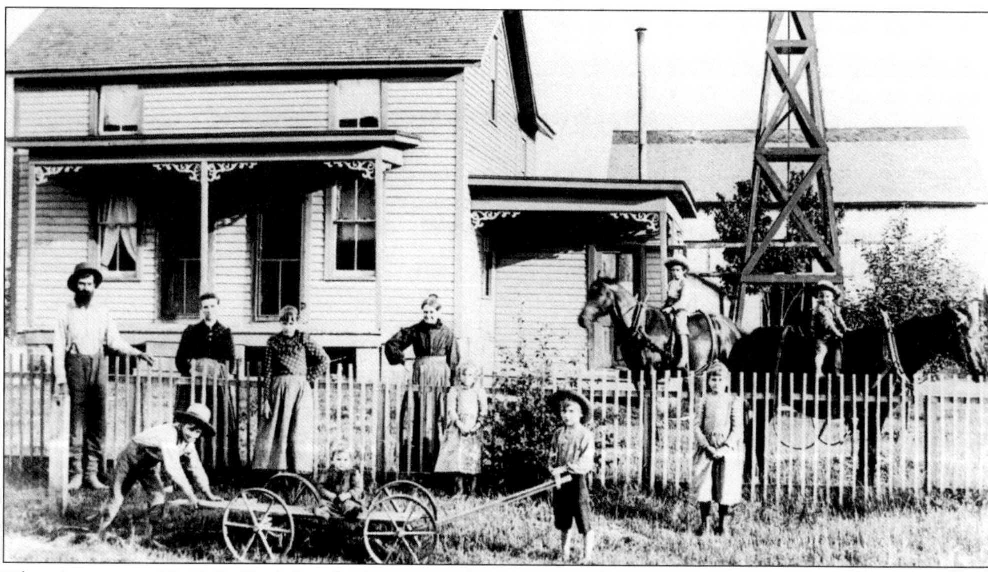

The Augustus G. Schalliol family homestead was located two miles east of Wyatt, Indiana, in Madison Township. Pictured here are, from left to right, Augustus G. Schalliol, Dorothea S. W. (Bollenbacher) Schalliol, Ida Schalliol, Margaret E. (Hauptreif) Schalliol (mother of Augustus), Amelia Schalliol, Nora Schalliol (with wagon), Victor Schalliol (pushing), Minnie Schalliol (riding), Thaddeus Schalliol (pulling), and Walter Schalliol and Grover Schalliol (both on the horses). Two more daughters were born after this 1895 picture, Elsie Schalliol and Mabel Schalliol. (Courtesy of Michael and Joyce Schalliol.)

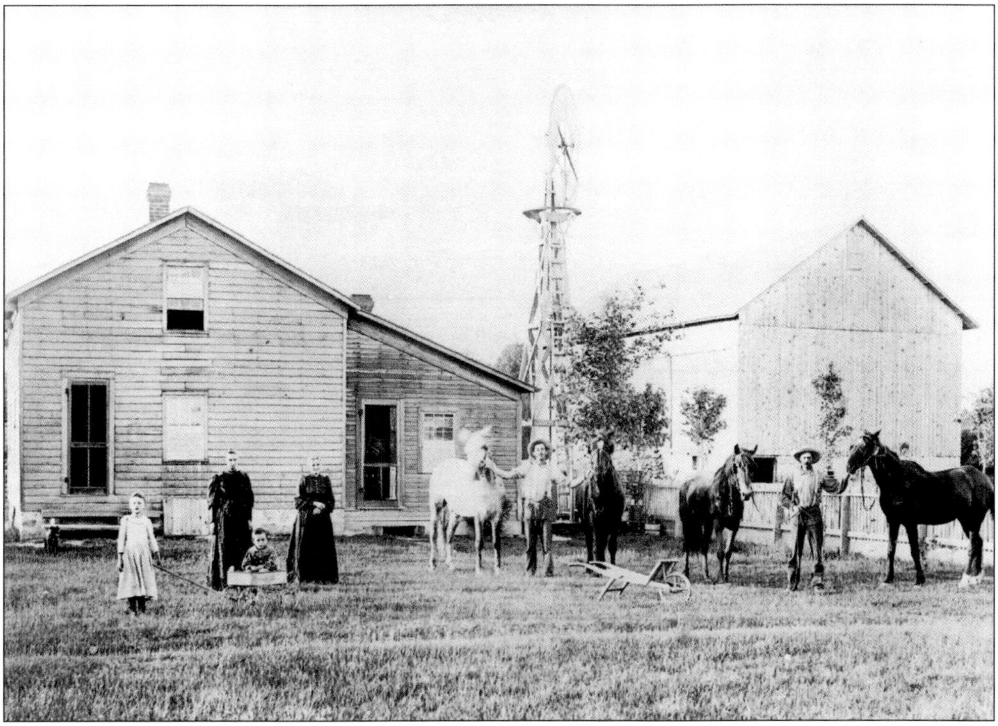

The original Marker homestead is pictured here. In the photograph, from left to right, are Nora Marker, Mary (Mason) Marker, Delbert Marker, Barbara Belser Mason, Charles Keil, and Christopher Frederick Marker. (Courtesy of John and Judy Marker.)

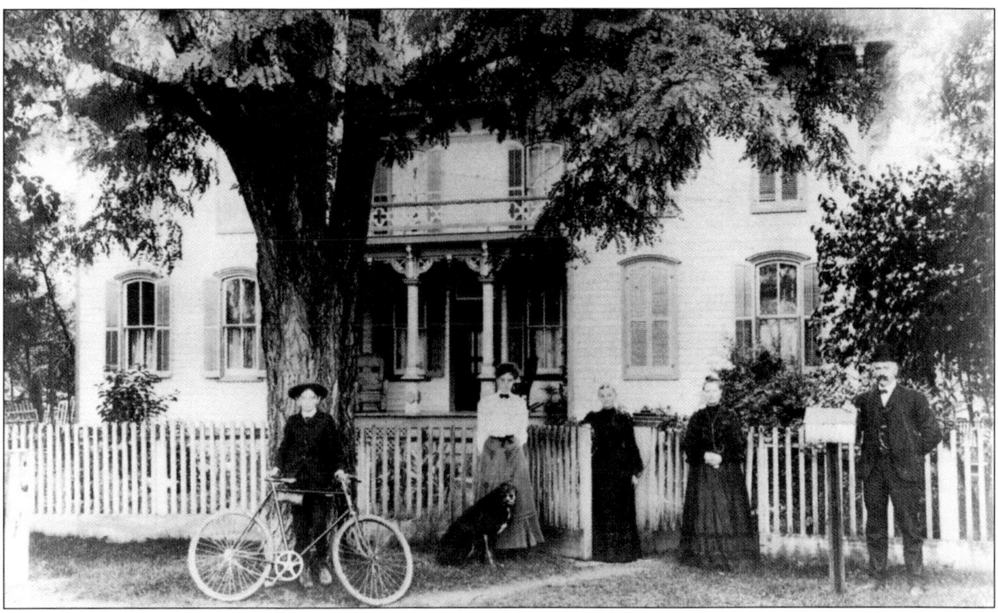

The newly rebuilt homestead of Christopher Frederick Marker is pictured here. The family lived on New Road between Fir Road and Madison Trail, in Madison Township. Pictured from left to right are Delbert Marker, Nora Marker, Barbara Belser Mason, Mary (Mason) Marker, and Christopher Frederick Marker. (Courtesy of John and Judy Marker.)

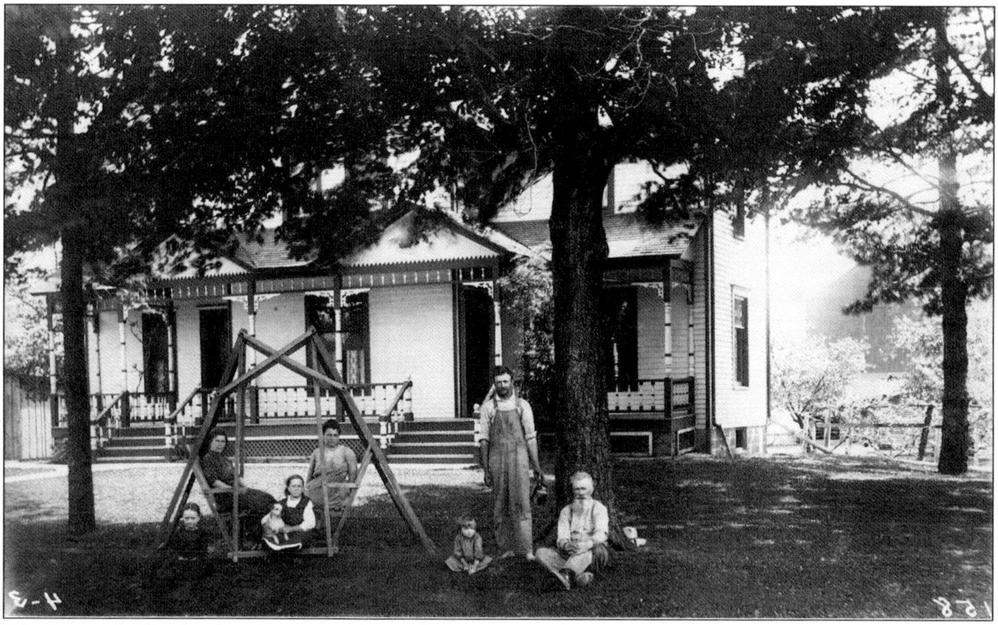

The Louis Bollenbacher homestead was located on Dogwood Road just south of Osborne Road. Pictured here in 1910, from left to right, are the following: (first row) Violet Martin, Nellie (Bollenbacher) Birk, Marie Martin, and Louis Bollenbacher; (second row) Nora (Bollenbacher) Martin, Anna Bollenbacher, and Weaver Martin. (Courtesy of Jeanette [Battles] Martin.)

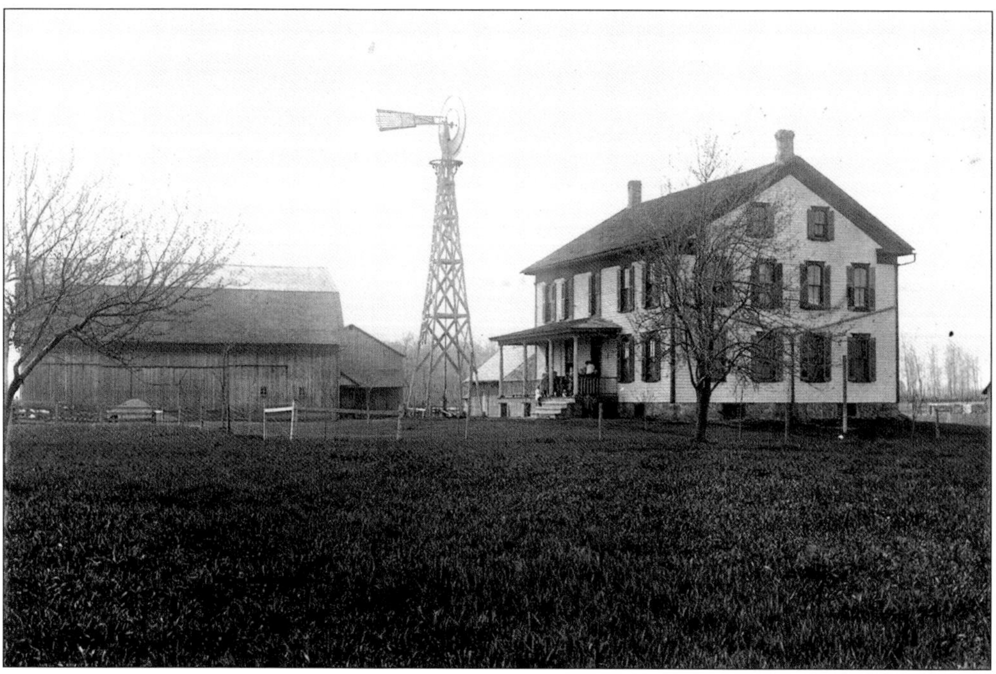

The homestead of Jake and Lena Berger was located on Madison Road between Beech and Cedar Roads. (Courtesy of Rosemary [Contat] Dixon.)

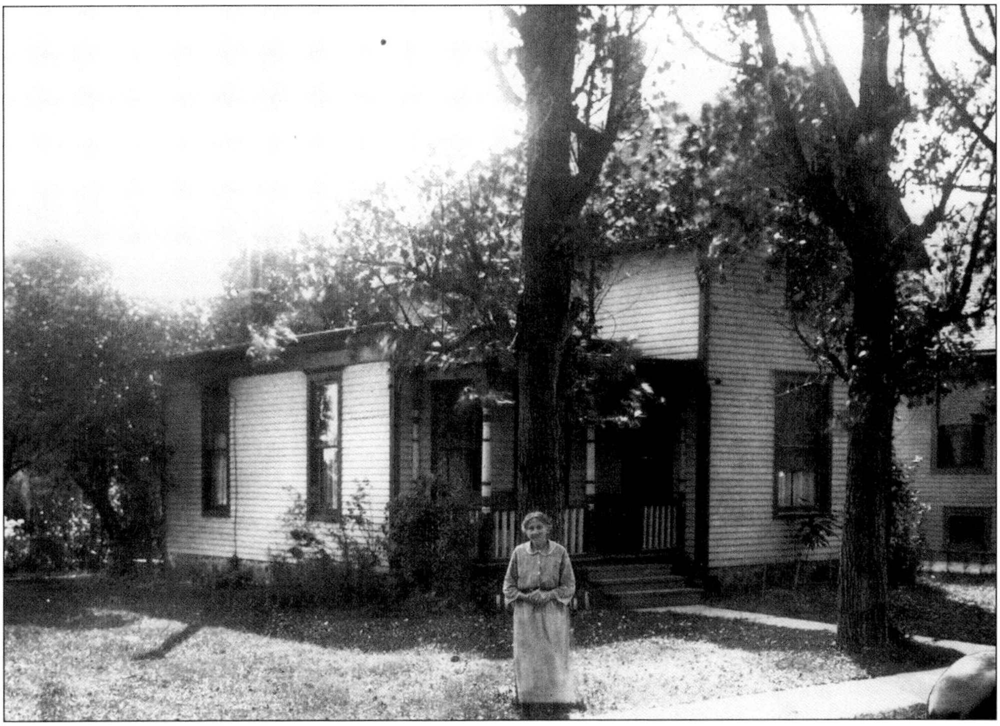

Sophia Aline (Juillerat) Bendit is photographed here at her home in downtown Wyatt, Indiana. (Courtesy of Vicki Berger.)

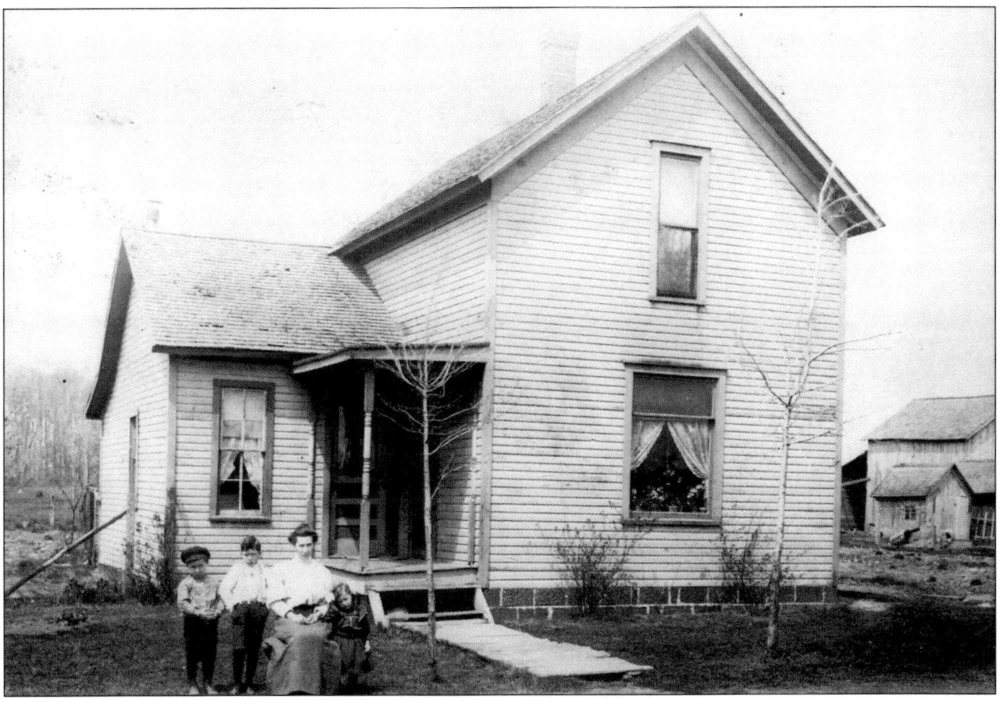

This photograph was taken in Wyatt, Indiana, at the home of, from left to right, Paul Berger, Albert Berger, Edith (Bendit) Berger, and Edna Berger. (Courtesy of Vicki Berger.)

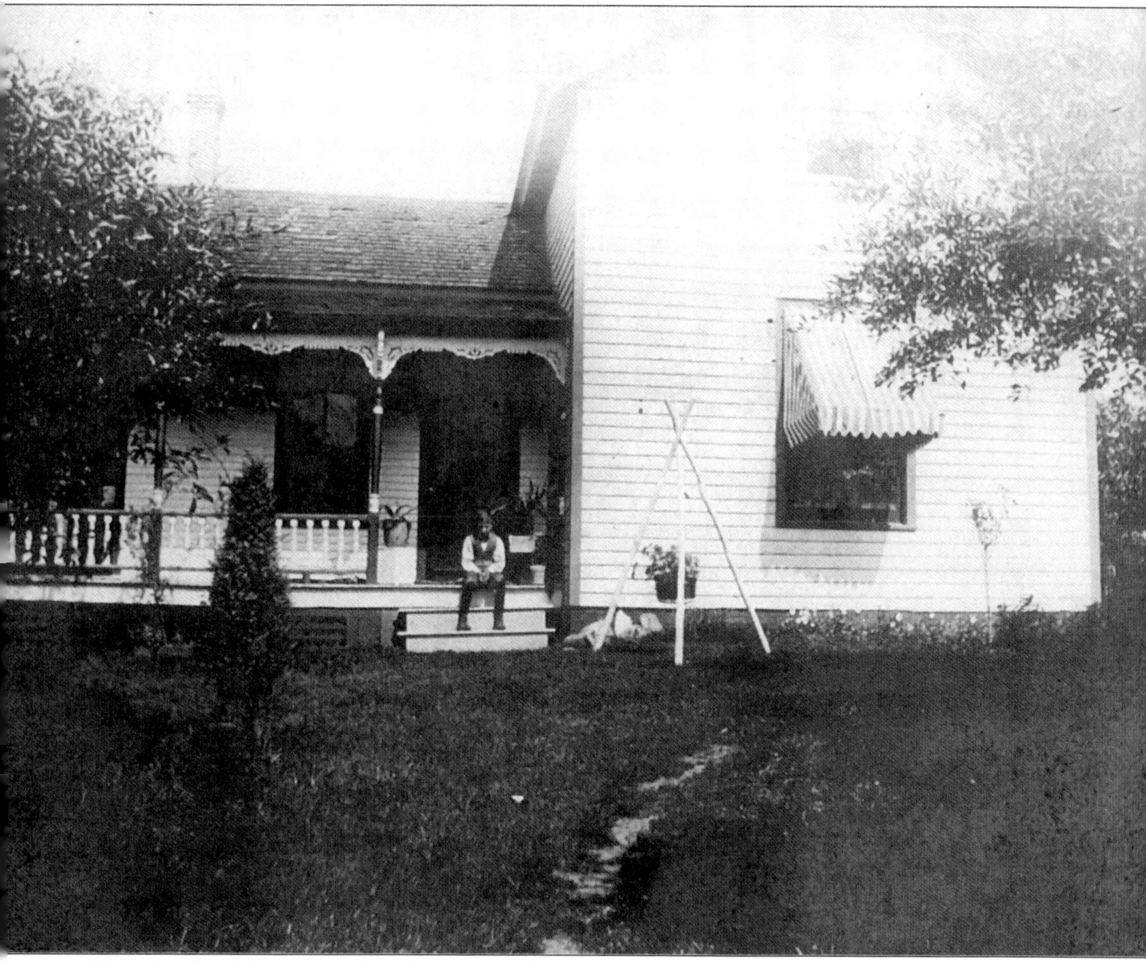

The Matz family homestead was located on the southeast corner of Blackberry and Harrison Roads, in Penn Township. This photograph was taken in 1902. (Courtesy of Rosemary [Contat] Dixon.)

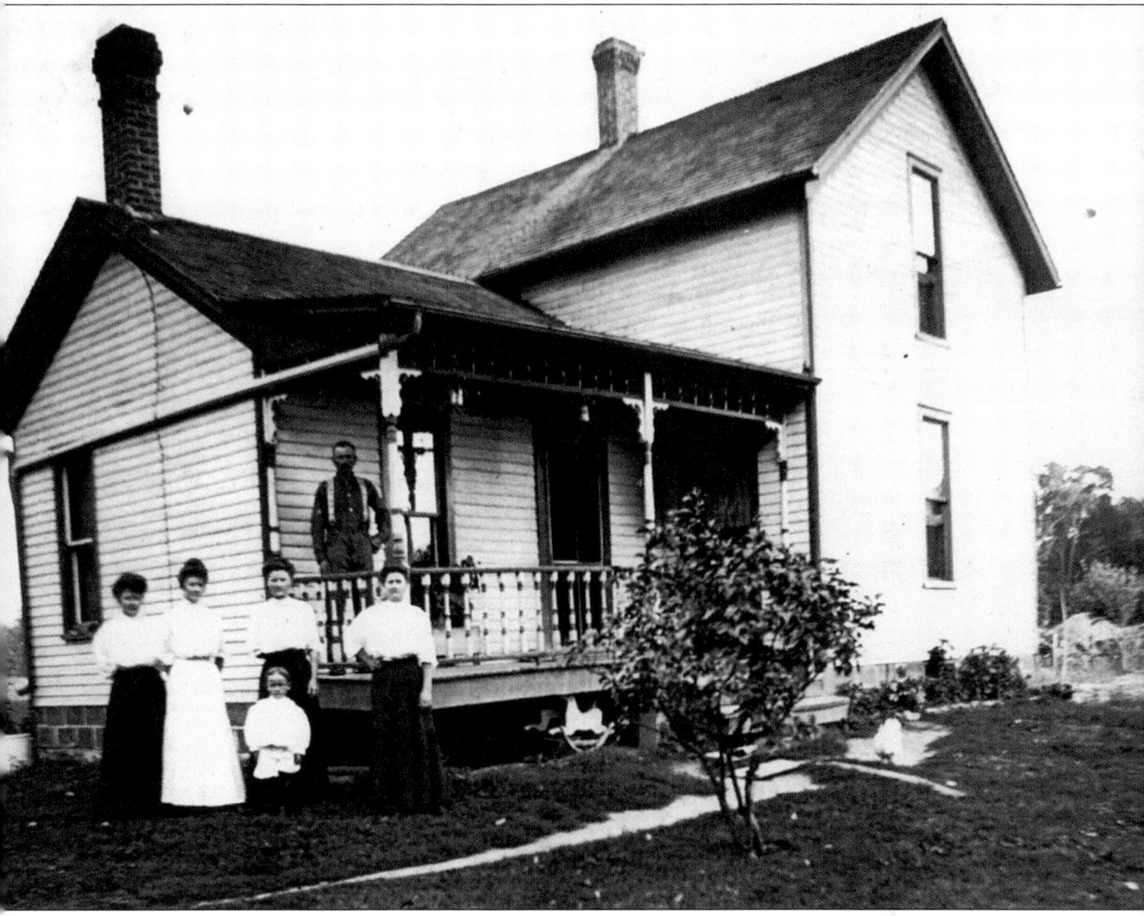

The Scheidegger family home was located on Fir Road. Pictured are, from left to right, Elizabeth (Scheidegger) Bendit, Anna Barbara (Scheidegger) Smith, Mary (Scheidegger) Gase, Emma (Scheidegger) Balmer (with her son Arthur Balmer), and Alexander Scheidegger (on the porch). (Courtesy of Vicki Berger.)

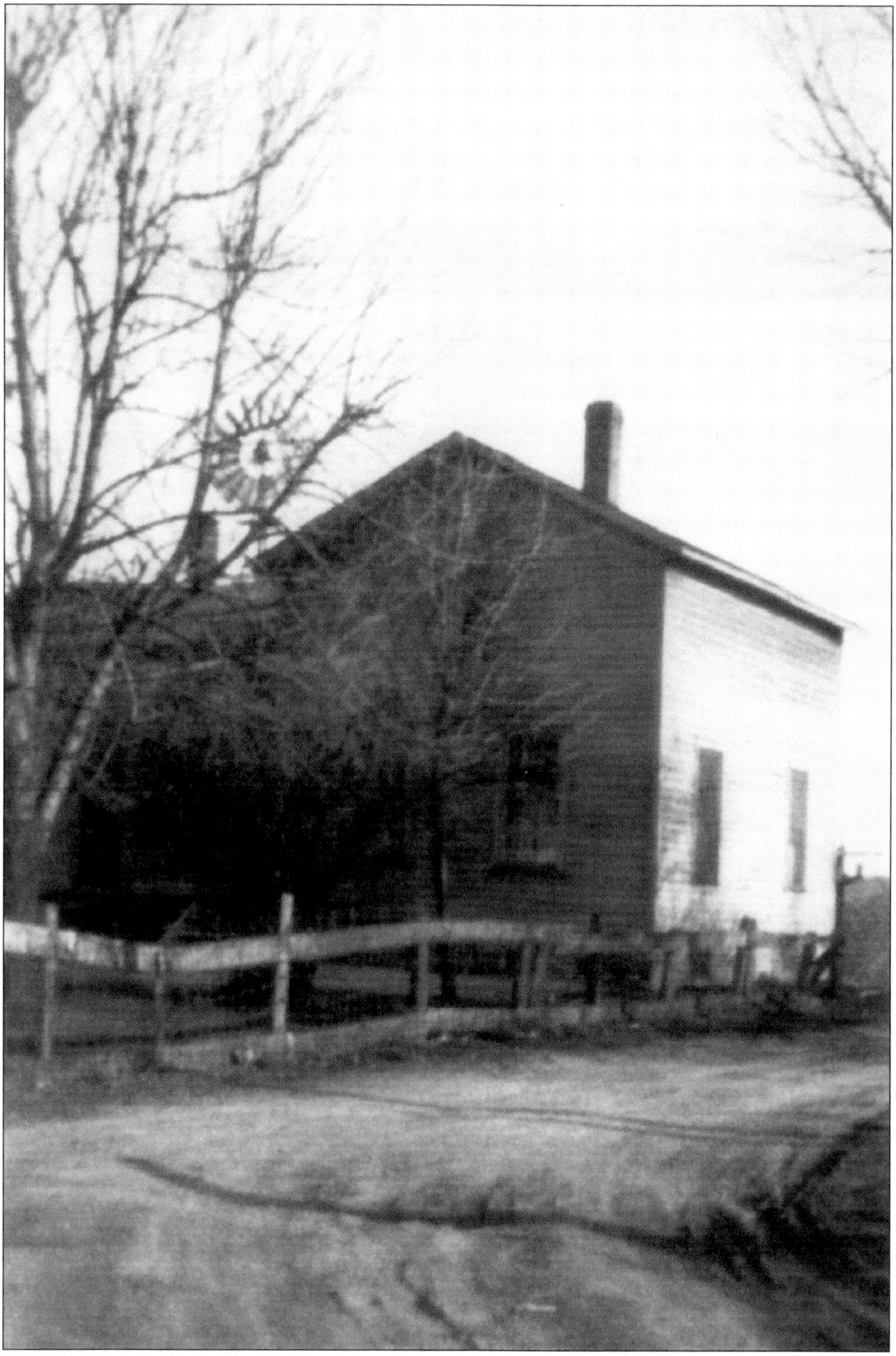

This photograph shows the former home of Emil Berger and Rosa (Rosti) Berger, located on Madison Road. (Courtesy of Vicki Berger.)

# *Three*

# CLASS PICTURES

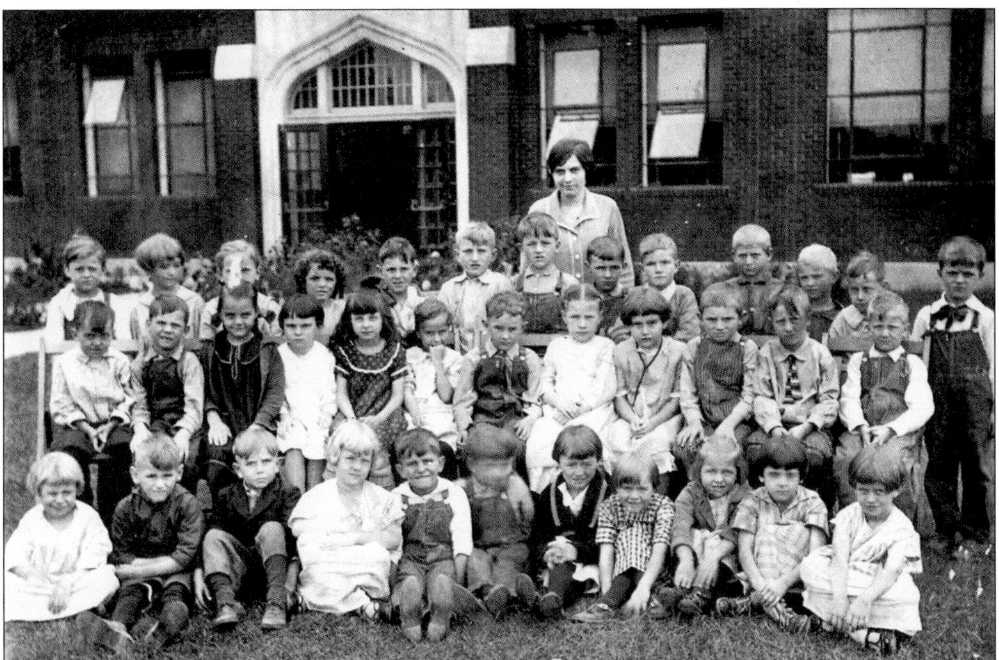

This is a 1920s class picture from the old Madison Township School. (Courtesy of the author.)

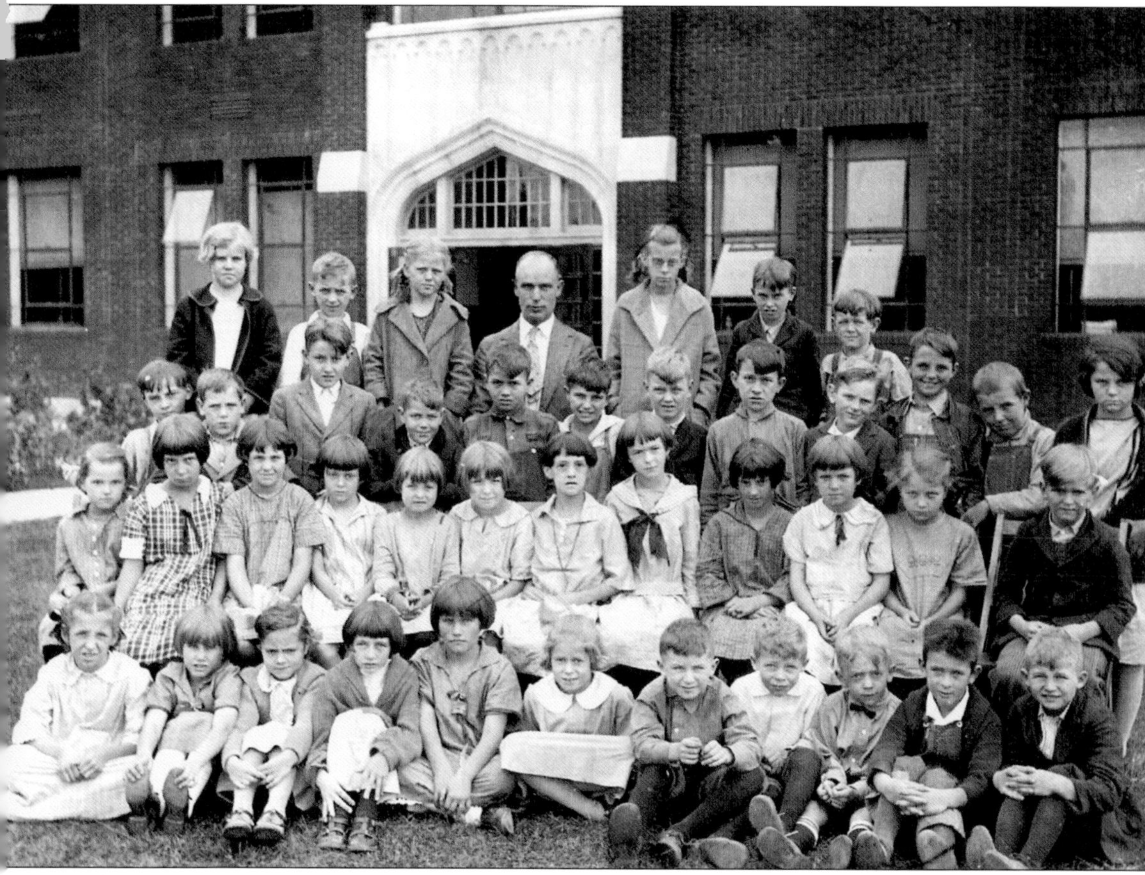

This class picture from Madison Township School was also taken in the 1920s. (Courtesy of the author.)

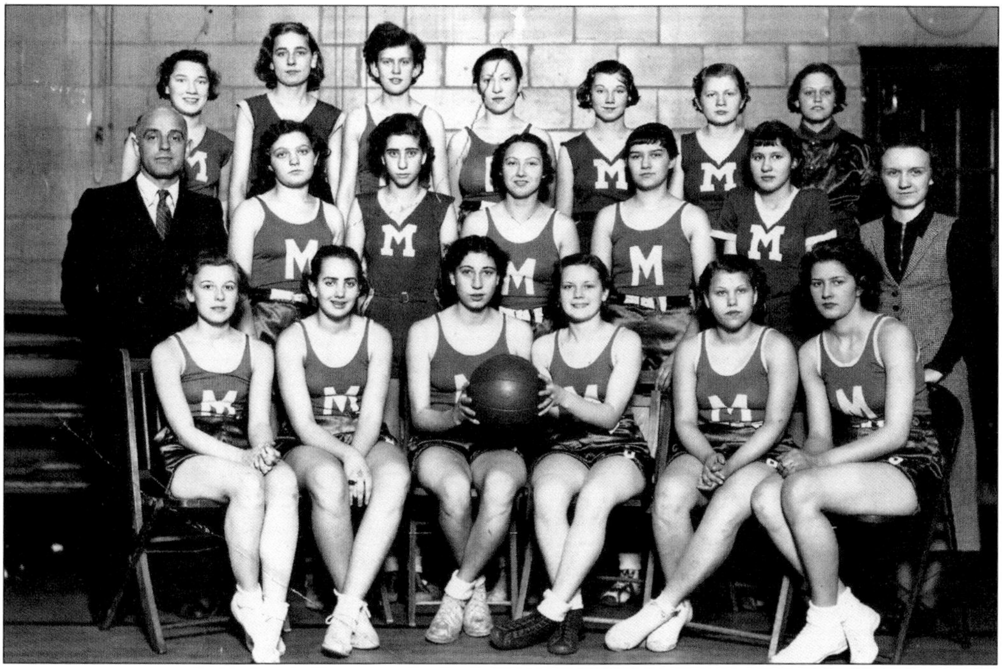

Taken during the 1936–1937 school year, this picture shows the Madison Township School girls basketball team. (Courtesy of the author.)

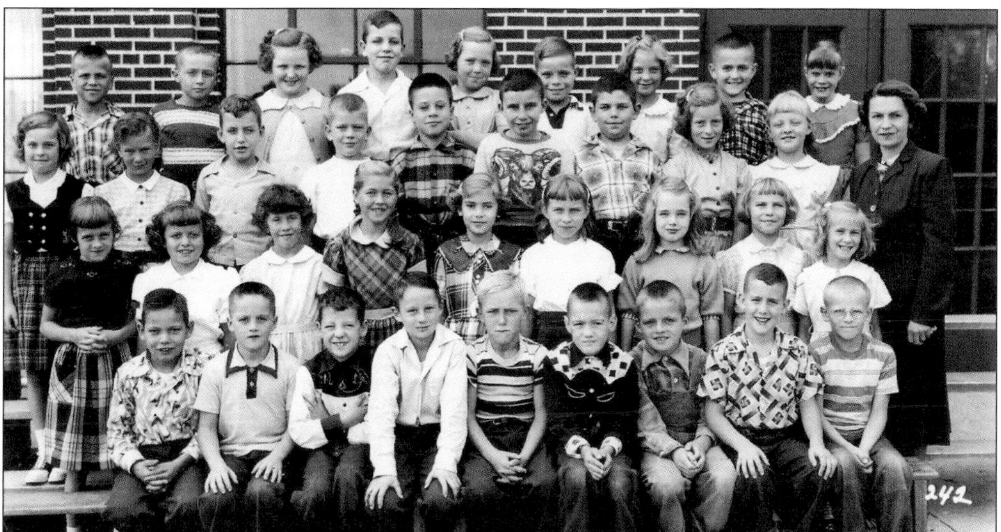

The 1953–1954 third-grade class from Madison Township School is pictured here. Shown, from left to right, are the following: (first row) Carl Moser, Terry Christman, Junior Kobold, Jim Dunkleberger, Larry Schutz, Richard Hunsberger, Robert Heltzel, Danny Shaw, and Terry Manges; (second row) Lynn Horvath, Ruthann Schweisberger, Marilyn Cook, Virginia Englehardt, Sharon Grise, Dion Schroder, Ann Wallace, Nancy Stahley, and Jane Whitehead; (third row) Charlene VanDeKeere, Dorothy Moser, LaVern Davidhizar, James Beehler, Wayne Fritz, Duane Fushs, Laurence Roeder, Kay Hayden, Annabell Barden, and Mrs. Eshelman (teacher); (fourth row) Ronald Holmes, Floyd Hummel, Irene Walters, Terry Wisler, Judy Huston, Gary Oswalt, Edith Stewart, Bobby Troxel, and Alliene Meeks. (Courtesy of the author.)

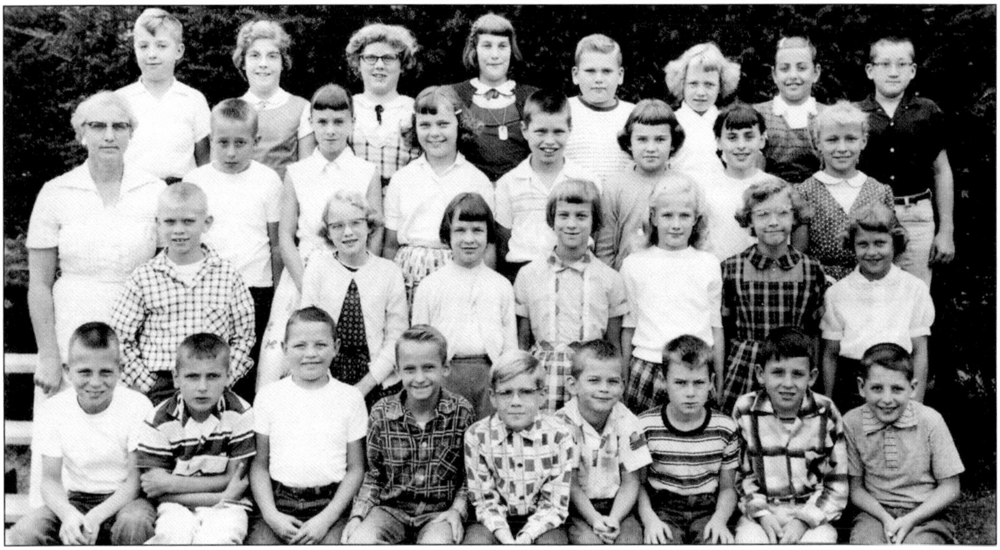

The fourth-grade class of 1957–1958 from Madison Township School is shown here. Pictured are, from left to right, as follows: (first row) Donald Holmes, Thomas Jordan, Thomas Sherk, Todd Horvath, Jerry Berger, Donald Horein, David Stuber, Roger Mutti, and Brian Henderson; (second row) Alan Beehler, Rebecca Laidig, Patricia Veheye, Shirlee Reed, Jill Frederickson, Sandra Tom, and Sharon DeLoddere; (third row) Mrs. Beehler (teacher), John Beer, Pamela Blue, Karen Hunsberger, Charles Johnson, Shela Conrad, Carol Duarte, and Lois Schutz; (fourth row) Maynard Hahn, Barbara Stiver, Starless Rader, Marilyn Hummel, Ronald Schriver, Albertha Brinkhoff, Roberta Davidhizar, and Dennis Flickinger. (Courtesy of the author.)

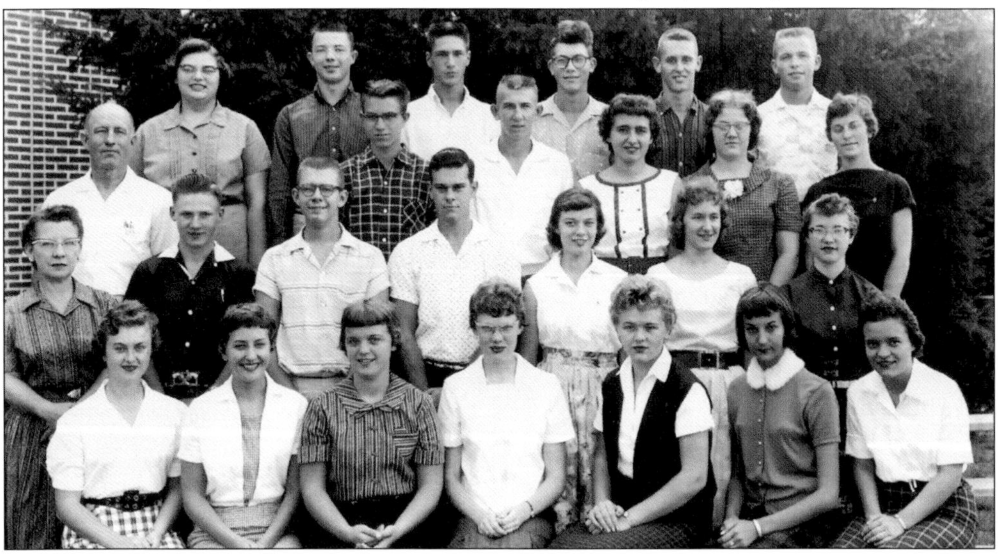

The junior class of 1959 from Madison Township School is featured here. Pictured are, from left to right, the following: (first row) Judy Horein, Kathryn Felton, Darlene Reum, Barbara Schrader, Carol Kobold, Donna Hummel, and Phyllis Hiatt; (second row) Marion Kintzel (sponsor), Donald Nettrour, Tom Hahn, Dennis McCormack, Patricia Beehler, Ruth Woods, and Janet VanDeKeere; (third row) Glenmore Horein (sponsor), William Mikel, Hal Whitehead, Judy Martin, Judy Stiber, and Sarah Englehardt; (fourth row) Minnie Roeder, Larry Fisher, Byron Blue, Lynn Becker, Dick Jordan, and Charles Selner. (Courtesy of the author.)

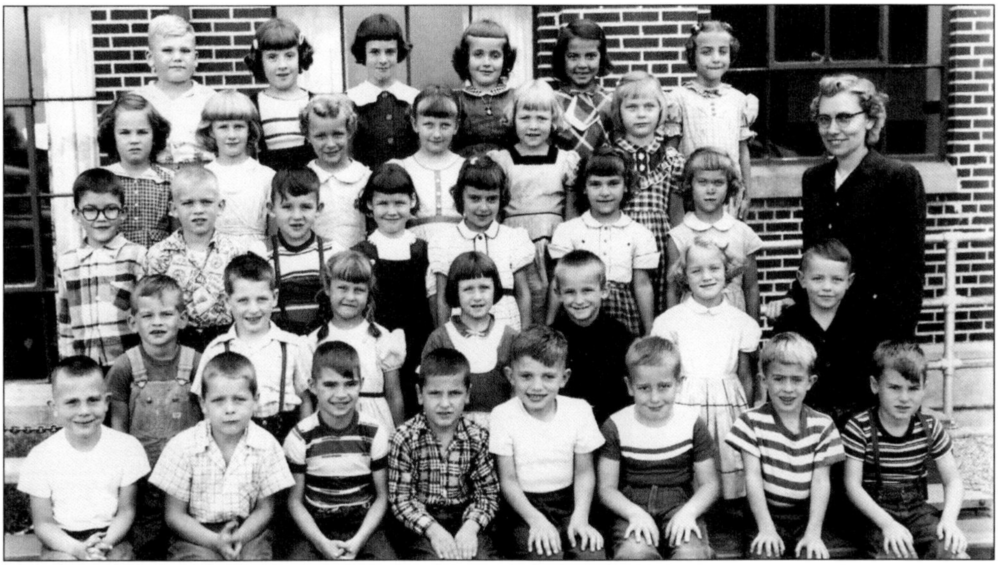

This is the first-grade class of 1954–1955 from Madison Township School. Pictured are, from left to right, the following: (first row) Donnie Holmes, Dick Johnson, Mark Schroeder, Tommy Jordan, Dennis Fox, John Beer, John Weil, and David Stuber; (second row) Donald Horein, Brian Henderson, Sharon DeLoddere, Nancy Hummel, Todd Horvath, Becky Laidig, Tommy Sherk, and Miss Eppley (teacher); (third row) David Schlarb, Alan Beehler, Roger Mutti, Patty Verheye, Diane Stuckey, Judy Hargus, and Shirlee Reed; (fourth row) Shela Conrad, Jill Frederickson, Lois Schutz, Mary Moser, Albertha Brinkhoff, and Karen Hunsberger; (fifth row) Ronnie Schriver, Barbara Stiver, Pamela Blue, Jill Gerber, Minnie Morrison, and Roberta Davidhizar. (Courtesy of the author.)

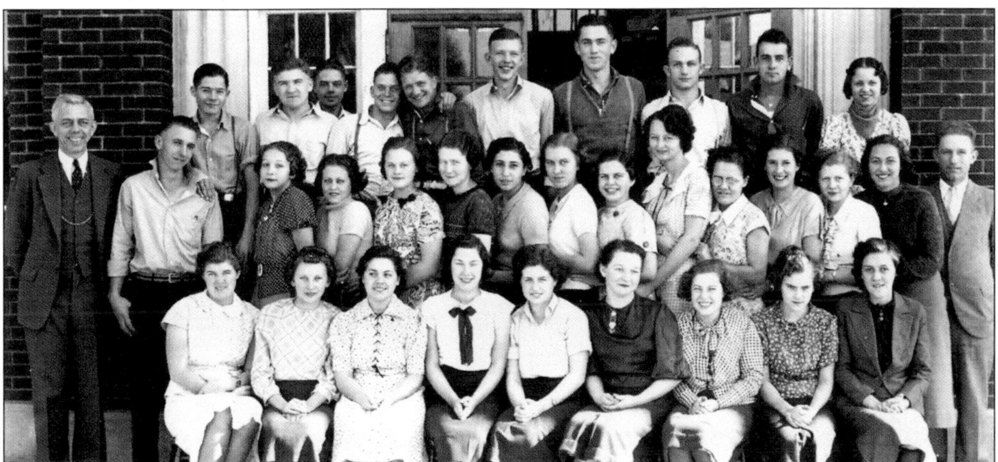

The senior class of 1938 from Madison Township School is pictured here. Shown are, from left to right, as follows: (first row) Evelyn Wolfe, Margaret Geyter, Inez Kline, Themla Geyer, Anna Hohl, Lora Contat, Edna Seese, Maribelle Fisher, and Vera Bixler; (second row) Mr. Newman (teacher), Dale Ehert, Delores Fox, Mabel Schweisberger, Mildred Germann, Bernice Johnson, Ruth Zeiger, Natalie Fredricks, Alice Heinke, Lucille Wagner, Jane Boner, LaVerna LaFree, Virginia Battles, Elnora Marburger, and Mr. Horein (sponsor); (third row) Keith Nash, Alfred LaVine, Preston Hagey, Arnold Stillson, Eugene Beehler, Arthur Schlifke, Forest Oakley, Kenneth E. Hummel, Kenneth S. Hummel, and Lois Godshalk. (Courtesy of the author.)

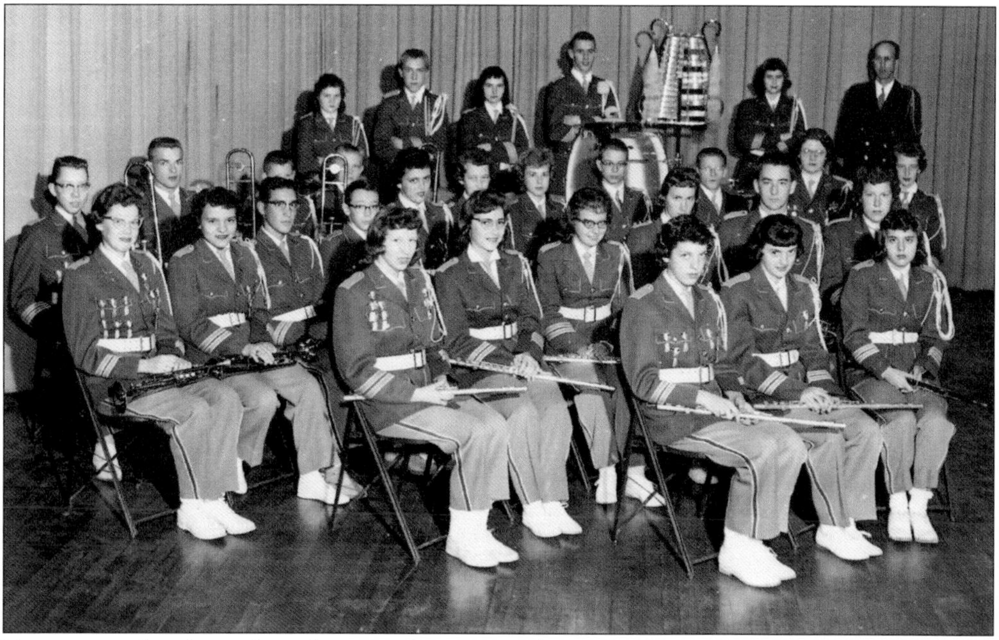

Twenty-nine band members from Madison Township School are shown in this photograph. (Courtesy of the author.)

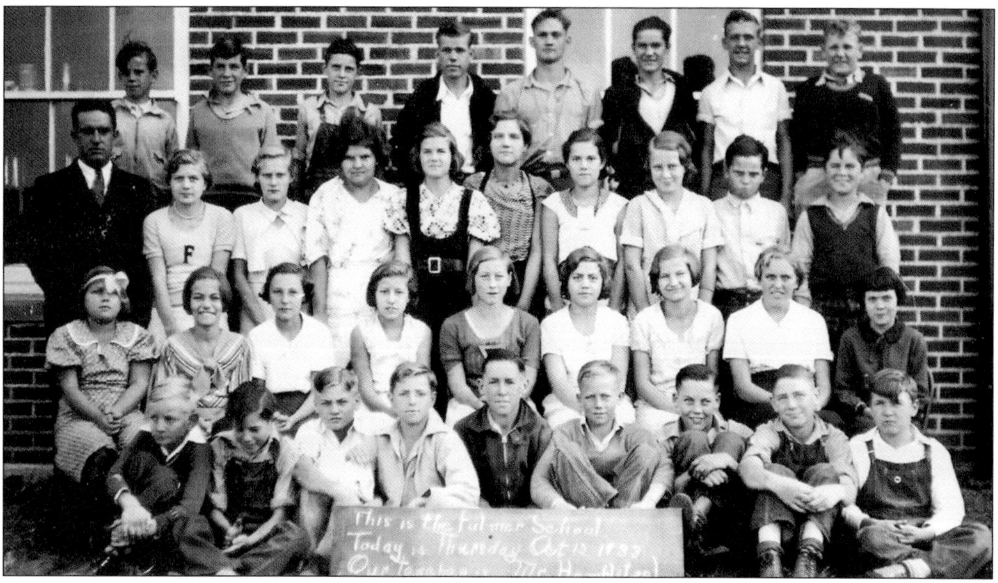


The seventh- and eighth-grade classes at Fulmer School were photographed on October 12, 1933. Pictured are, from left to right, the following: (first row) Robert Harlin, Keith Nash, Paul Knapp, Worthy Rowe, Frank Besinger, James Sellers, Dick Anderson, Omar Hunsberger, and Alfred LaVine; (second row) Emily Hawkins, Margaret Puller, Elouise Kloppenstien, Isabell Williams, Merion Hawkins, Inez Kline, France Taruineer, Anna Pollitt, and Mariyln Seybold; (third row) Mr. Deuwaine Hawblitzel (teacher), Virginia Battles, June Weiss, Carol Miller, Evelyn Wolfe, Wilma Richards, June Wellman, Esther Collins, Lawrence Britton, and Billy Geist; (fourth row) Darrell Matchett, Robert Kloppenstein, Eugene Kloppenstein, Harley Andrews, Loyd Richards, Lewis Manuwal, George Andrews, and Delmer Lundstrom. (Courtesy of the author.)

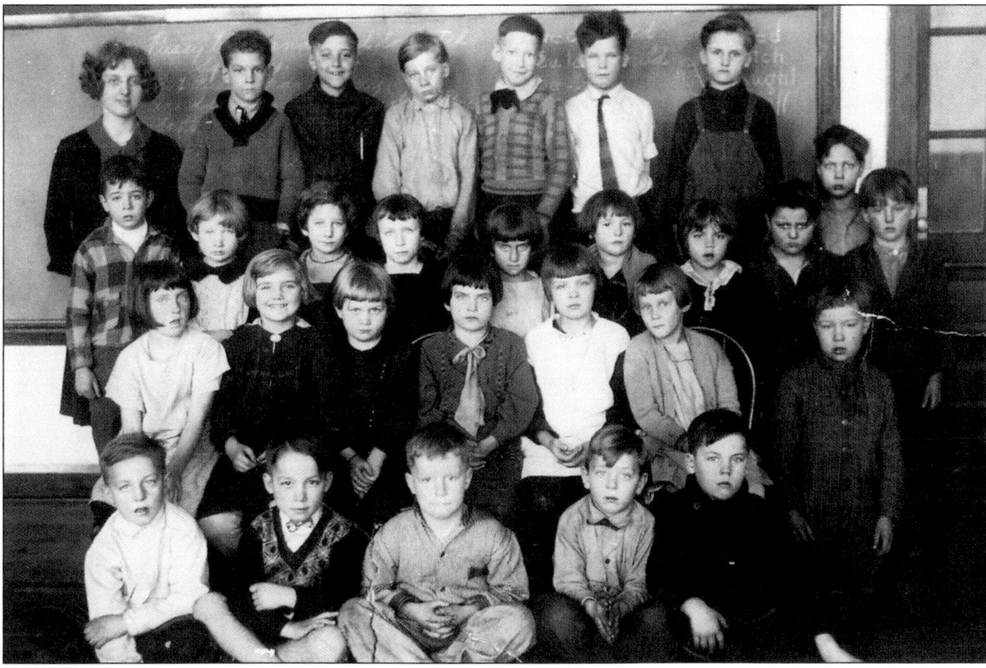
A class from the Fulmer School is shown here. (Courtesy of the author.)

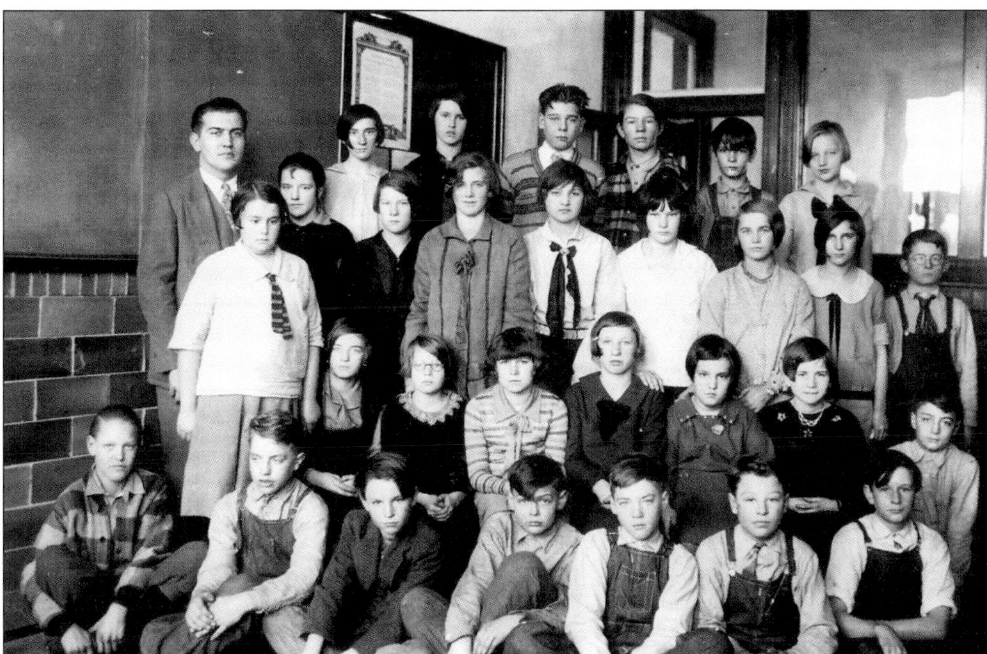
Another class from the Fulmer School is also pictured. (Courtesy of the author.)

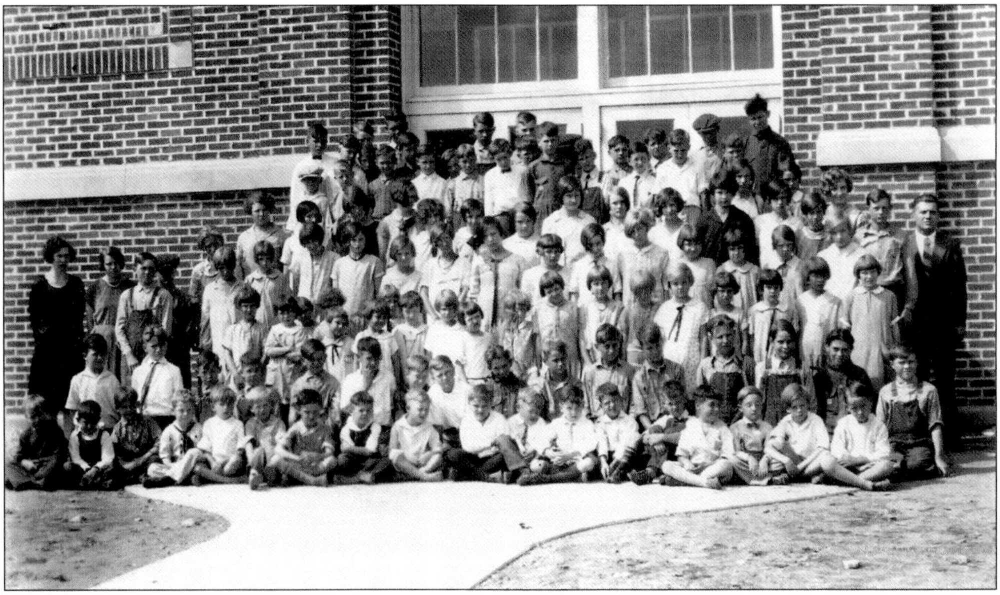

A class from the Fulmer School is pictured here around 1932. (Courtesy of the author.)

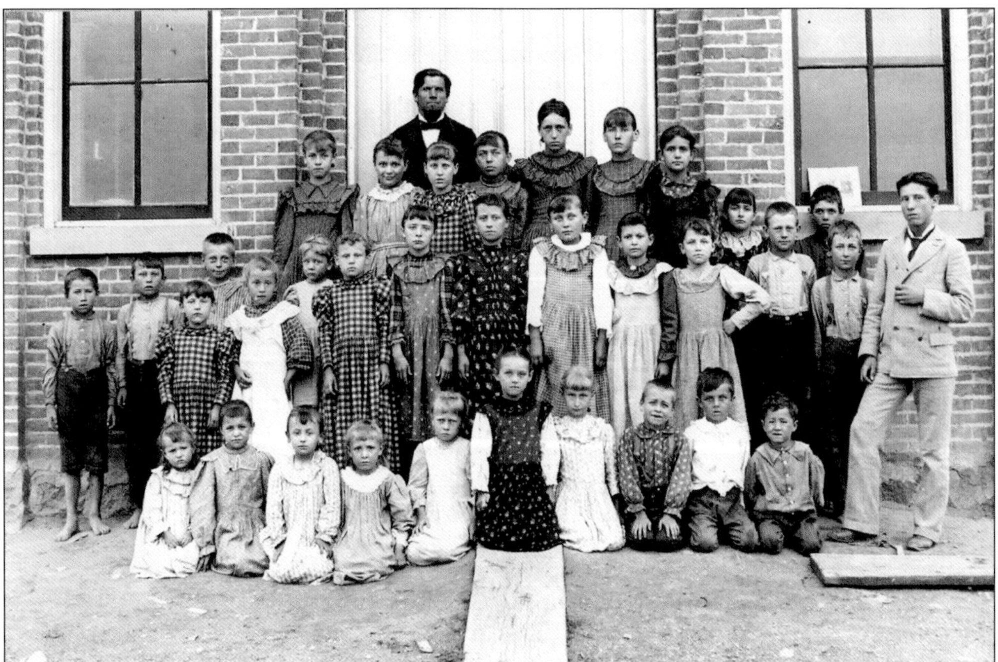

Taken around 1900, this photograph is of the one-room Brenneman schoolhouse, located on the corner of Beech and New Roads in Madison Township. (Courtesy of the author.)

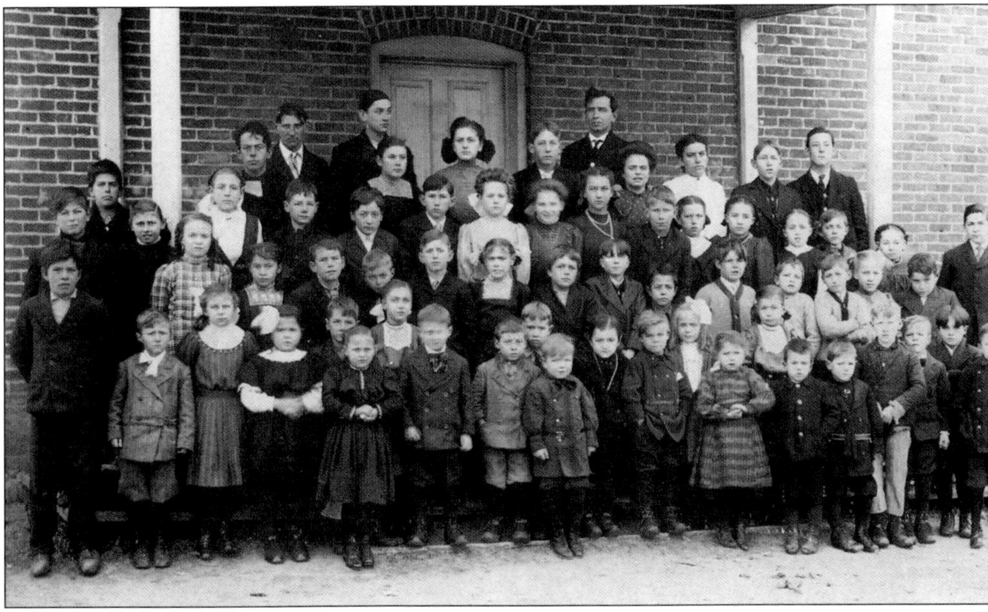

This photograph of the one-room Brenneman School in Madison Township was taken in 1910. Charles J. Conrad was the teacher at the school for 30 years. (Courtesy of the author.)

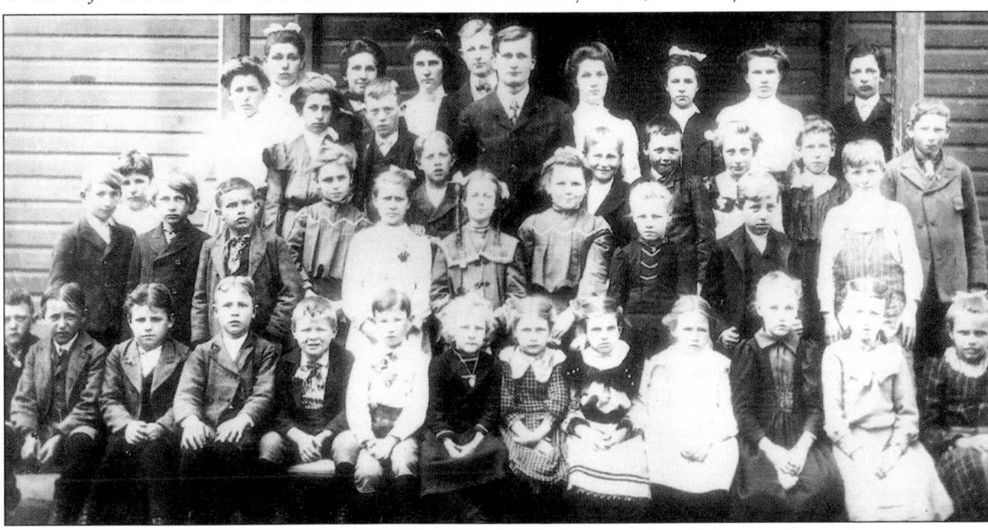

This class picture was taken in 1904 at Fred Esenwein School, located on the corners of Dogwood and Shively Roads. Pictured are, from left to right, the following: (first row) Willard Pittman, Victor Beehler, Lloyd Smith, Wallace Boocher, Oscar Mutti, Walter Strahler, Bertha Leatherman, Yetta Zimmerly, Sophia Hummel, Helen Starrett, Laurie Abbiehl, Grace Pittman Kiefer, and Emmy Schlemmer Weaver; (second row) Jean Wordinger, Raymond Abbiehl, Ray Neff, Helbert Schlemmer, Hattie Fredricks Gordon, Laurie Zimmerly, Hazel Wickizer Lehr, Grace Fredericks Lehman, Goldie Leatherman, Ernest Baumgartner, and Ralph Wordinger; (third row) Lula Smith Schilt Heinke, Audrey Neff, Jess Pittman, Harry Kling, Clarence Strahla, Robert Mutti, Mabel Baumgartner, Minnie Strahla, and Glen Strahla; (fourth row) Susie Schemmer Ringle, Bess Boocher Simon, Elsie Abbiehl Keck, Clem Wickizer, Lovina Grunawald Holderman, Myrtle Starrett, and Pauline Schlemmer Grove. (Courtesy of Clifford and Janet [Abbiehl] Holderbaum.)

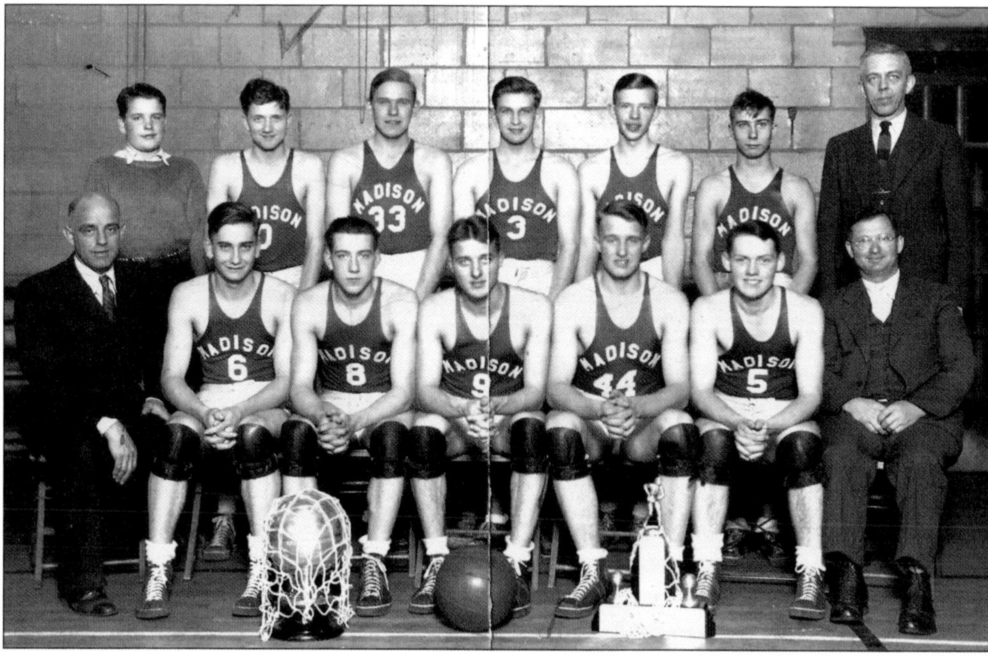

In 1936, the Madison Township School boys basketball team was the St. Joseph County championship team. (Courtesy of Dennis and Rae Beehler.)

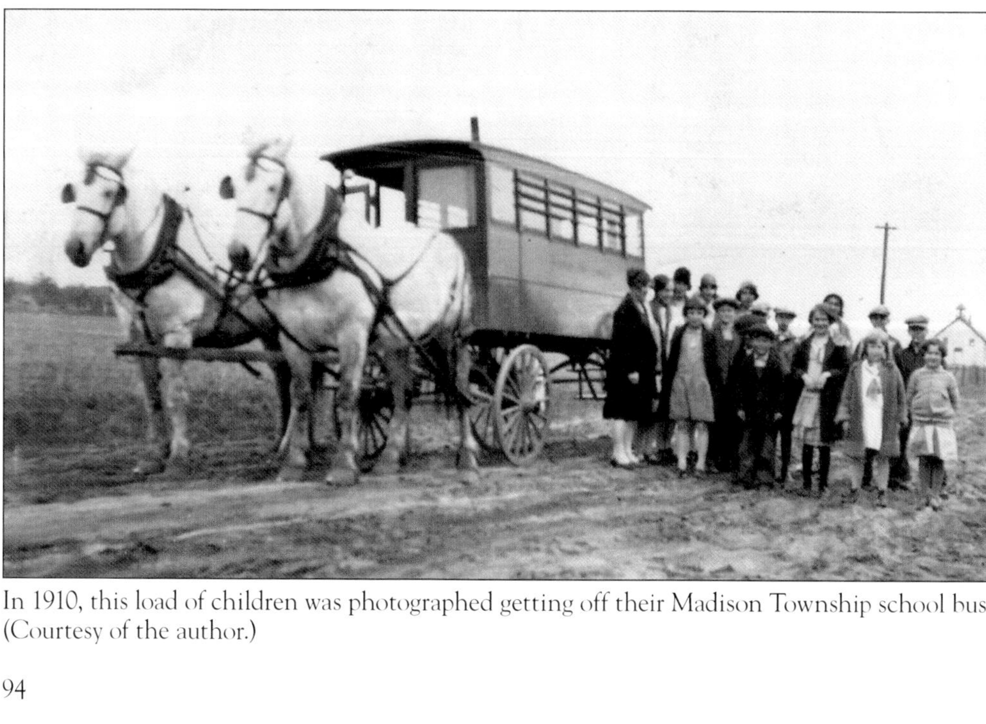

In 1910, this load of children was photographed getting off their Madison Township school bus. (Courtesy of the author.)

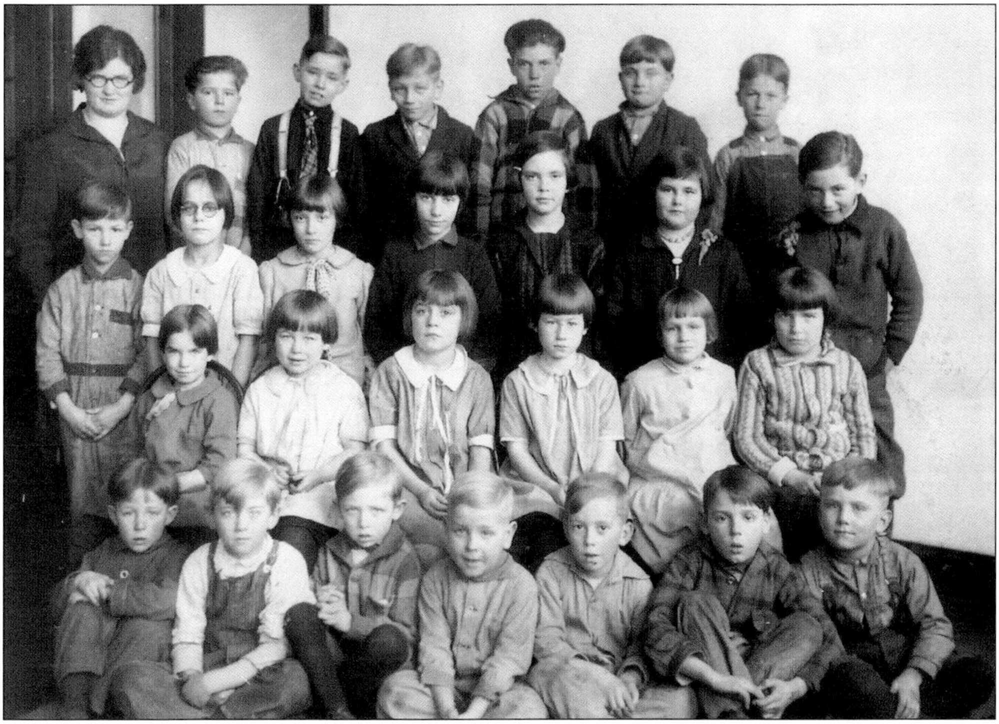

A class from the Boner School is pictured here. Boner was located on Kern Road at the Cedar Road dead end in Penn Township. (Courtesy of Dale Hahn.)

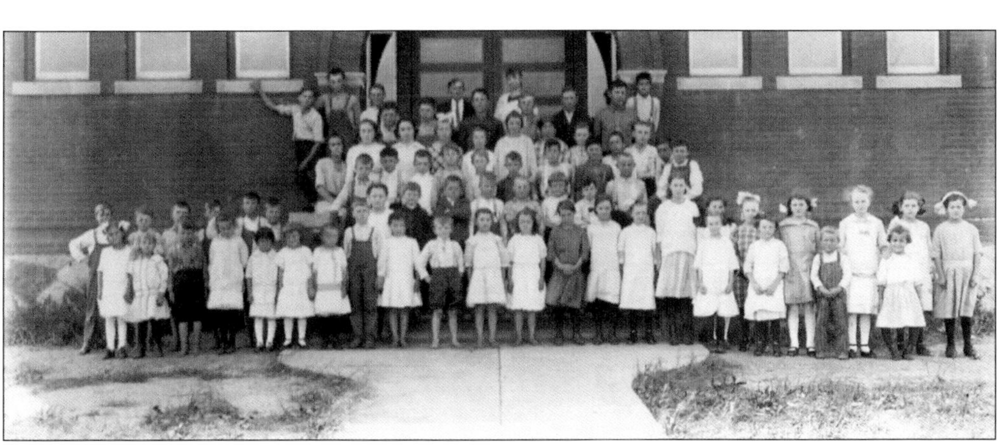

A class picture from Wyatt School is depicted here. Wyatt School was destroyed by the 1965 Palm Sunday tornadoes. (Courtesy of Helen [Rader] Marker.)

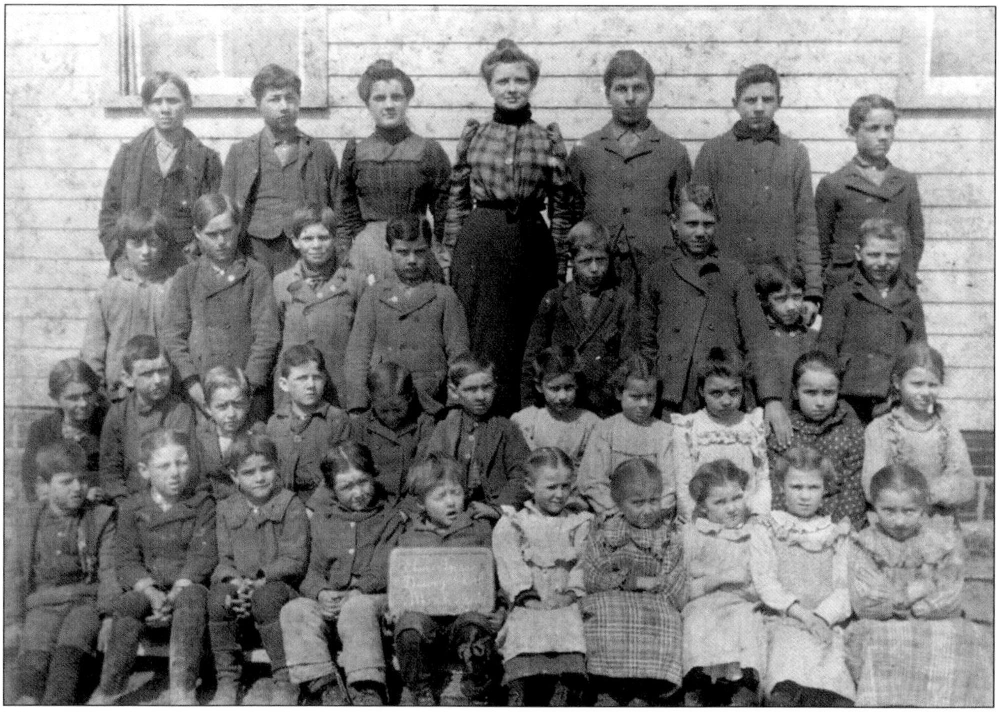

This 1901 class picture is from Dewey School. Dewey was located on Shively Road and Oak Grove Road, which is now known as Beech Road. (Courtesy of Helen [Rader] Marker.)

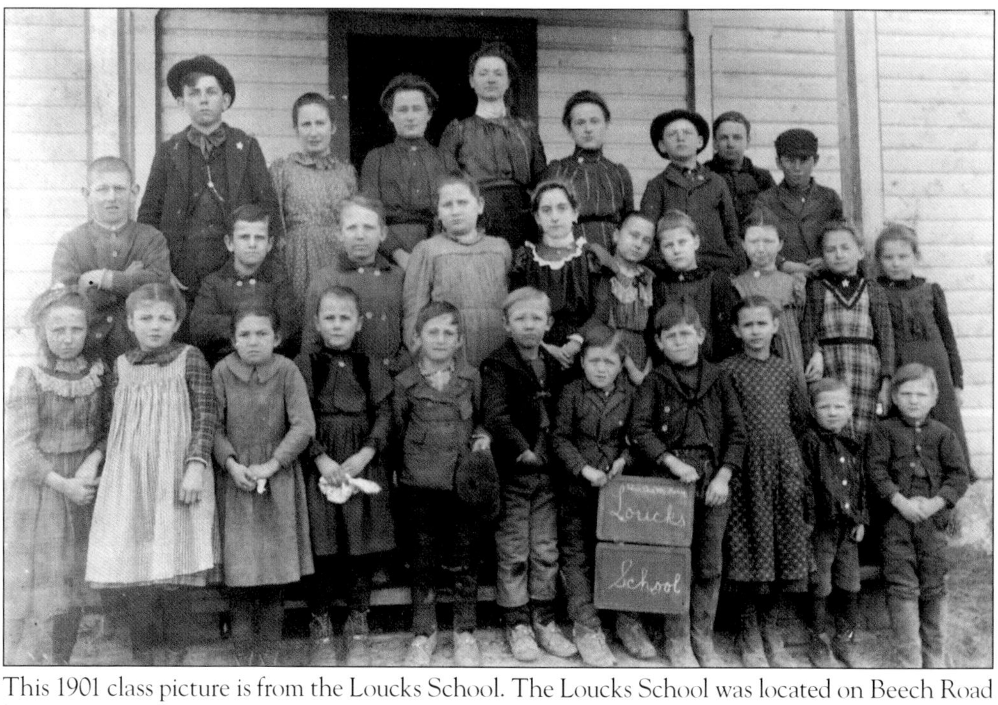


This 1901 class picture is from the Loucks School. The Loucks School was located on Beech Road between Pierce and Patterson Roads, in Madison Township. (Courtesy of Helen [Rader] Marker.)

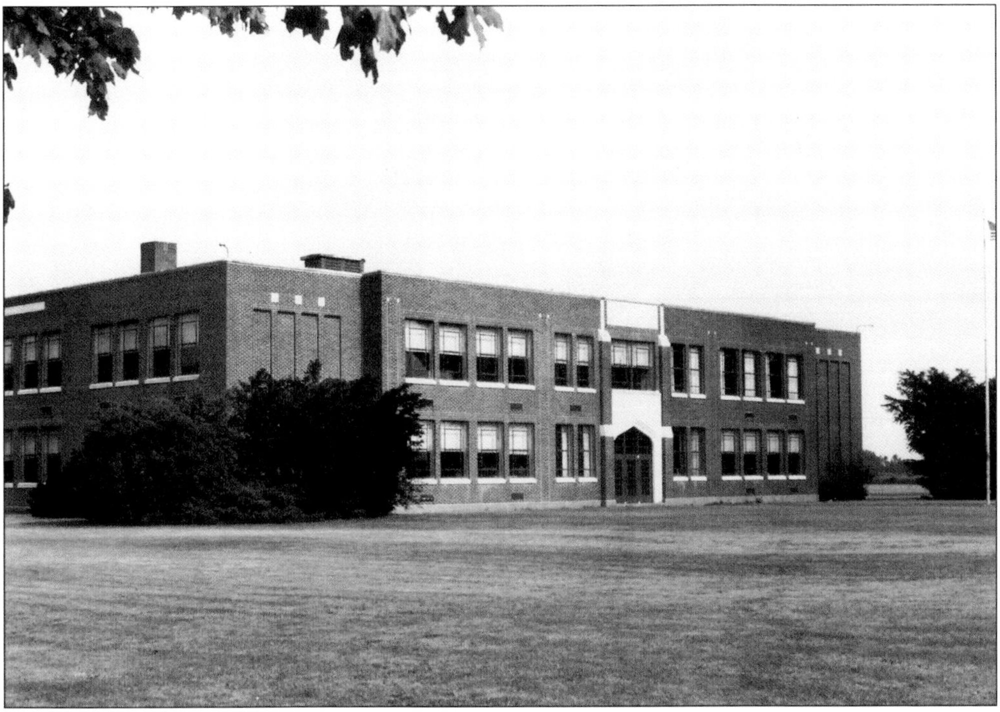

In the fall of 1900, during the administration of George A. Birk, a township trustee, a two-story school building opened at the southeast corner of Dogwood and Pierce Roads. It was the first Madison Township School, pictured here. (Courtesy of Harold and Verdene [Gerber] Hunke.)

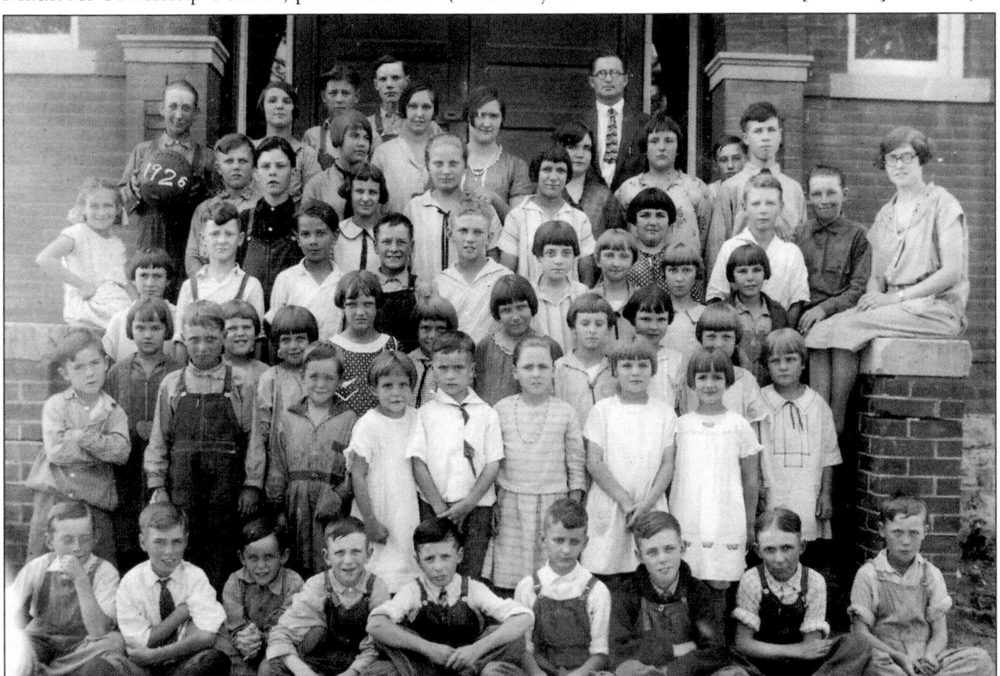


This school photograph was taken at the Wyatt School in Madison Township in 1926. (Courtesy of Harold and Verdene [Gerber] Hunke.)

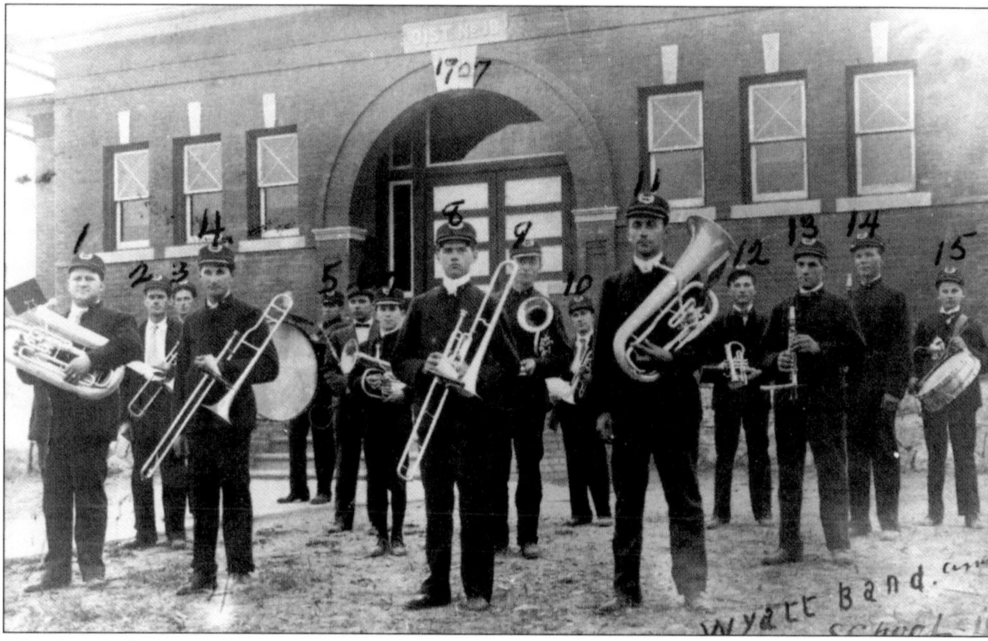

This band photograph was taken in 1907 in front of the Wyatt School. Identified by number in this picture are the following: (1) Berton Shenefield, (2) Ford Shenefield, (3) Chester Kettring, (4) Amos Bendit, (5) John Felton, (6) Otto Felton, (7) Clinton Felton, (8) Harrison Shearer, (9) Albert Enders, (10) Lewis Bendit, (11) Harvey Shearer, and (12) Joseph Bendit. (Courtesy of Harold and Verdene [Gerber] Hunke.)

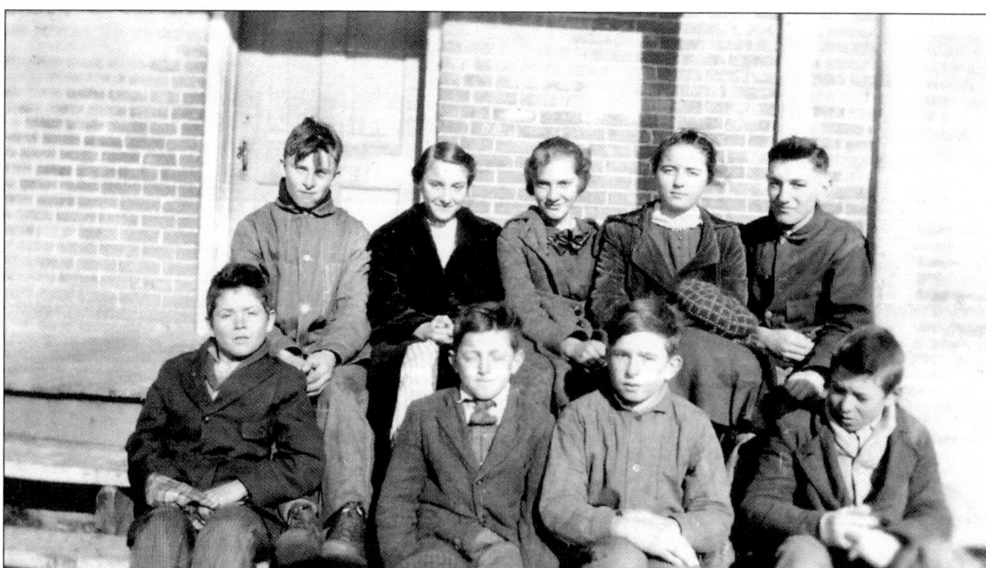

This photograph was taken in 1919 at the Brenneman/Clodville School. Pictured are, from left to right, as follows: (first row) Cecil Wisler, Floyd Hartman, Ralph Hahn, and Roland Troxel; (second row) Harold Hahn, Ethel Klein, Dora (Schalliol) Fredericks, Bernice Martin, and Willis Barkey. (Courtesy of Dora [Schalliol] Fredericks.)

Bernice Martin (left) and Dora Schalliol are photographed in 1919 after their final exam for eighth grade at the Brenneman/Clodville schoolhouse. (Courtesy of Dora [Schalliol] Fredericks.)

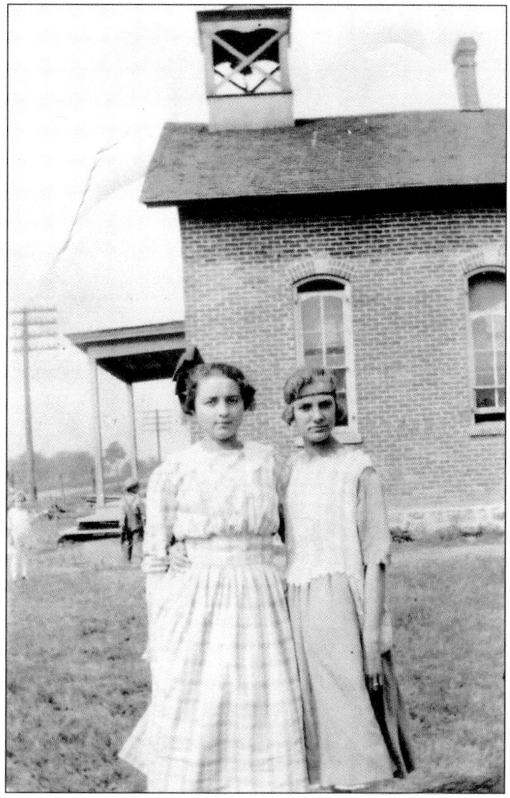

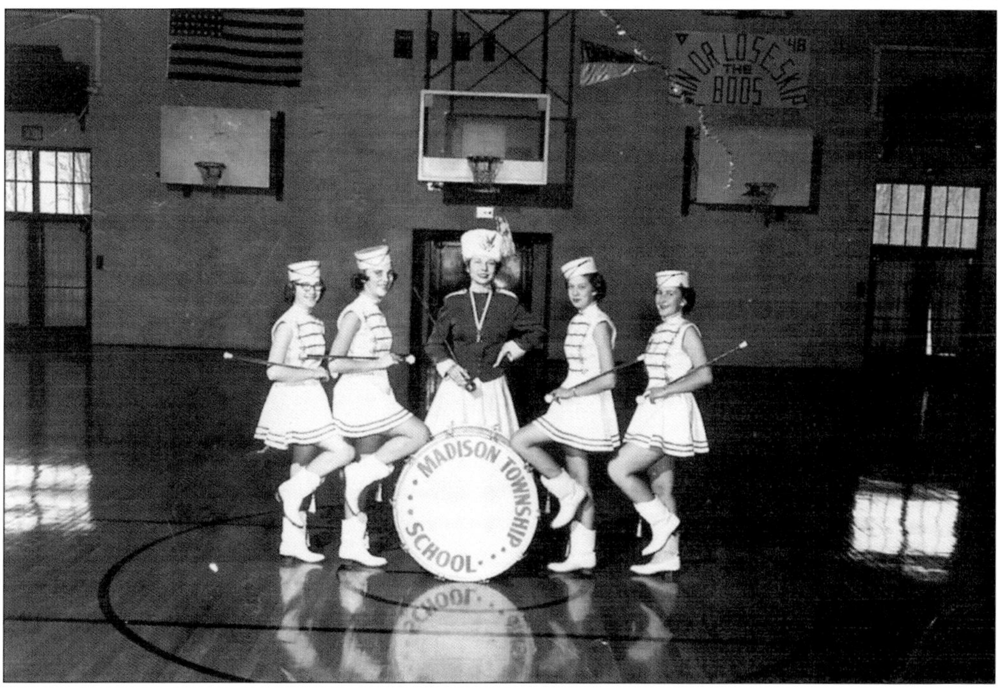


This photograph shows drum majorettes from Madison Township School. (Courtesy of the author.)

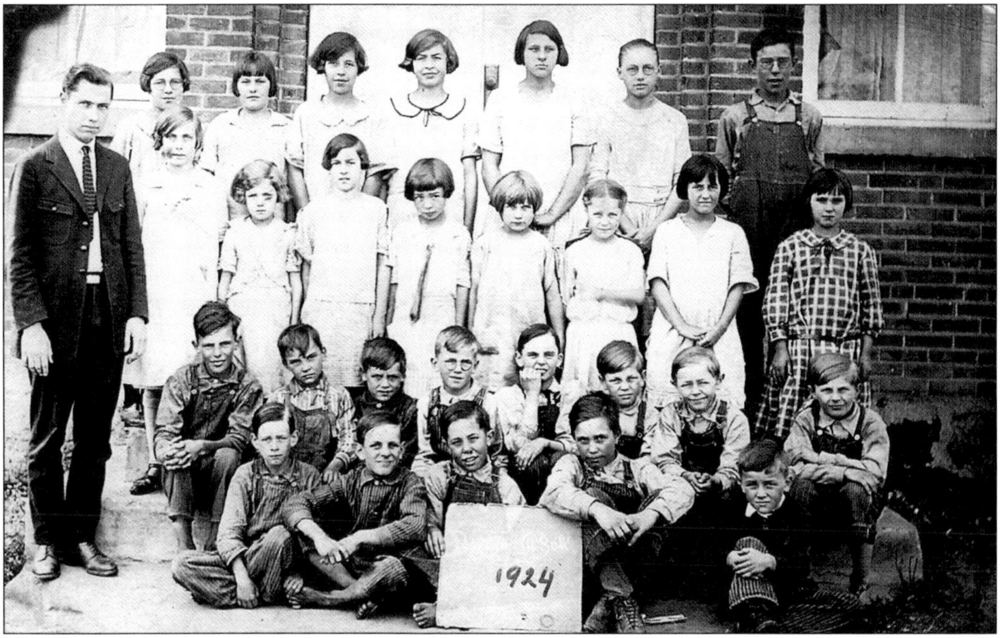

A 1924 school picture depicts the Daughtery School, located on the corner of Dogwood and New Roads in Madison Township. (Courtesy of Charles and Dorothy [Reum] Neer.)

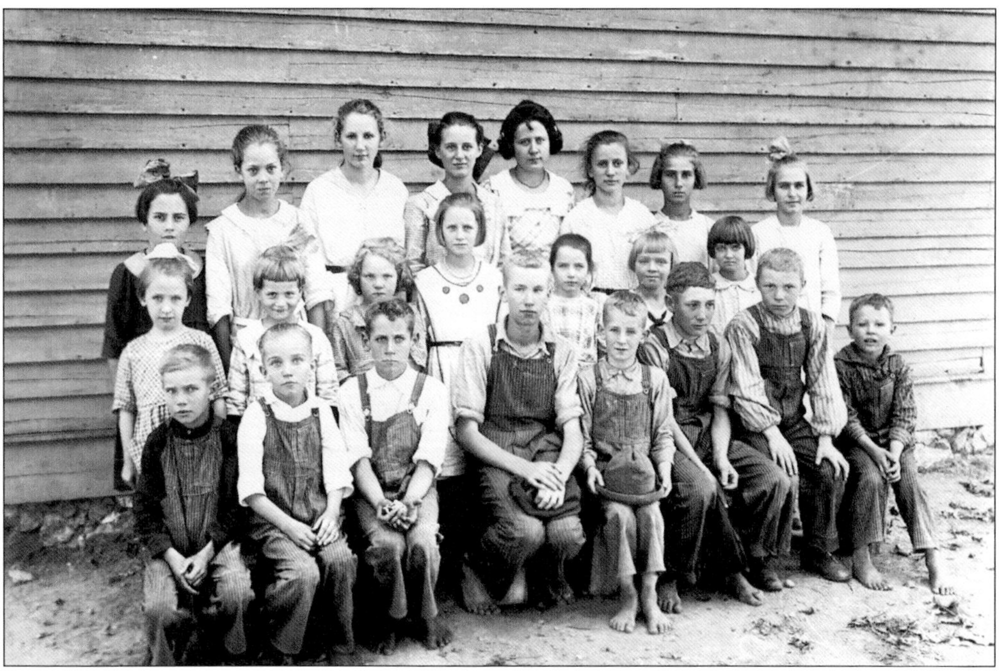

This 1922 school picture is from the Van Burskit School in Penn Township. The school was located on Ironwood and Roosevelt Roads. Pictured are, from left to right, the following: ? Nemeth, ? Nemeth, ? Nemeth, ? Wallace, ? Wallace, Carl Dutoi, Alfons Dutoi, and Albert Beutter; (second row) Ruth Myers, Jeanette Battles, ? Knott, ? LaClase, unidentified, ? Nemeth, and ? Nemeth; (third row) Helen Battles, Bealuh Knott, unidentified, Elsie LaClase, Ruby Schafer (teacher), Martha Myers, ? Nemeth, and ? Nemeth. (Courtesy of Jeanette [Battles] Martin.)

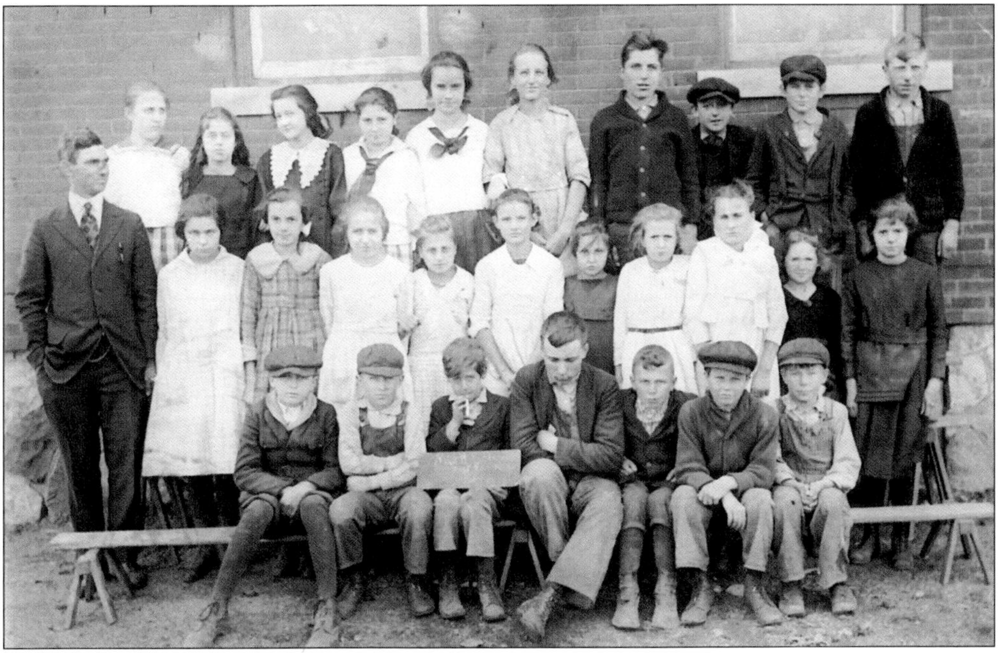

Here is a 1920 class picture from the first-grade room at Wyatt School in Wyatt, Indiana. Pictured are, from left to right, the following: (first row) Clem Fox, Harris Hawkins, Lewis Jacobson, Linden Shearer, Harry Berger, Wilbur Conrad, and Oswald Hummel; (second row) unidentified, Irene Shearer, Edna Berger, Dora Pehlke, Ruth Hawkins, Ida Baumgartner, Edith Moser, Ion Smith, Lucille Grose, Gladys Mottice, and Evelyn Kuhn; (third row) Laura Kaiser, Erma Jacobson, Lena Kuhn, Alta Clark, Pearl Pehlke, Esther Moser, Clayton Fitz, Claude Grose, Albert Hummel, and Richard Fitz. (Courtesy of Vicki Berger.)

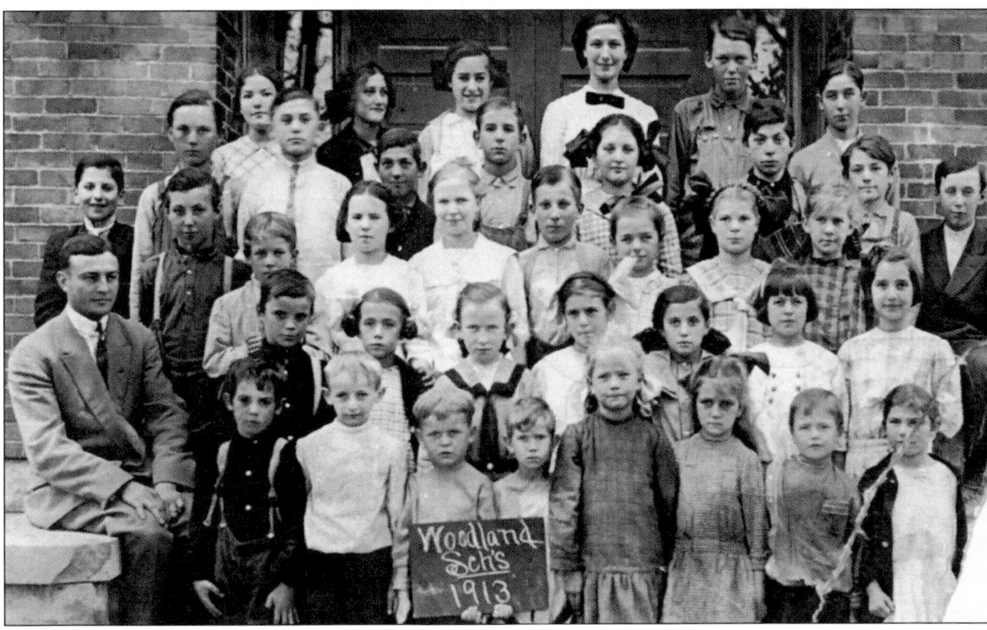


This class photograph was taken in 1913 at the Woodland School in Woodland, Indiana. (Courtesy of Vicki Berger.)

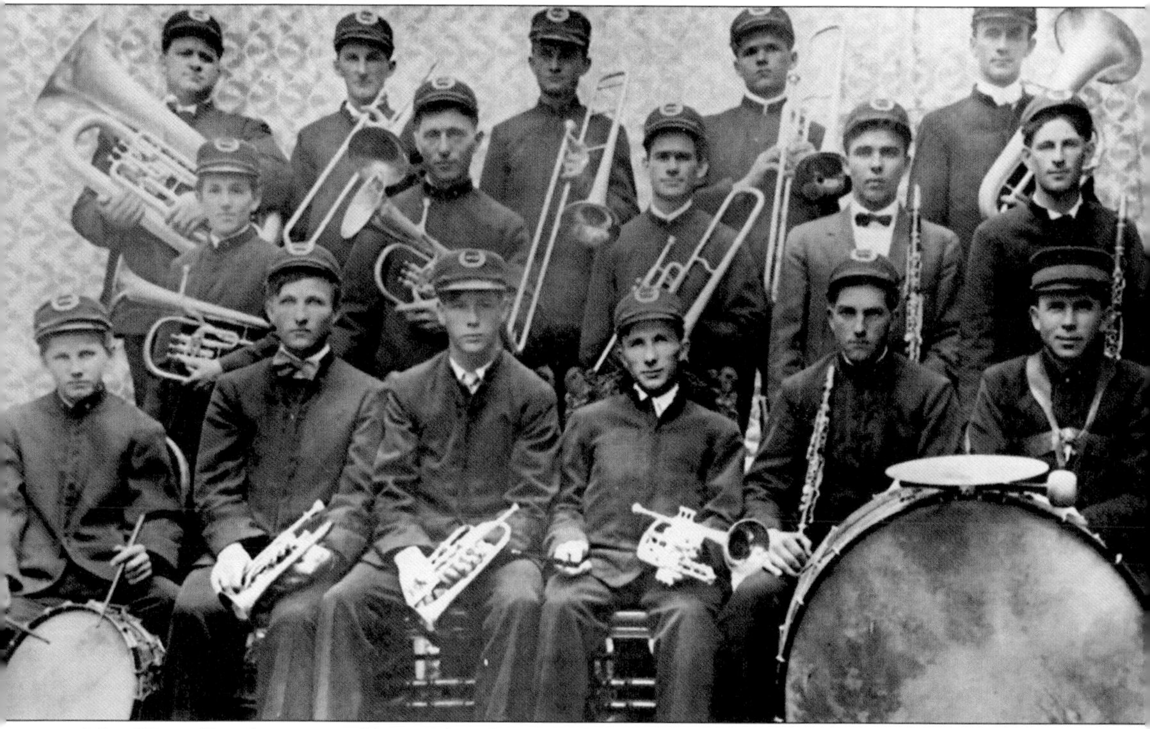

The Wyatt Band is pictured here. The photograph includes, from left to right, the following: (first row) Albert Bendit, Joe Bendit, George Beron, Lewis Bendit, Harvey Kolby, and John Felton; (second row) Clint Felteu, Albert Enders, Ford Shurefield, Otto Felture, and Chet Kettring; (third row) Berton Shurefield, Amos Bendit, Homer Barnhart, Harrison Shearer, and Harve Shearer. (Courtesy of Vicki Berger.)

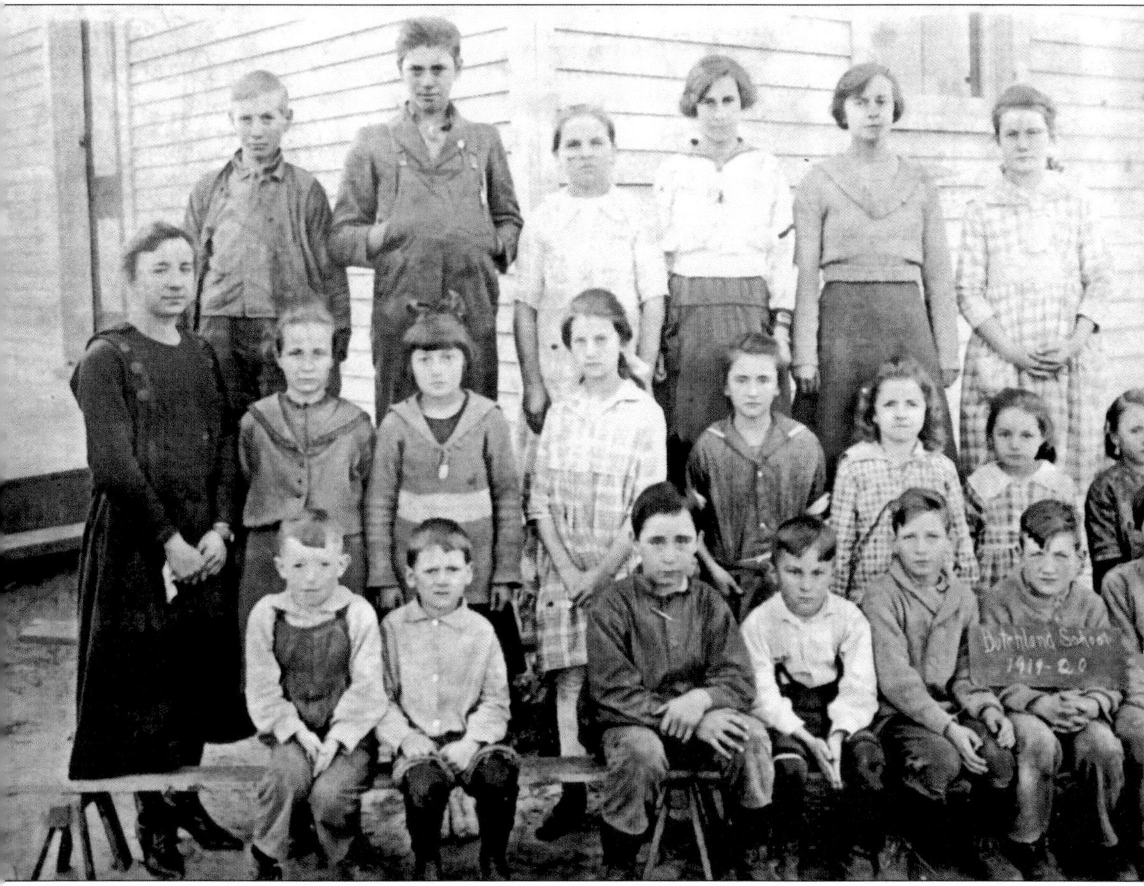


This school picture from the Dutchland School in Madison Township was taken in 1919 or 1920. (Courtesy of Vicki Berger.)

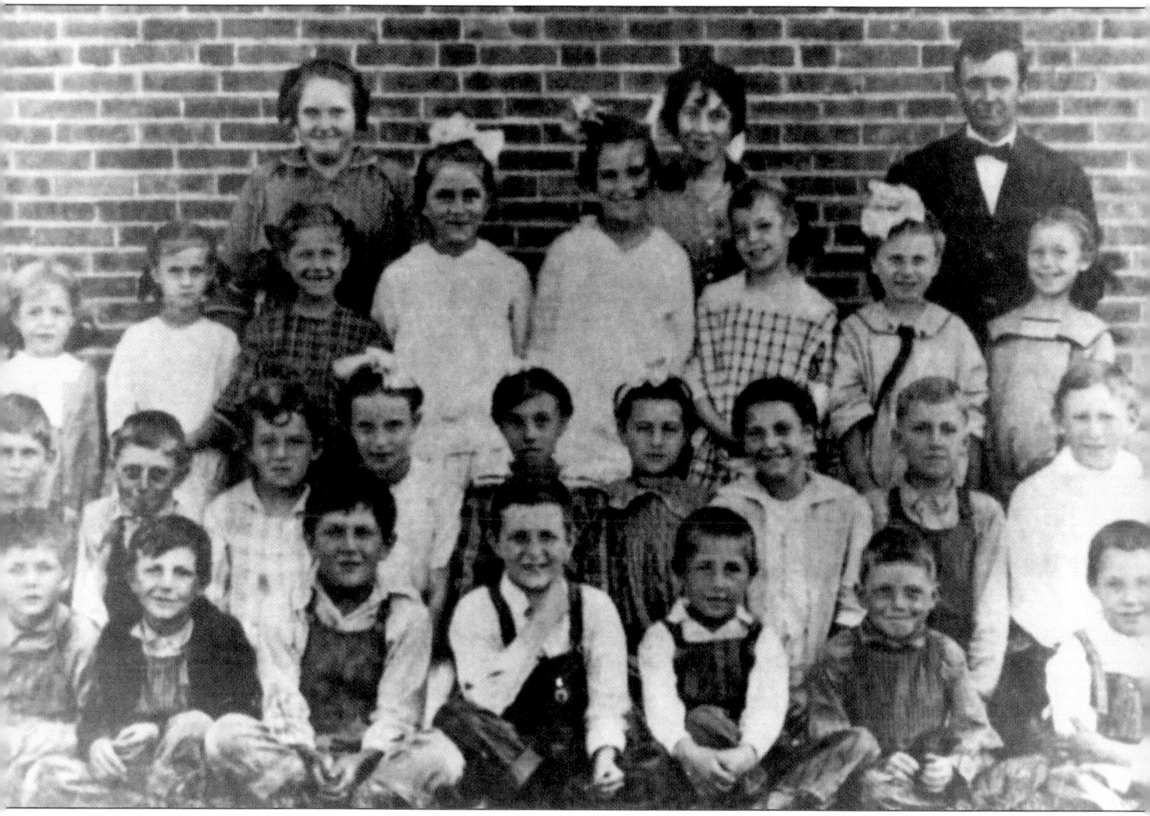

A school picture was taken at the Daugherty School in 1916 or 1917. Pictured are, from left to right, the following: (first row) Victor Andrews, Wilbert Beehler, Ted Grob, Allen Seifert, Herbert Schmeltz, Delbert Schlarb, and Wilbur Schmeltz; (second row) Walter Kline, Vernon Schlarb, Paual Grob, Fern Marker, Arvilla Keil, Laura Schlarb, Dorothy Schmeltz, Ralph Kirk, and Rudolph Grob; (third row) Sophia Berger, Mabel Keil, Marie Birk, Grace Andrews, Frieda Andrews, Ida Berger, Carrie Zeiger, and Minnie Berger; (fourth row) Nellie Fredericks, Florence Kline, and Charles Schurr (teacher). (Courtesy of Vicki Berger.)

## *Four*

# Business

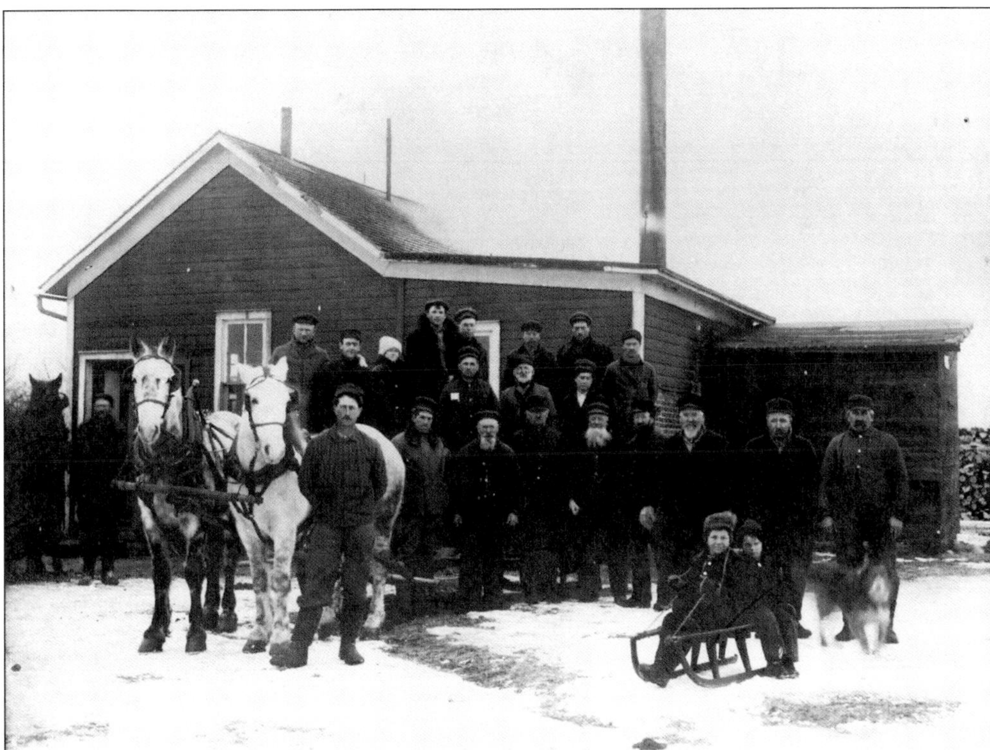

This creamery was located on the northwest corner of Osborne and Dogwood Roads. Some of the regular customers were Louis Bollenbacher, Adam Beehler, Peter Beehler, Augustus Schalliol, and Julius Schalliol. (Courtesy of the author.)

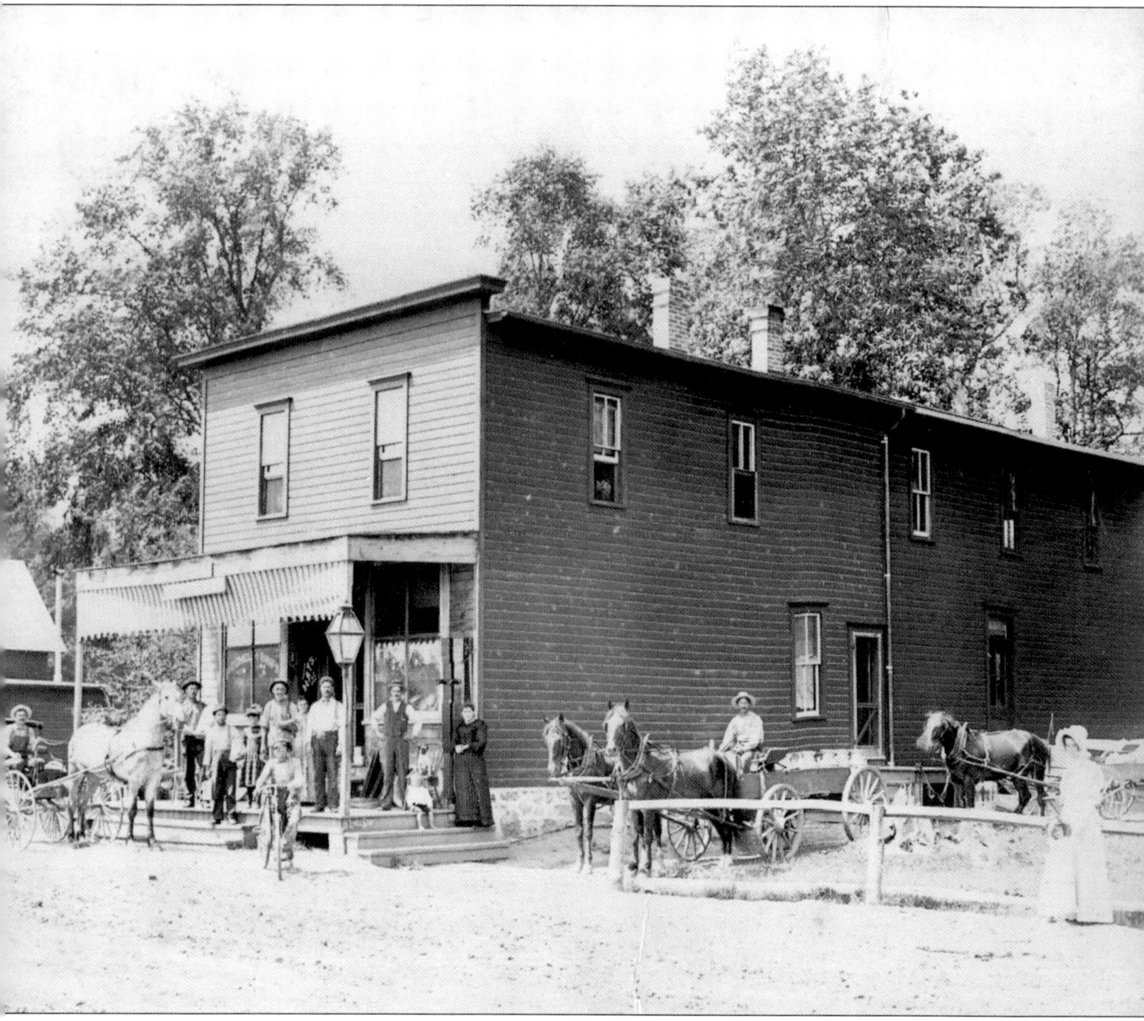

The Mochel Brothers store was located in Wyatt, Indiana. Many of the local farmers bought goods there. Marie Mochel and Myrtle Mochel were born on the second floor of this building. (Courtesy of Evelyn [Beehler] Salyer.)

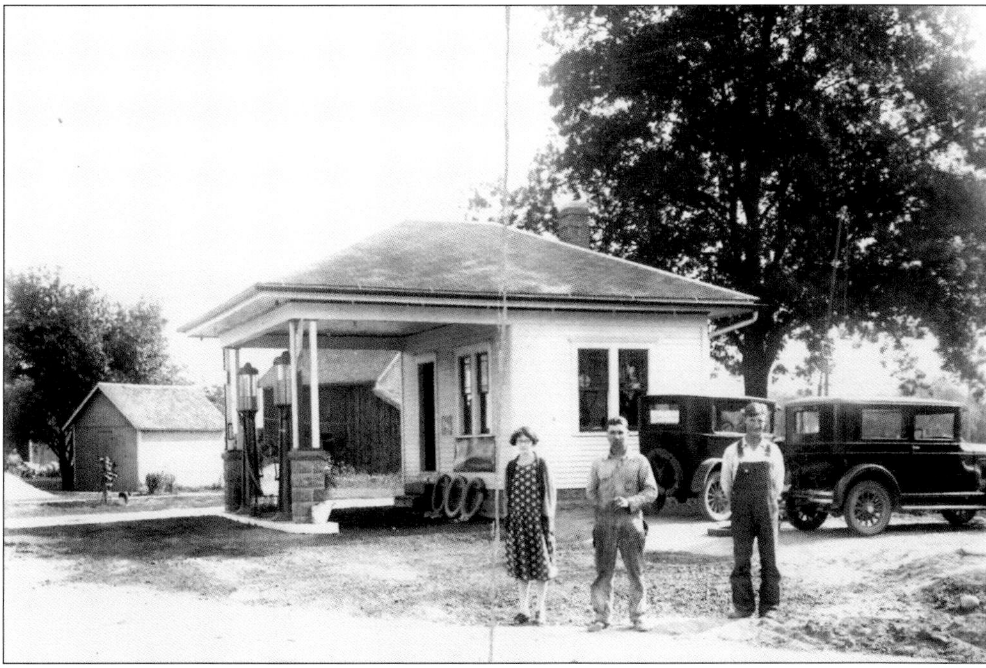

From left to right, Russell Pletcher, Loneda Pletcher, and Carl Roeder are pictured standing in front of the first filling station in Wyatt, Indiana. (Courtesy of Helen [Rader] Marker.)

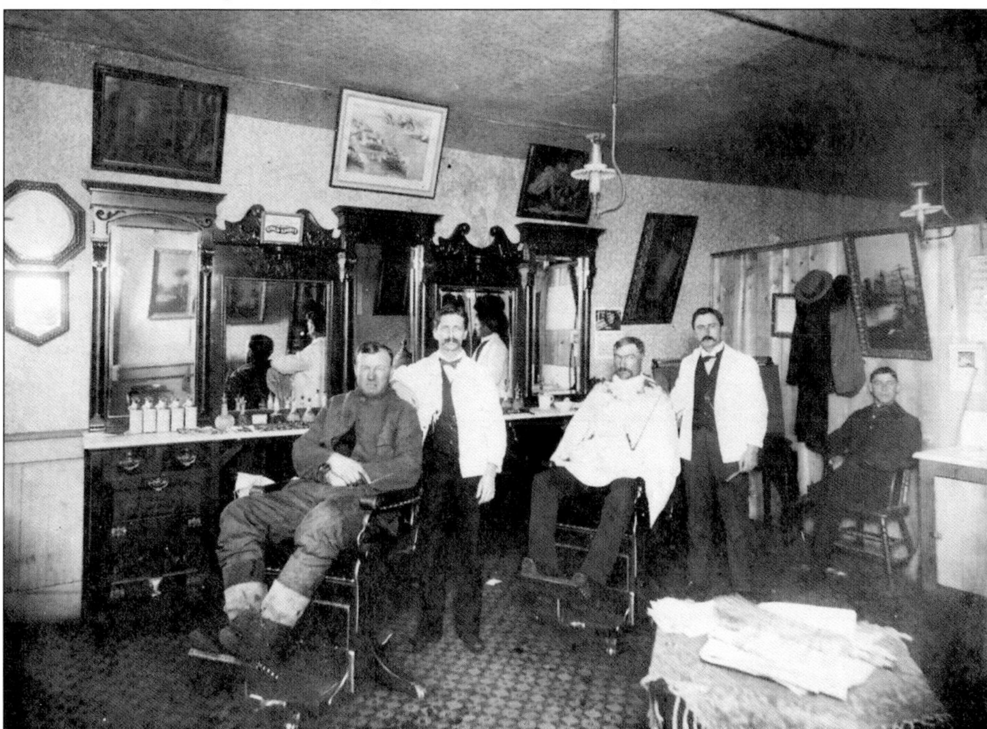

Men from the surrounding area gathered in the barbershop in Wyatt, Indiana, in this photograph. Albert K. Boss is in the middle seat. (Courtesy of Helen [Rader] Marker.)

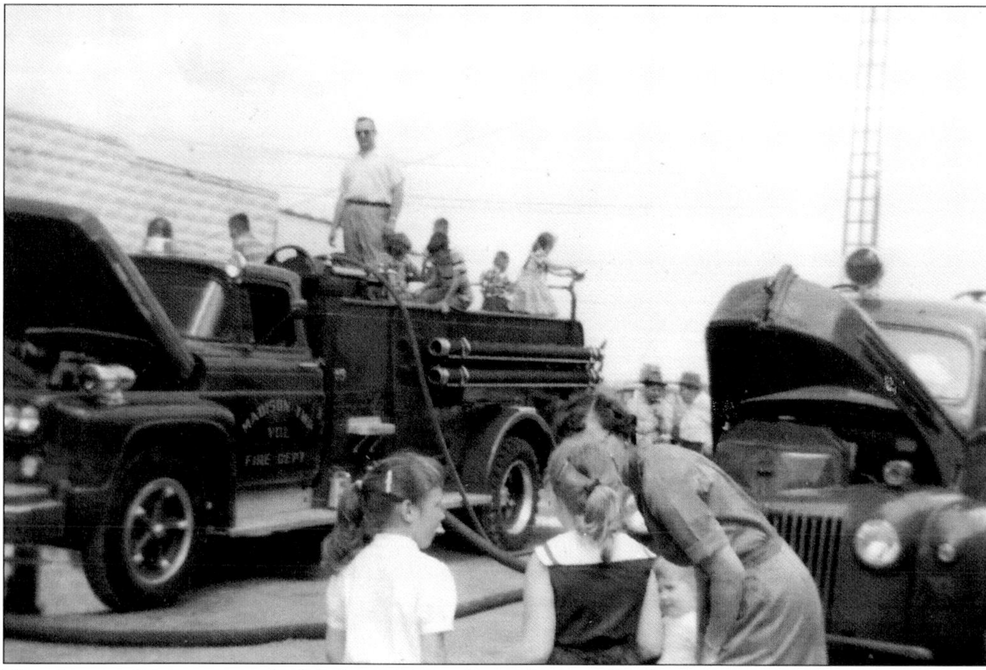

This fire truck was new to the Madison Township volunteer fire department when this photograph was taken. (Courtesy of Harold and Verdene [Gerber] Hunke.)

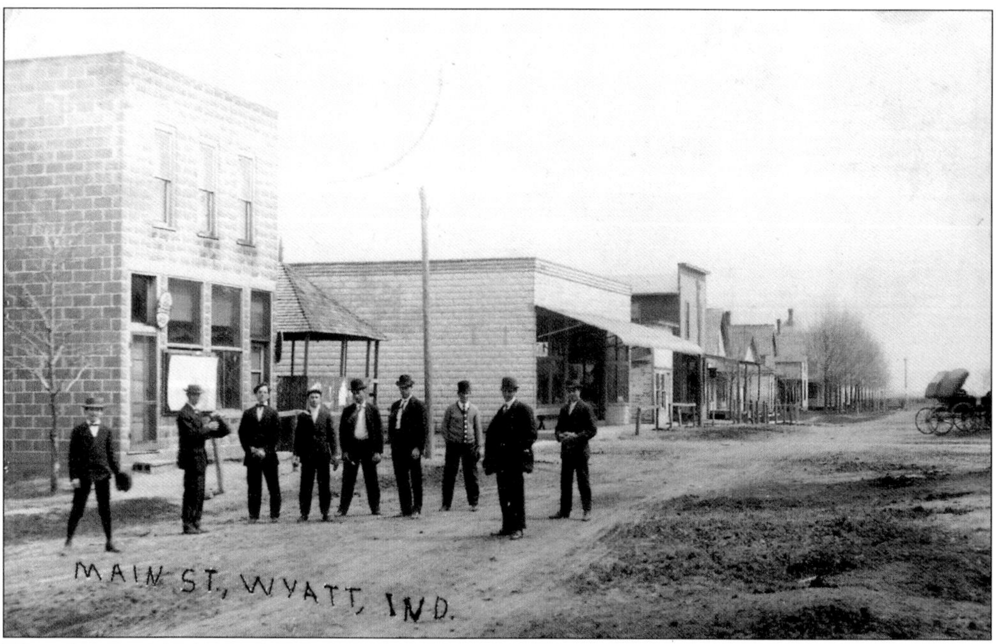


This photograph shows the Wyatt, Indiana, baseball team in uniform, posing on Main Street. (Courtesy of Harold and Verdene [Gerber] Hunke.)

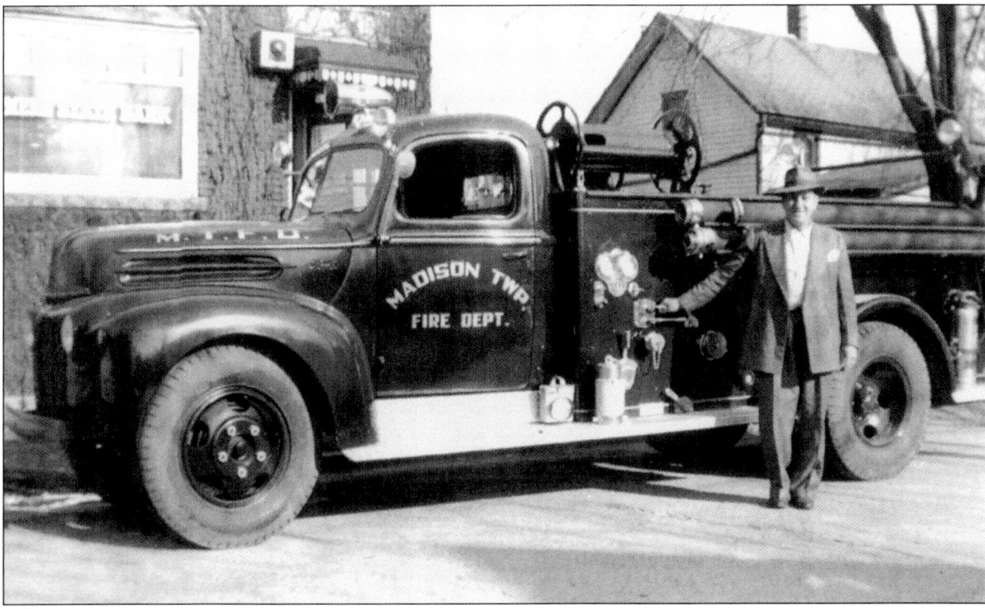


This picture shows the first fire truck in Madison Township. (Courtesy of Harold and Verdene [Gerber] Hunke.)

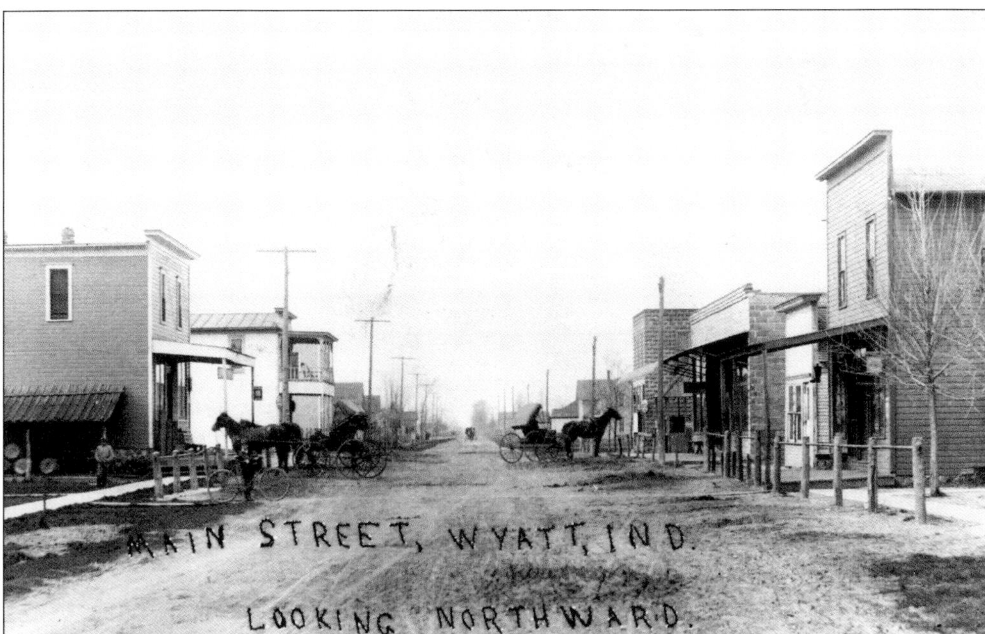


An old view shows Main Street in Wyatt, Indiana, looking northward down what is now known as Bremen Highway. (Courtesy of Harold and Verdene [Gerber] Hunke.)

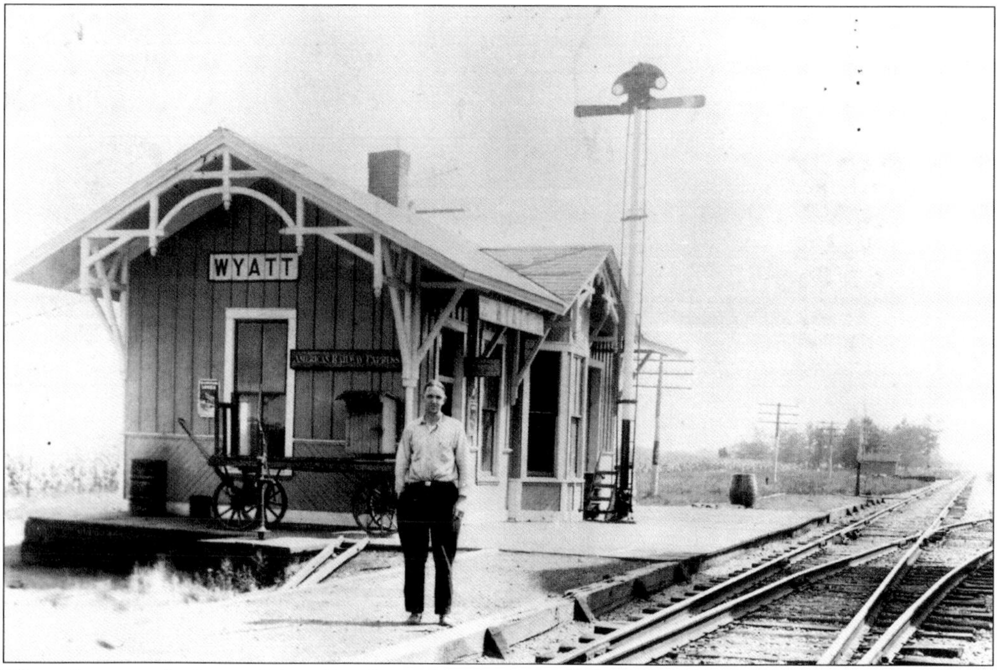


This photograph shows John Smith standing at the Wyatt Train Depot, where the Wabash Railroad came through the town. (Courtesy of Harold and Verdene [Gerber] Hunke.)

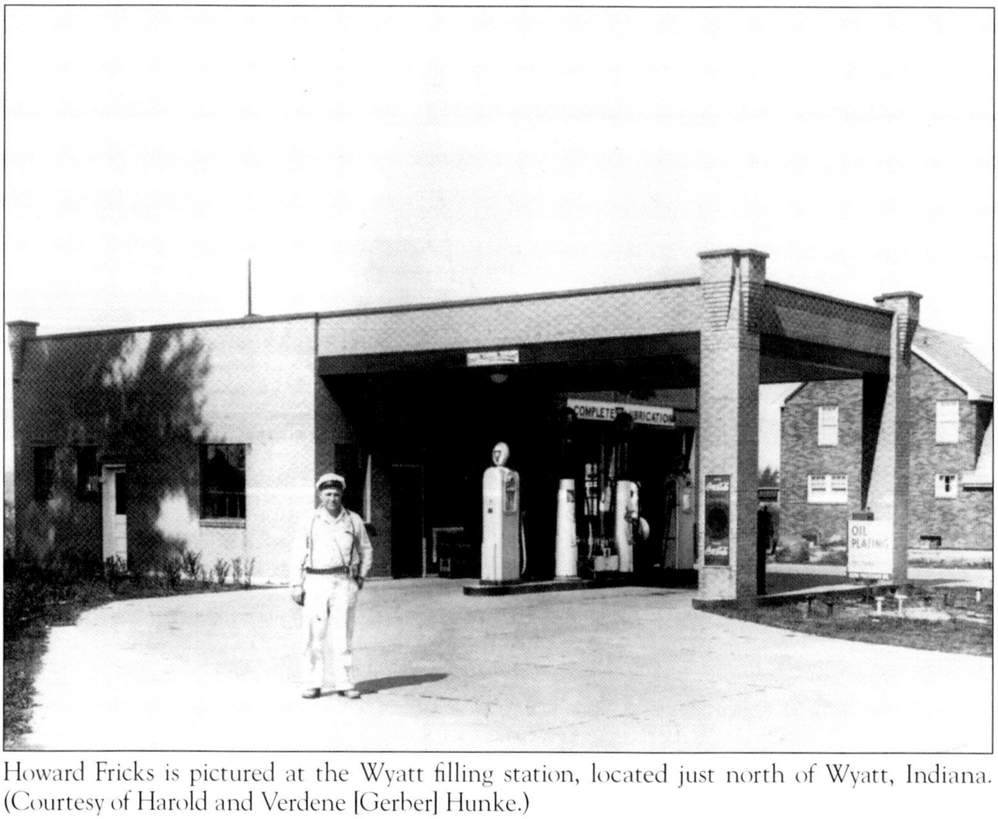


Howard Fricks is pictured at the Wyatt filling station, located just north of Wyatt, Indiana. (Courtesy of Harold and Verdene [Gerber] Hunke.)

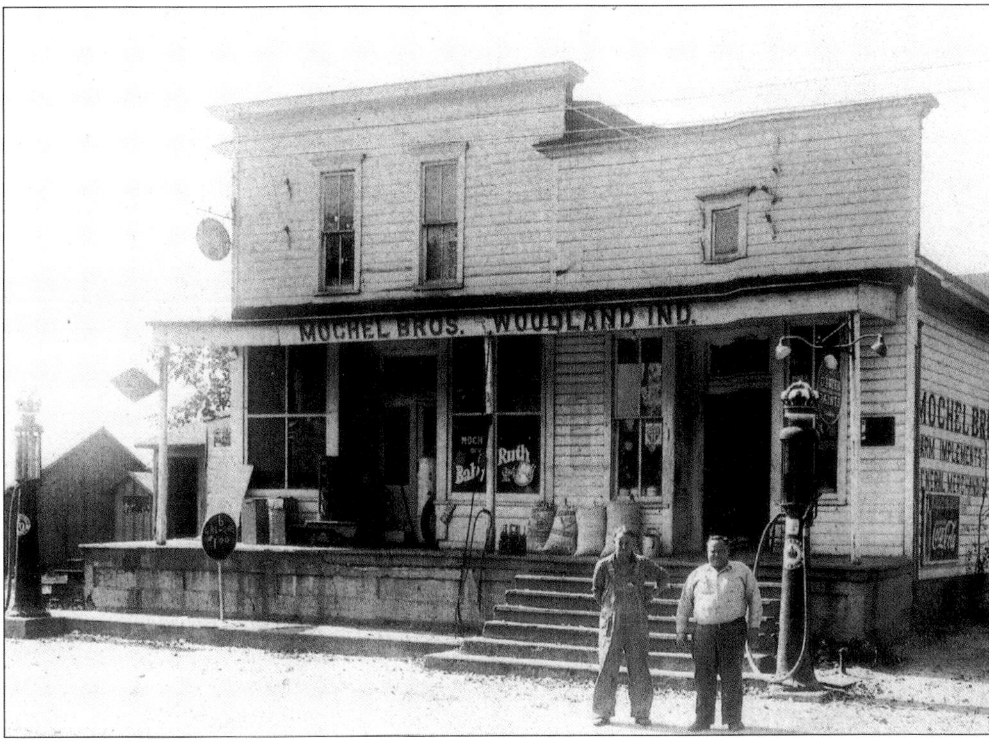


Michael Mochel (left) and Omer Mochel (right) are pictured at the Mochel Brothers Store in Woodland, Indiana. (Courtesy of Richard Mochel.)

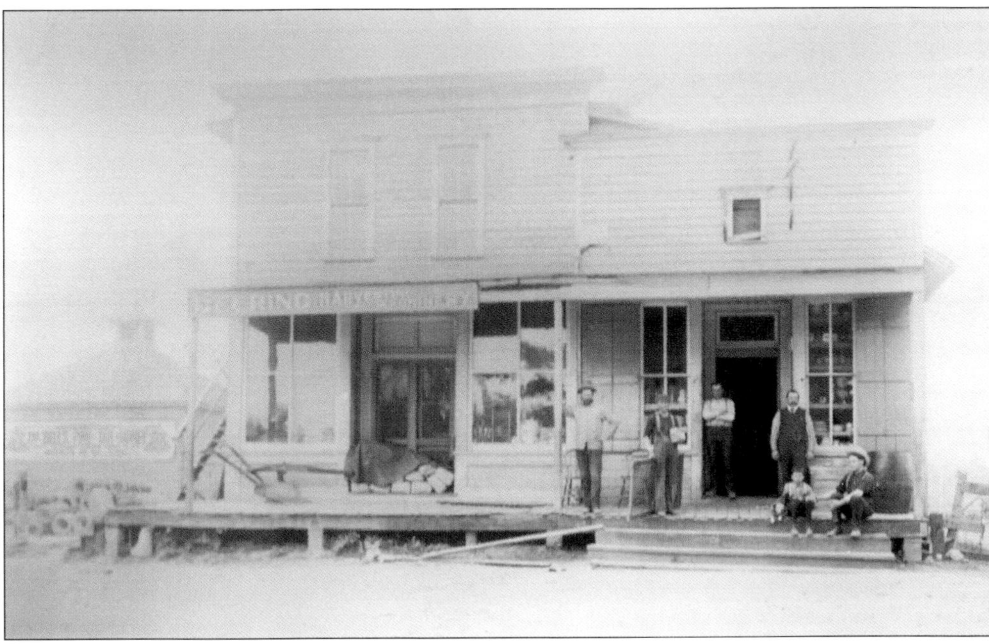

Clem Mochel is pictured with his dog, "Date," at the Deering Harvesting Machinery store in Wyatt, Indiana. Martin Mochel is standing to the right of the door. (Courtesy of Richard Mochel.)

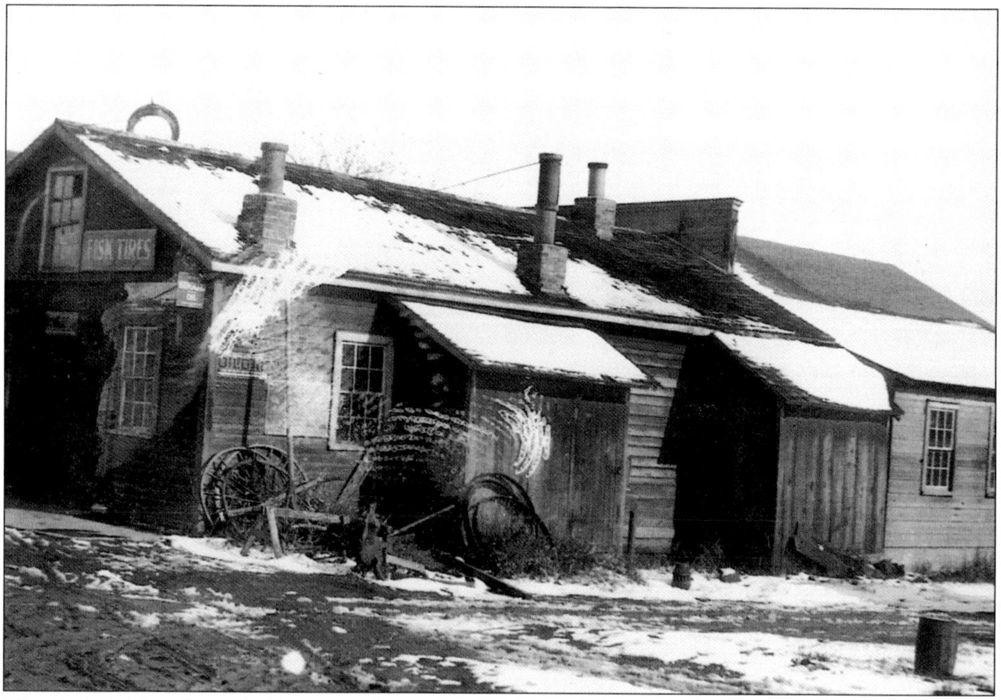


The Kobold Blacksmith Shop was located next to Phillip Marker's home, on the east side of State Road 331, in Woodland, Indiana. (Courtesy of Richard Mochel.)

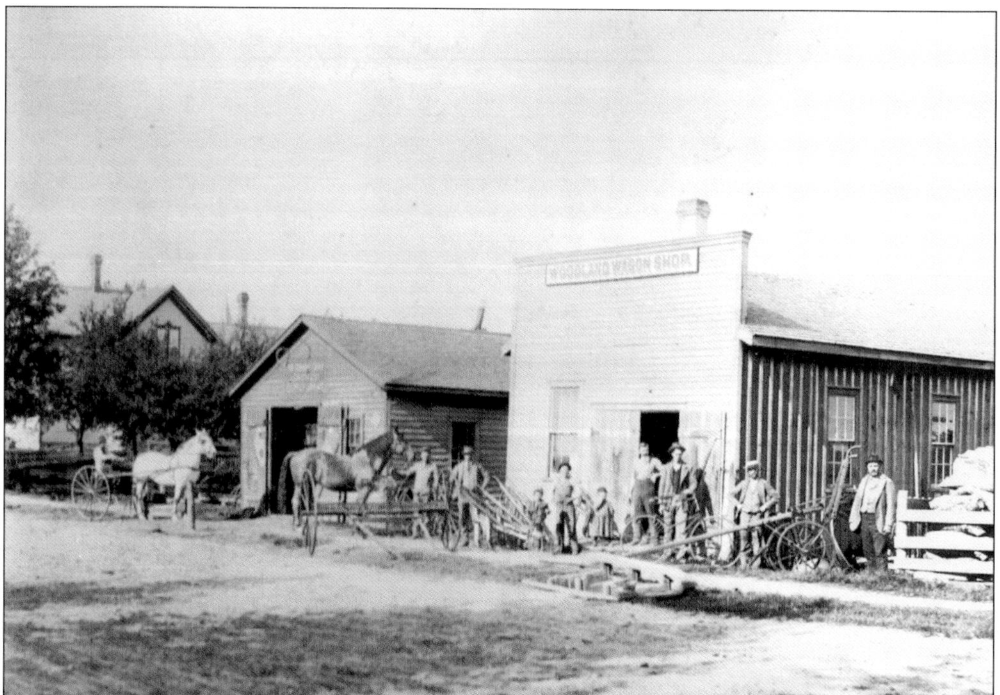


This photograph shows the Wagon Shop in Woodland, Indiana. (Courtesy of Richard Mochel.)

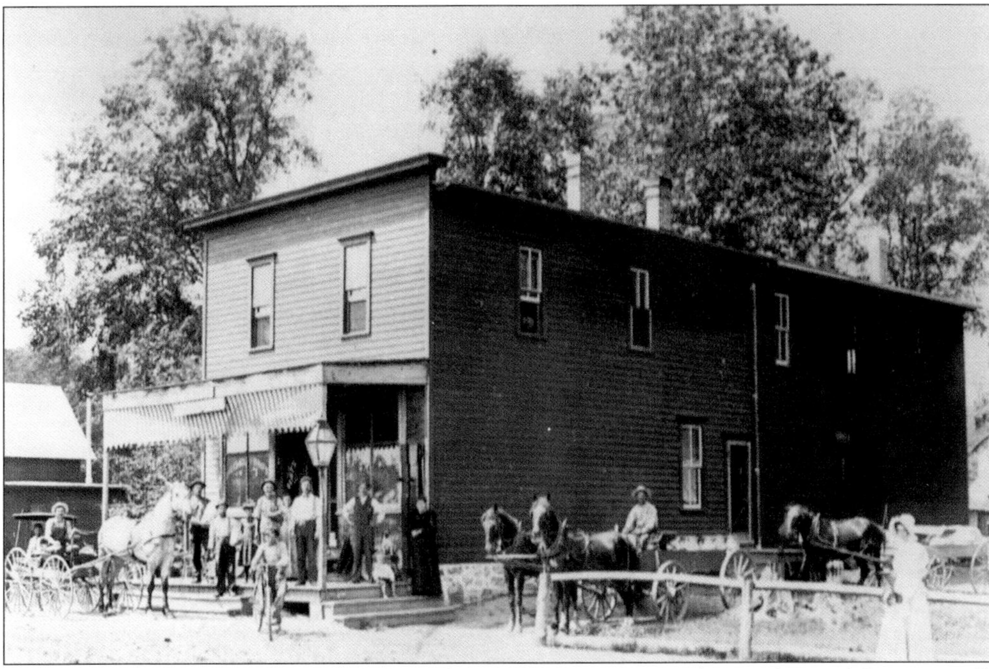

Photographed in front of the Mochel Brothers Store, a Wyatt resident is shown delivering milk and cream from the one of the many local creameries. (Courtesy of Richard Mochel.)

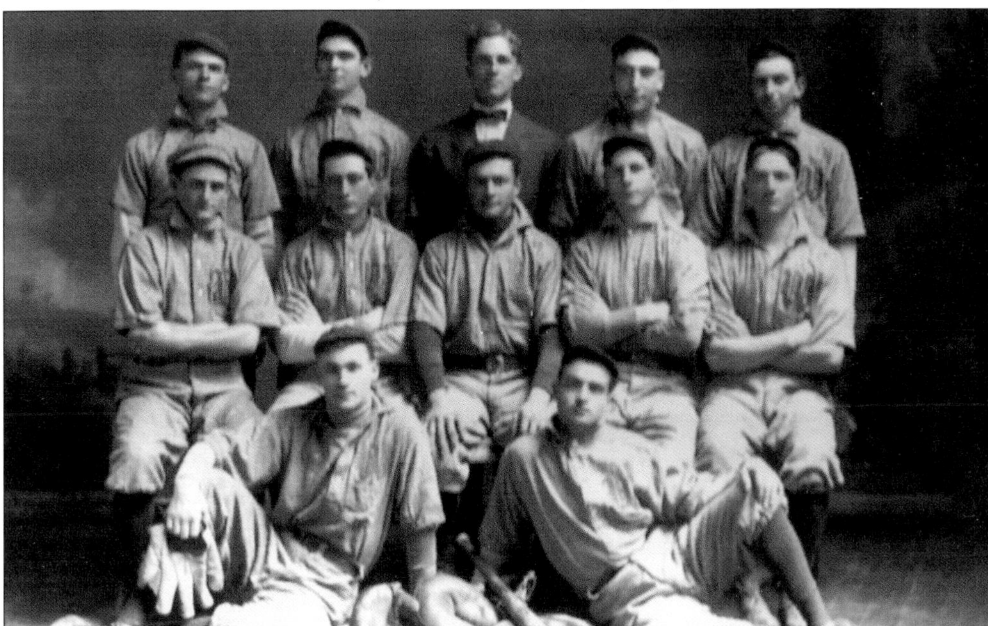

The 1911, the Woodland Greys were the St. Joseph County baseball champions. Pictured are, from left to right, the following: (first row) E. Weber (second base and catcher) and Clem Mochel (center field); (second row) O. Kelley (short stop), D. Marker (right field), O. J. Kelley (captain, catcher, pitcher), D. Flory (first base), and W. Geyer (third base); (third row) H. Shearer (short stop, second base), C. Shearer (pitcher), H. Layer (umpire), J. Zeiger (left field), and R. Kelley (left field). (Courtesy of Richard Mochel.)

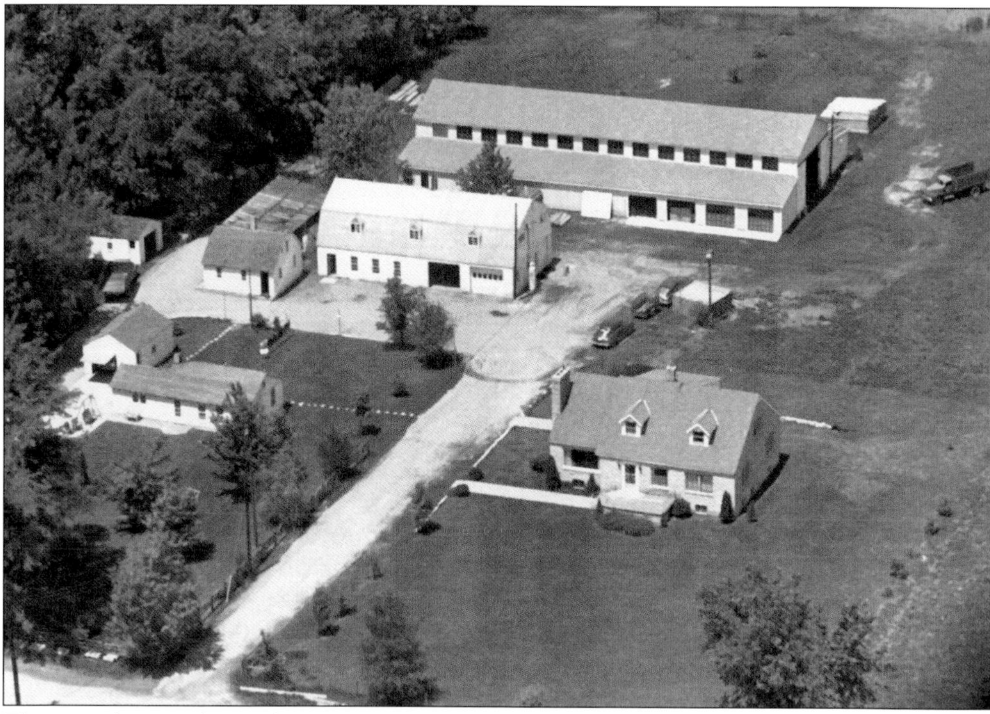

This aerial view shows the Contat Lumber Company on Kelley Road in Penn Township. (Courtesy of Rosemary [Contat] Dixon.)

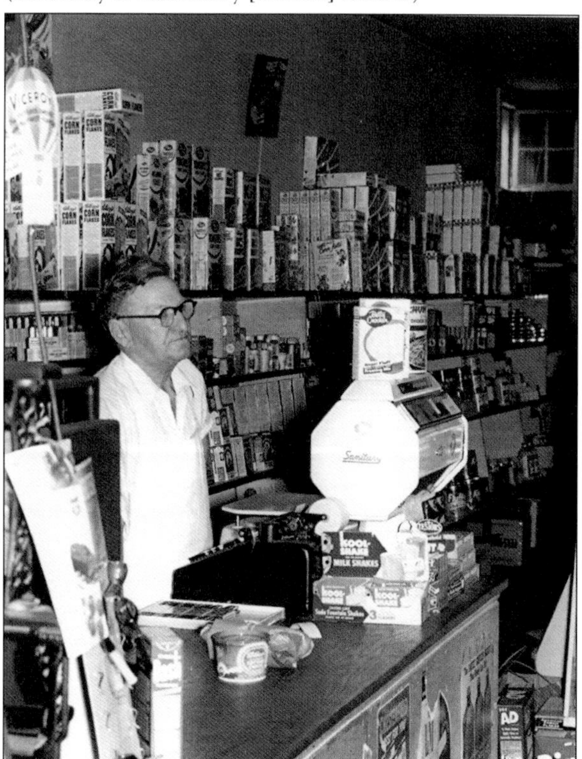

Joseph Bendit owned and operated Bendit's IGA Grocery Store in Wyatt, Indiana, for many years. (Courtesy of Vicki Berger.)

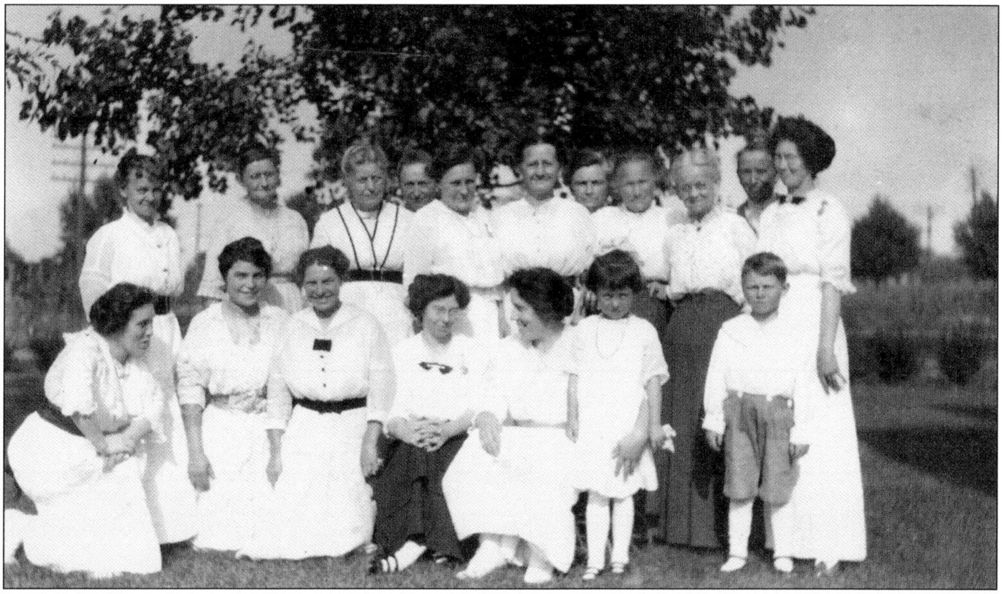

This photograph shows the St. Joseph County Busy Bee Club in Penn Township in 1914. (Courtesy of Rosemary [Contat] Dixon.)

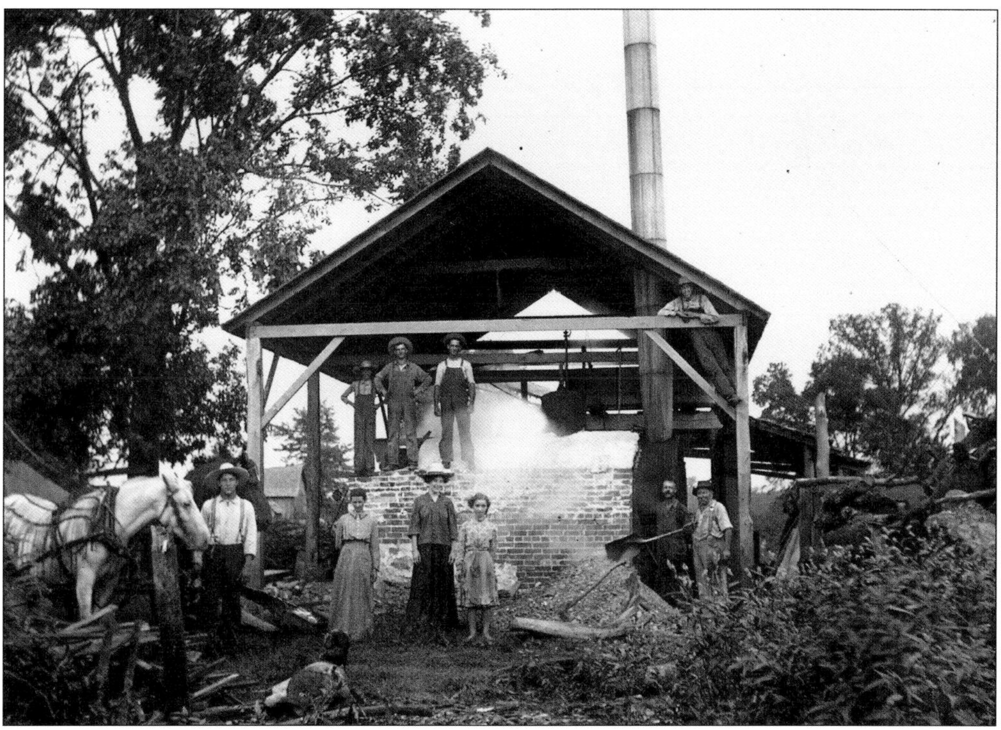

The mint still owned and operated by George and Charlotte Matz is located on the southeast corner of Blackberry and Harrison Roads in Penn Township. (Courtesy of Rosemary [Contat] Dixon.)

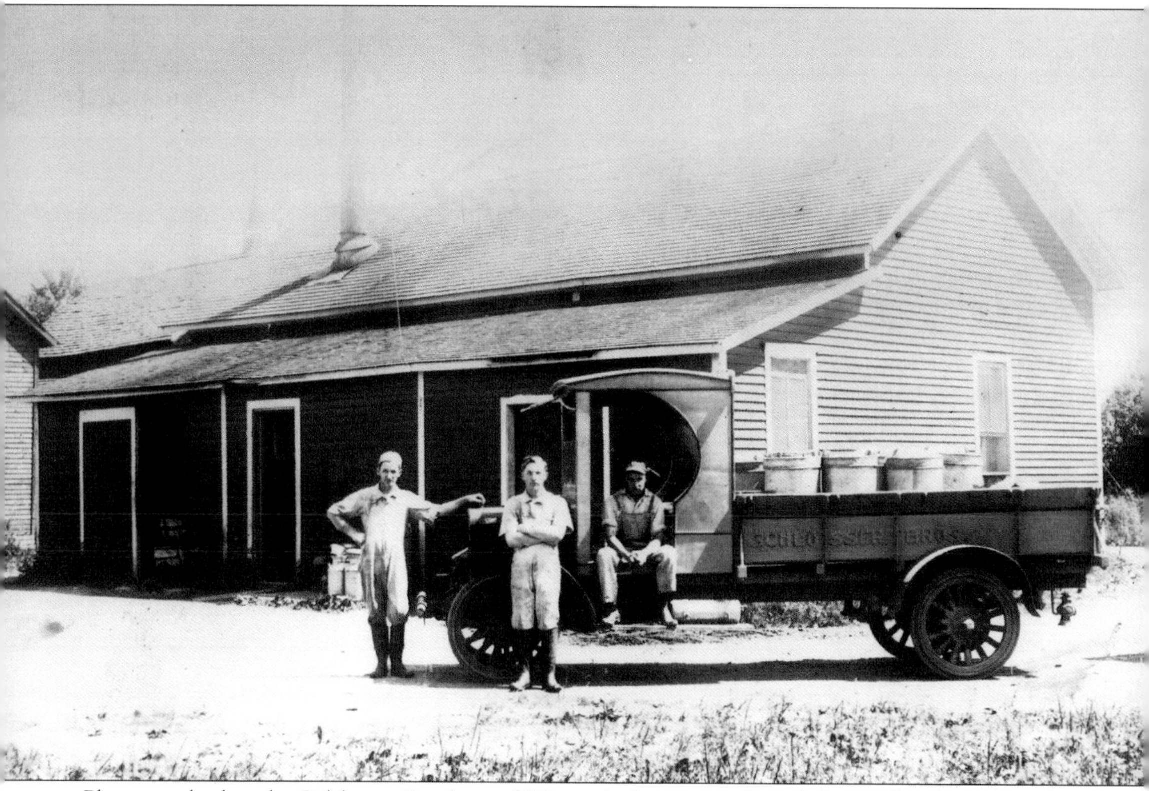

Photographed at the Schlosser Brothers of Wyatt, Indiana, are, from left to right, Amos Bendit, Joseph Bendit, and Albert Bendit. (Courtesy of Vicki Berger.)

# *Five*

# Rural Living

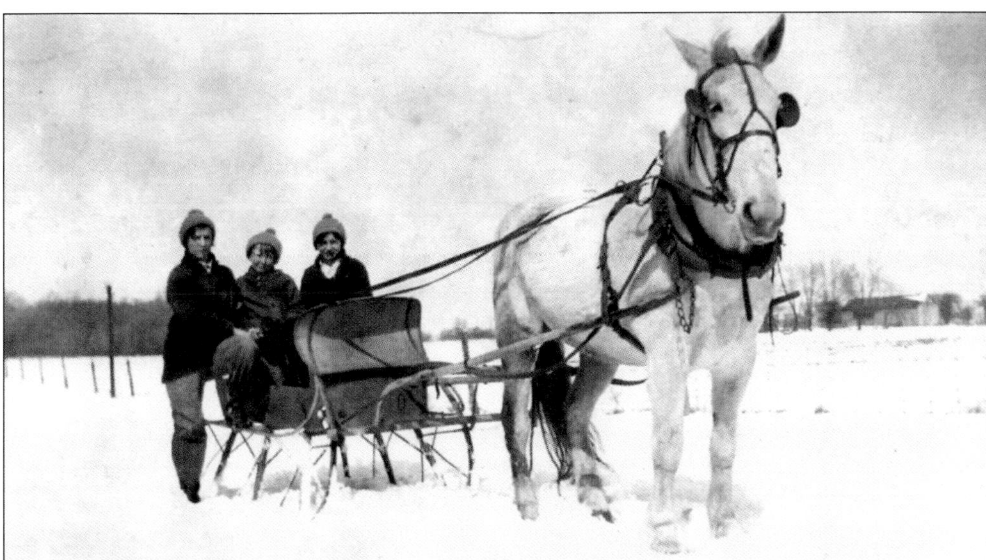

In the past, travel during the winters in Penn and Madison Townships necessitated a horse and sleigh. A mother and two children are shown here enjoying a sleigh ride with their Belgian horse. (Courtesy of the author.)

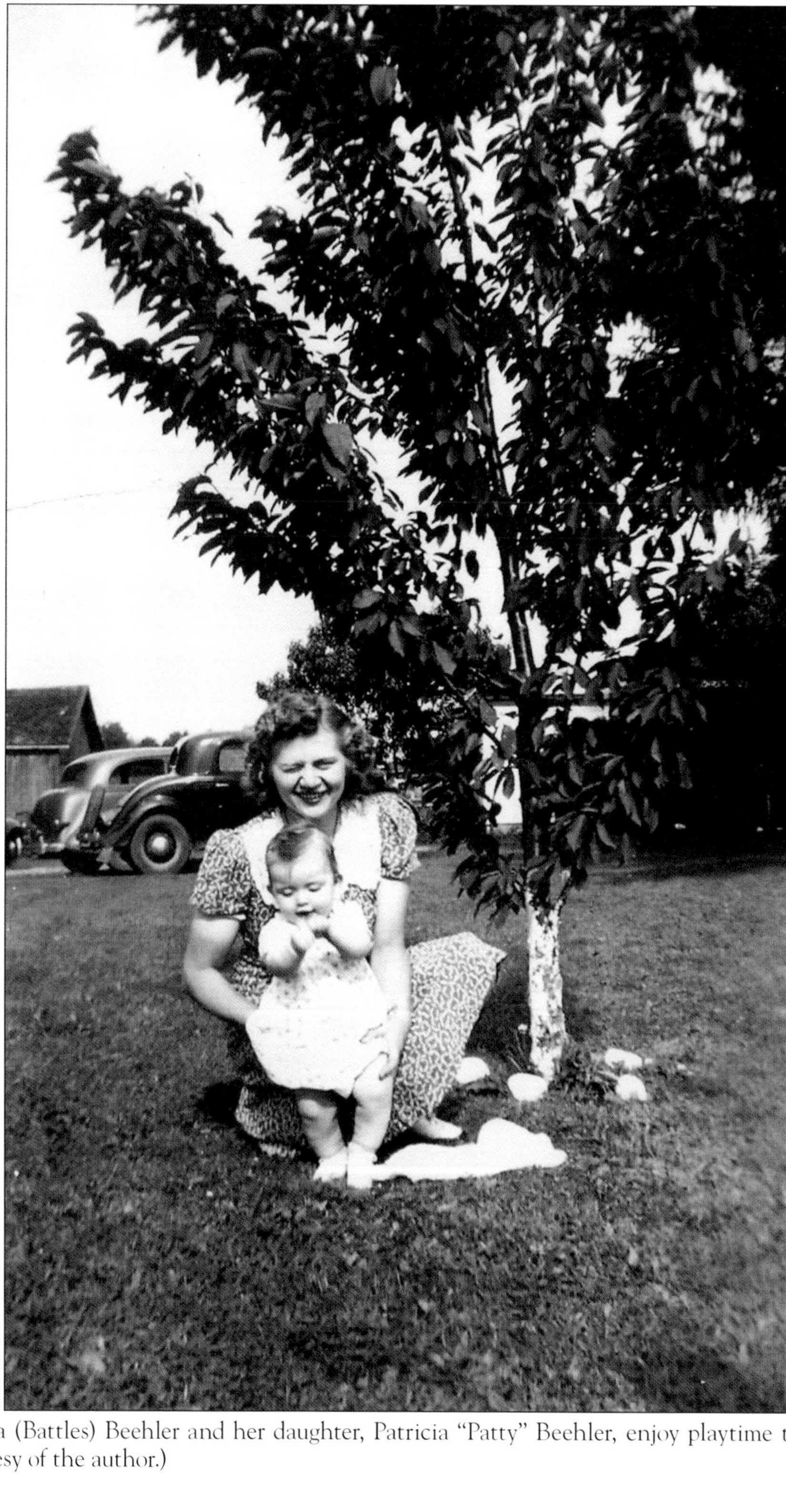

Virginia (Battles) Beehler and her daughter, Patricia "Patty" Beehler, enjoy playtime together. (Courtesy of the author.)

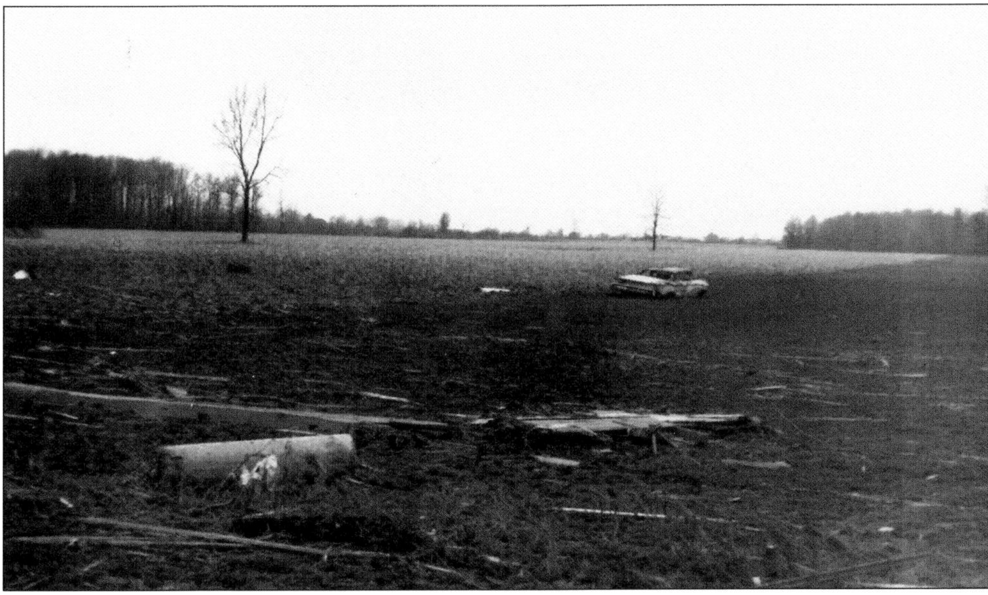

On April 11, 1965, many lives were changed in Madison Township by the Palm Sunday tornadoes. This car was on Pierce Road and was blown out into the field. Also note the chassis of Herb Schmeltz's school bus—parts of the body of the bus were found more than 20 miles away, in Goshen, Indiana. (Courtesy of the author.)

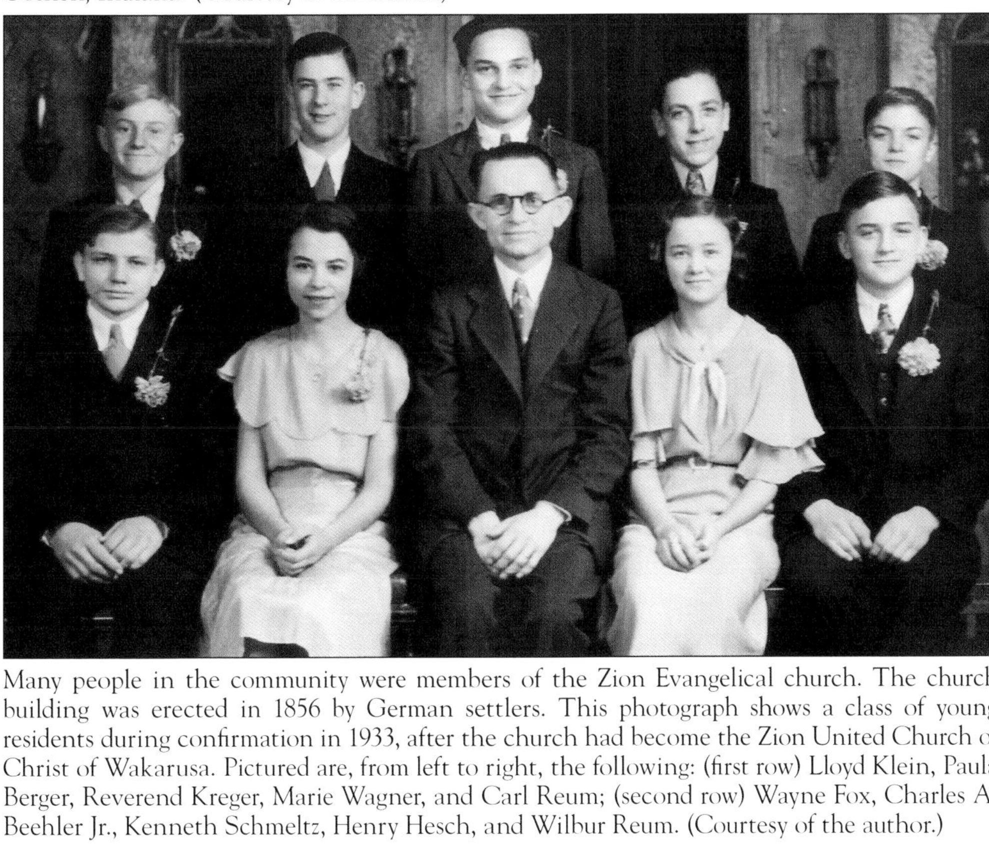

Many people in the community were members of the Zion Evangelical church. The church building was erected in 1856 by German settlers. This photograph shows a class of young residents during confirmation in 1933, after the church had become the Zion United Church of Christ of Wakarusa. Pictured are, from left to right, the following: (first row) Lloyd Klein, Paula Berger, Reverend Kreger, Marie Wagner, and Carl Reum; (second row) Wayne Fox, Charles A. Beehler Jr., Kenneth Schmeltz, Henry Hesch, and Wilbur Reum. (Courtesy of the author.)

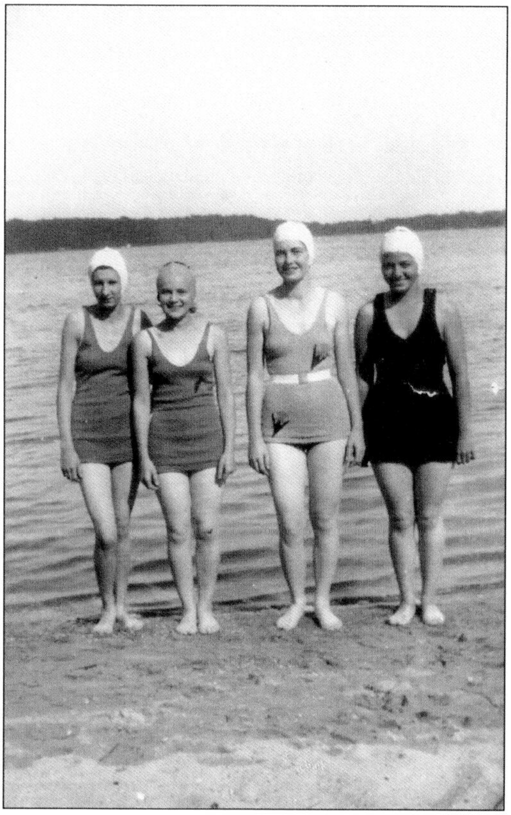

Four Madison township women are pictured in their swimsuits having a great time. They are, from left to right, Phyllis Sauer, Marie Shearer, Fern Pittman, and Verna Marburger. (Courtesy of Fern [Pittman] Beehler.)

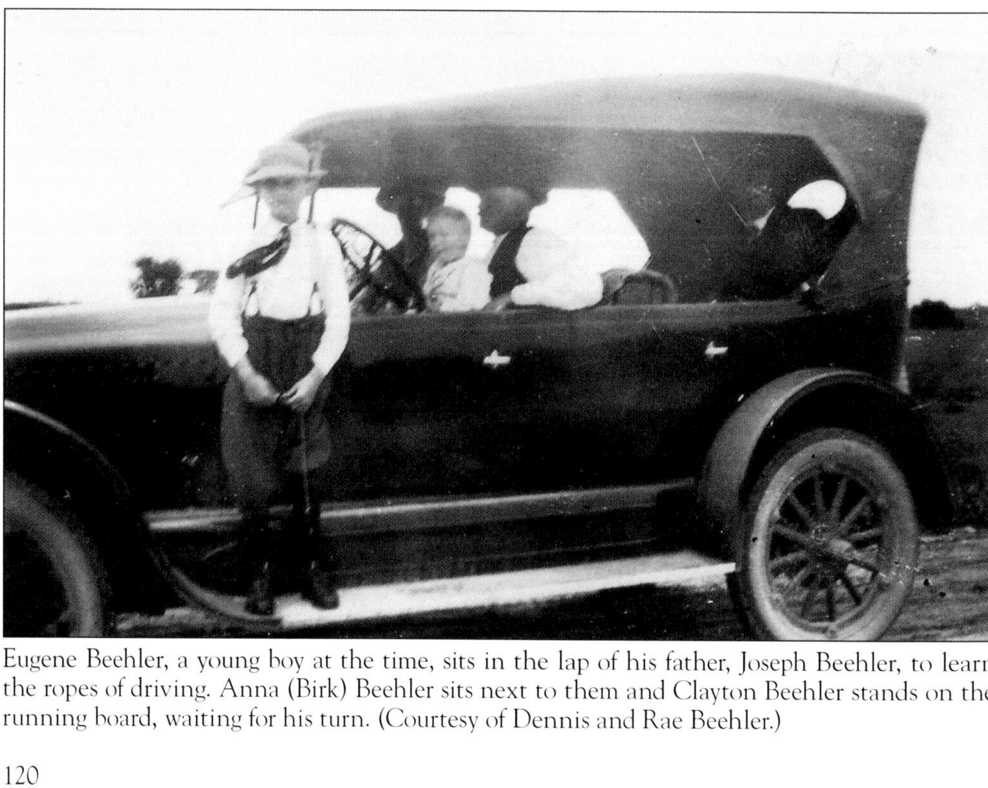

Eugene Beehler, a young boy at the time, sits in the lap of his father, Joseph Beehler, to learn the ropes of driving. Anna (Birk) Beehler sits next to them and Clayton Beehler stands on the running board, waiting for his turn. (Courtesy of Dennis and Rae Beehler.)

Jesse Groose is shown flying above the farms of Madison Township in his very own plane. In 1925, Jesse purchased a second plane from a St. Louis firm. For delivery to his father's home on Pierce Road, it was piloted by the now world-famous Charles Lindbergh. (Courtesy of Dennis and Rae Beehler.)

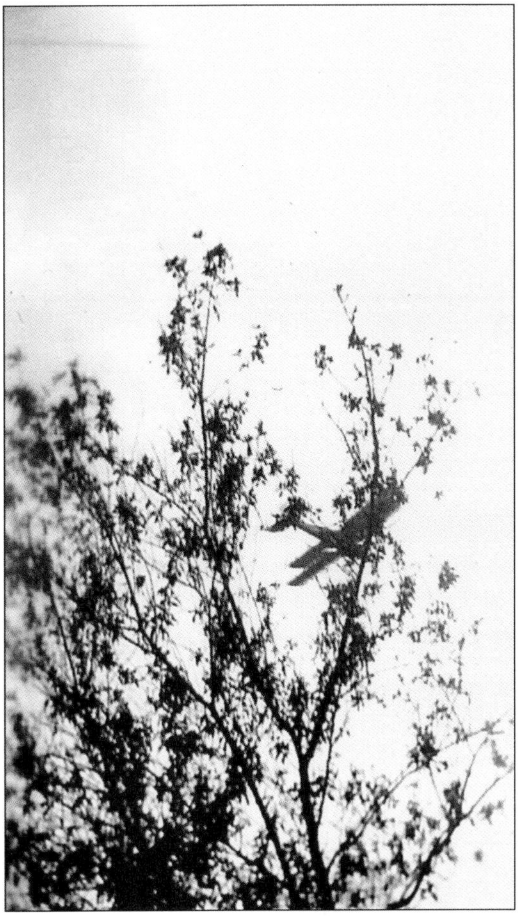

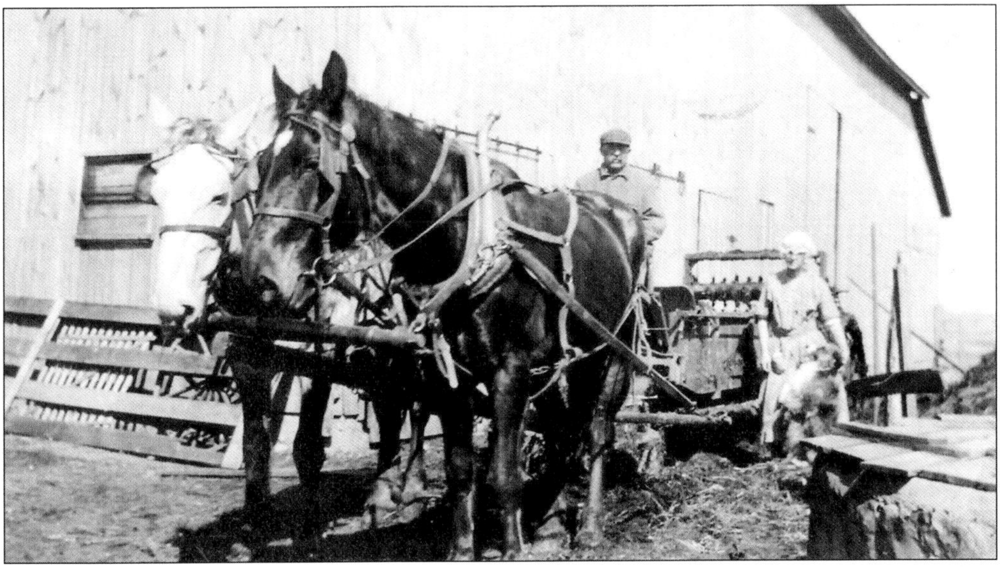

Leander Hahn is pictured getting ready to work in the fields of his farm. His farm was located on the corner of Kern and Elm Roads in Penn Township. (Courtesy of Dale Hahn.)

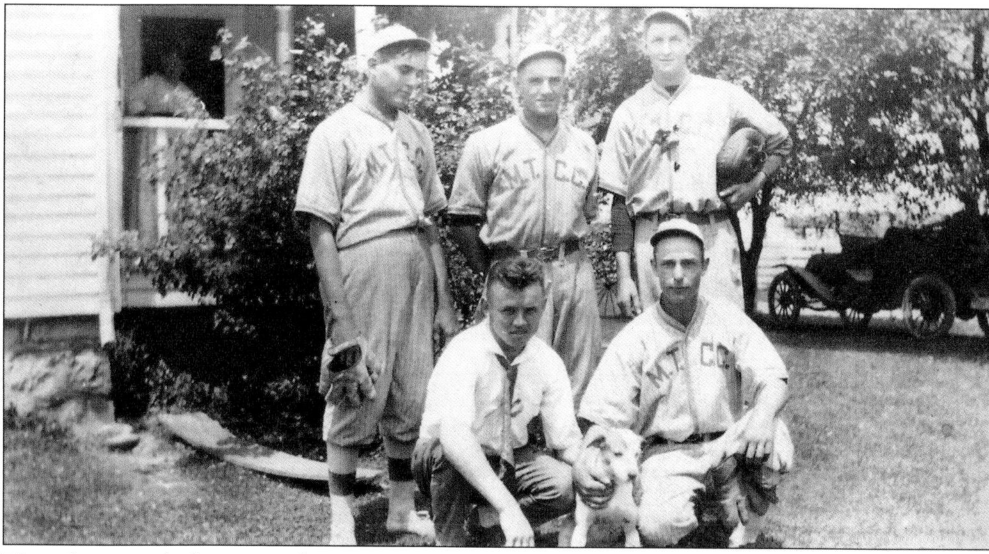

This photograph shows people getting ready for a day of baseball. Pictured are, from left to right, the following: (first row) Richard Beehler, and Ivo Marker; (second row) Rueben Marker, Sam Marker, and Stanley Kelley. (Courtesy of Evelyn [Beehler] Salyer.)

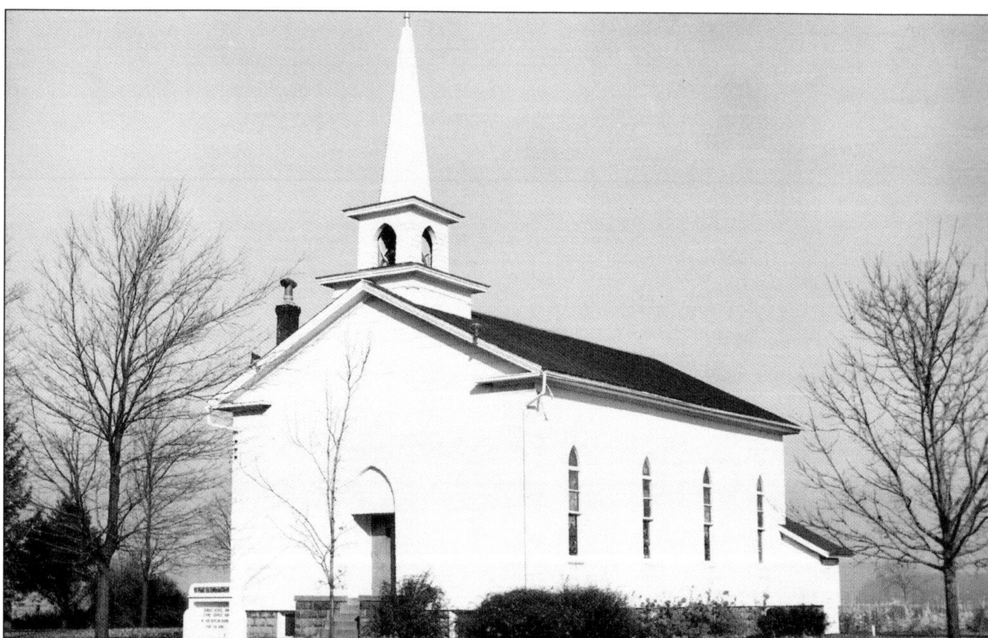

This photograph shows the Zion United Church of Christ in Wakarusa, Indiana, originally constructed out of logs on the corner of Cedar and New Roads in 1856. Charter members included Philip Beehler, Peter Beehler, Peter Bollenbacher, John Schafer, Nickalaus Schlarb, Philip Schlarb, Jacob Schlarb, Matthias Klein, John Marker, Godfred Bernhard, Anton Albert, Peter and John Hoos, Christian Hinze, Mr. Ramsey, Jacob Getz, K. Spohn, Philip Fries, Christian Horein, and Philip Marker. In 1868, the members decided to erect a new house of worship. Today it stands only 100 yards farther down New Road, on the south side. (Courtesy of Helen [Rader] Marker.)

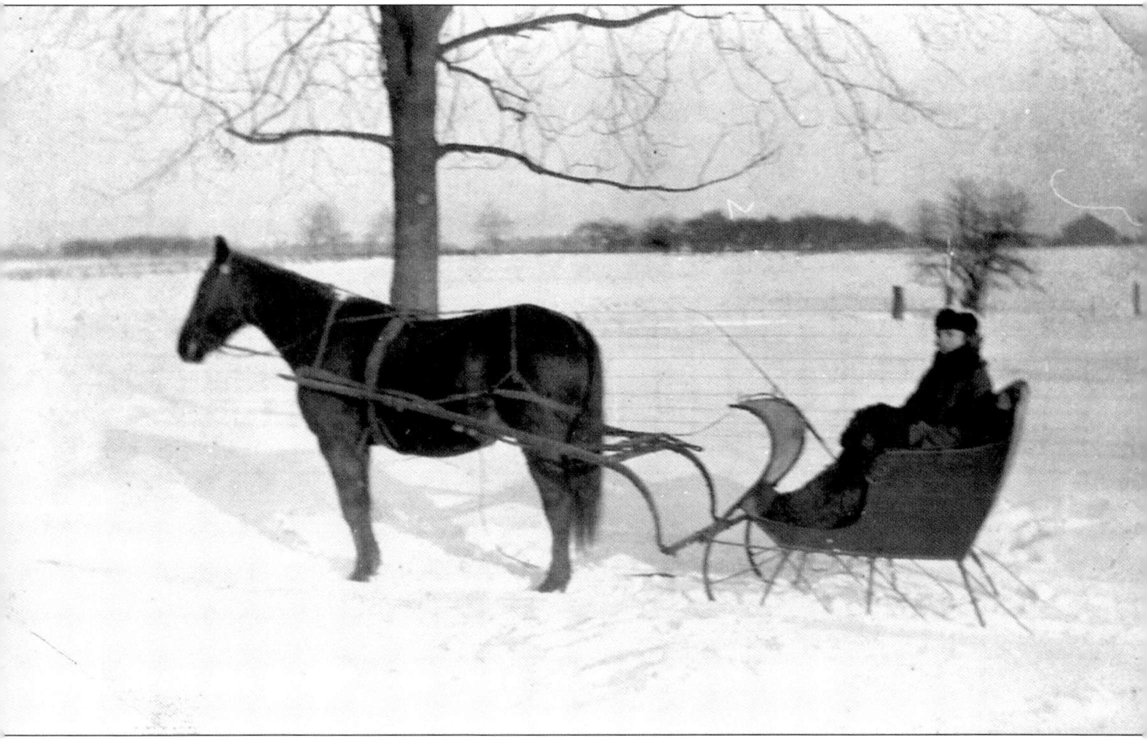

Dora Schalliol poses in a sleigh. She is getting ready to enjoy a beautiful winter day. (Courtesy of Dora [Schalliol] Fredericks.)

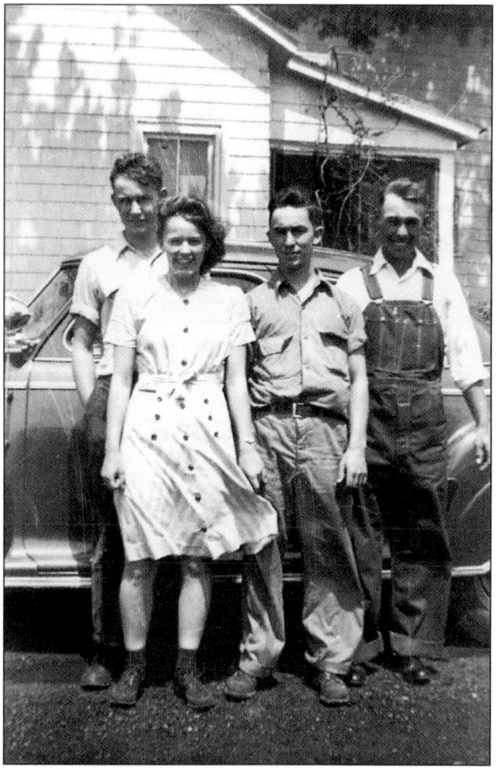

The Roeder children pose on the family homestead on Elm Road. Pictured are, from left to right, Thomas Roeder, Elnora (BeMiller) Roeder, Wayne Roeder, and Ralph Roeder. (Courtesy of Susie [Roeder] Pogue.)

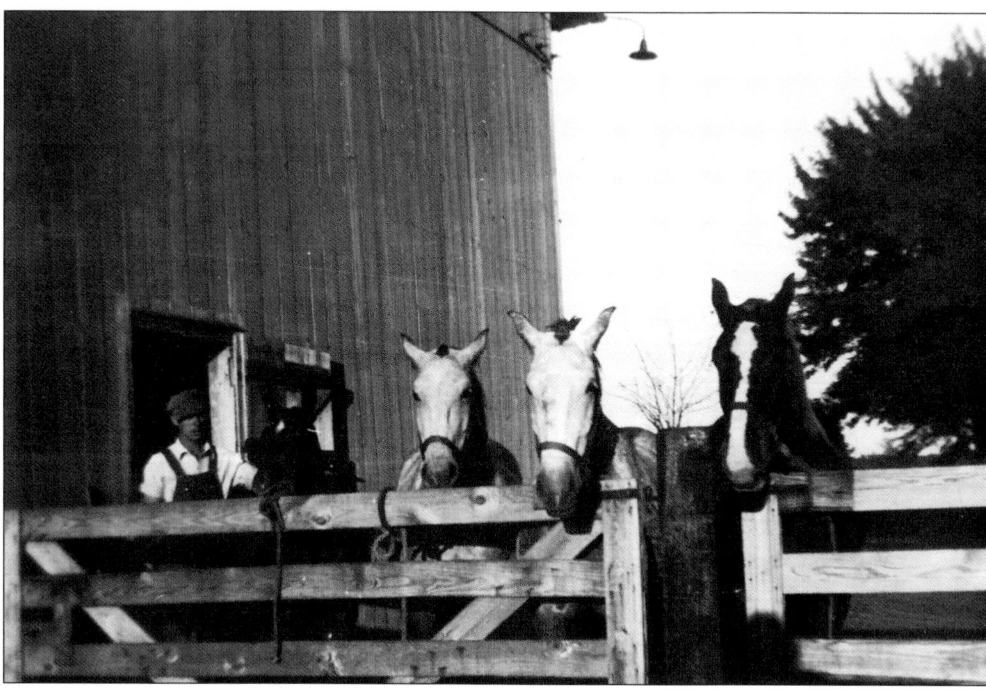

In 1948, one farmer, Ralph Roeder, used Belgian horses to work the fields of his farm. Ralph Roeder is pictured here with some of his young horses. His farm was located on Elm Road just north of Osborne Road, on the west side. (Courtesy of Susie [Roeder] Pogue.)

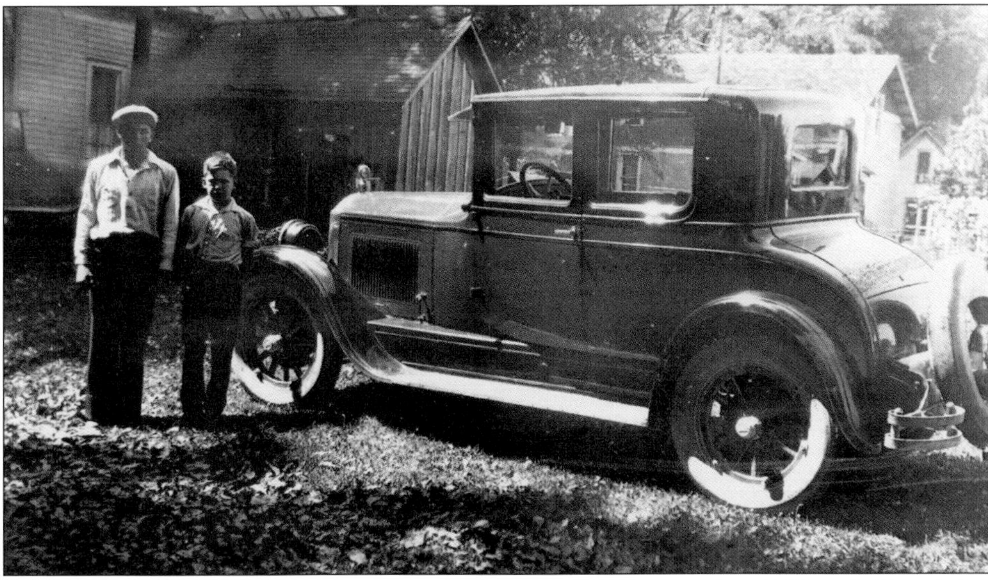

Harry Joseph Berger (left) and George Christian Berger are pictured in 1927, with Harry's first car. Harry was a hot-rodder in the town of Wyatt, Indiana, and eventually became a test driver for Bendix Corporation. (Courtesy of Vicki Berger.)

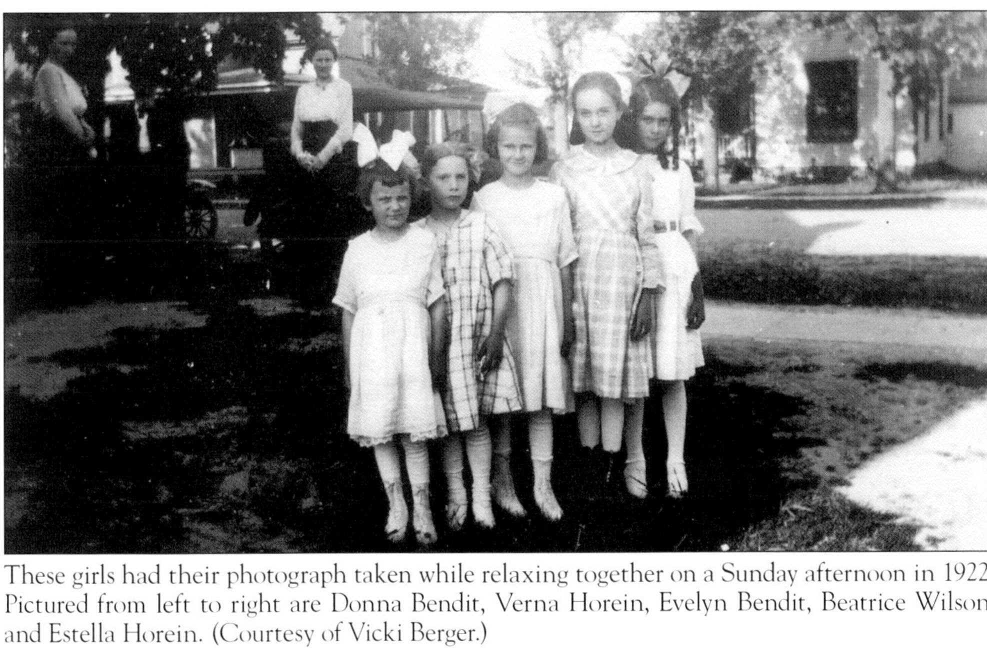

These girls had their photograph taken while relaxing together on a Sunday afternoon in 1922. Pictured from left to right are Donna Bendit, Verna Horein, Evelyn Bendit, Beatrice Wilson, and Estella Horein. (Courtesy of Vicki Berger.)

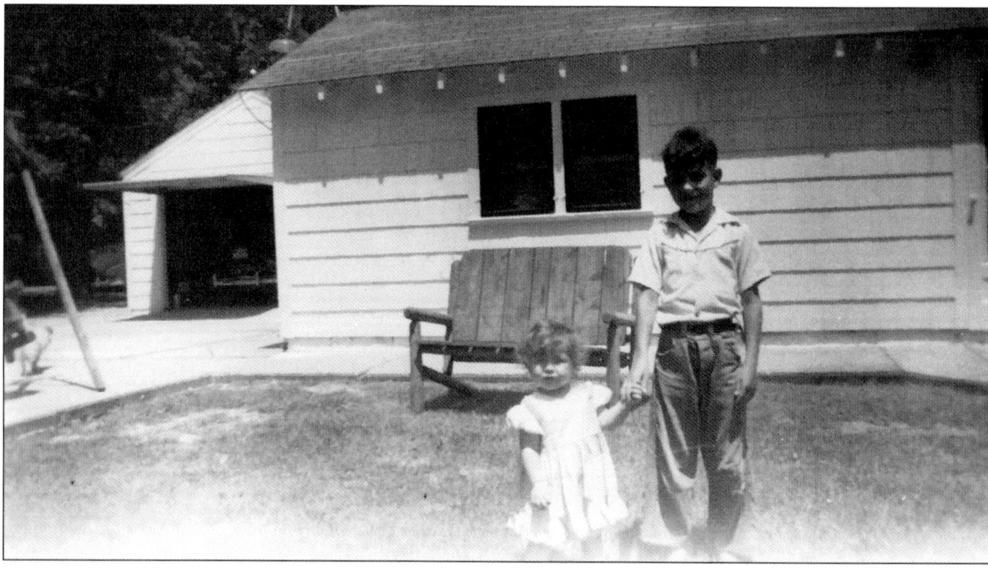

Rosemary Contat and her big brother, Larry Contat, are photographed on the family homestead on Kelley Road in Penn Township. (Courtesy of Rosemary [Contat] Dixon.)

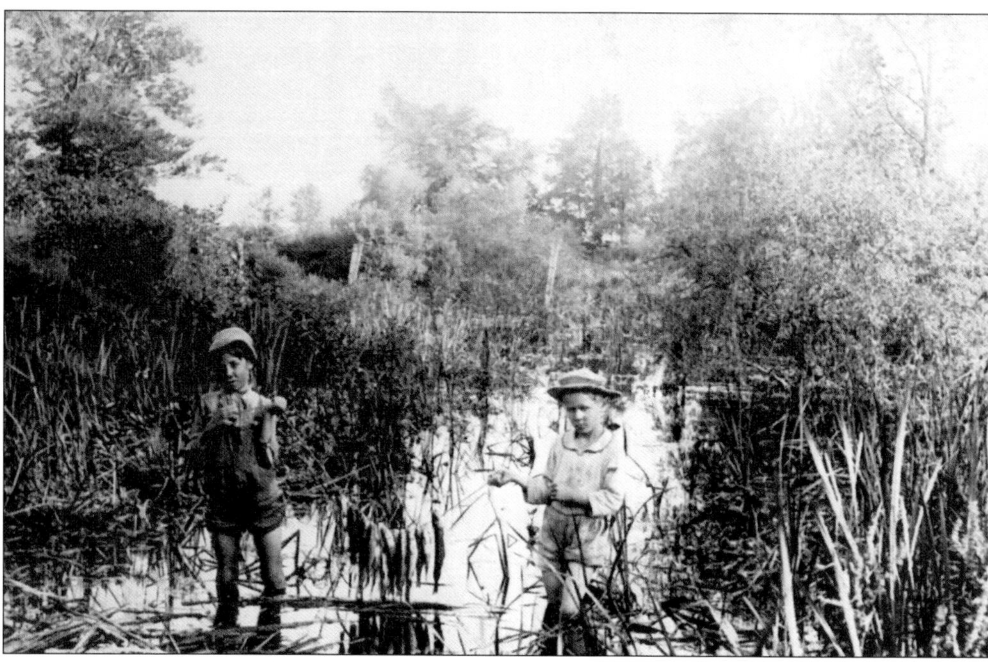

After a day of fishing in Madison Township, Adam Emil Berger (left) and his brother Joseph Herman Berger are photographed showing their catches for the day. (Courtesy of Vicki Berger.)

Standing in front of the largest tree on the Shaffer-Berger farm in Madison Township are Jacob Shaffer, Walter Shaffer, Margaret Berger, Anna Berger, Zulma Shaffer (sitting on the log), Harold Shaffer, Kathryne Berger, Lena Berger, John Shaffer, and Abraham "Jim" Berger. (Courtesy of Ann [Kovach] Fette.)

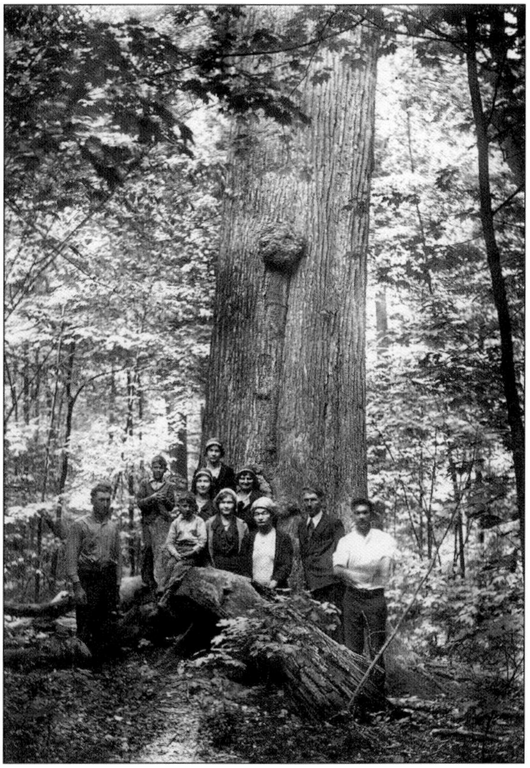

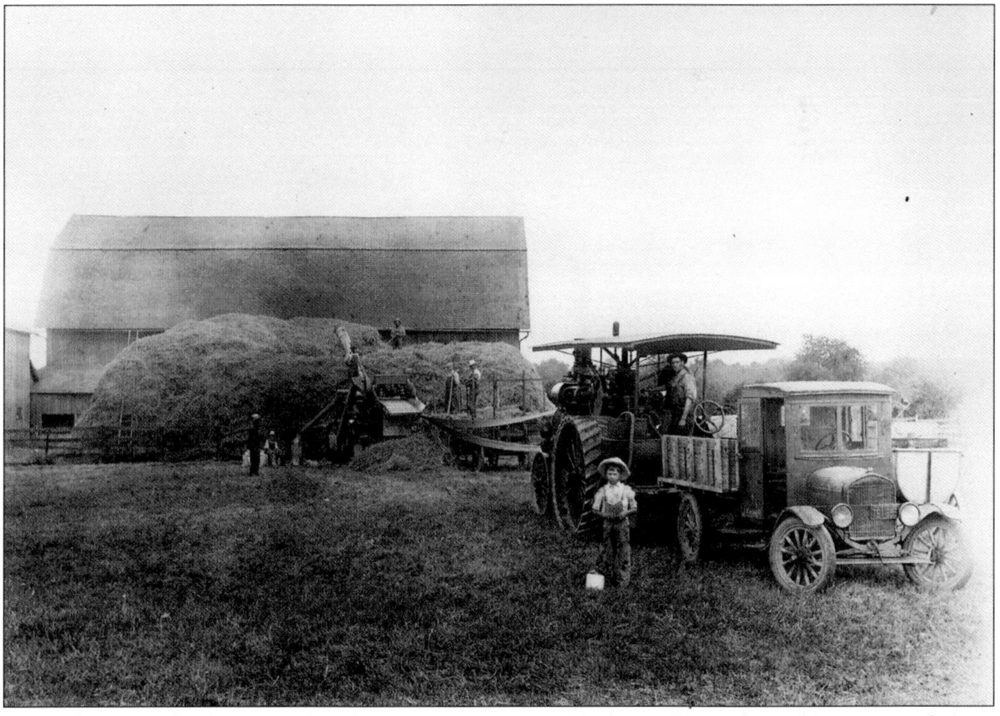

This photograph shows a threshing operation in Madison Township. (Courtesy of Ann [Kovach] Fette.)

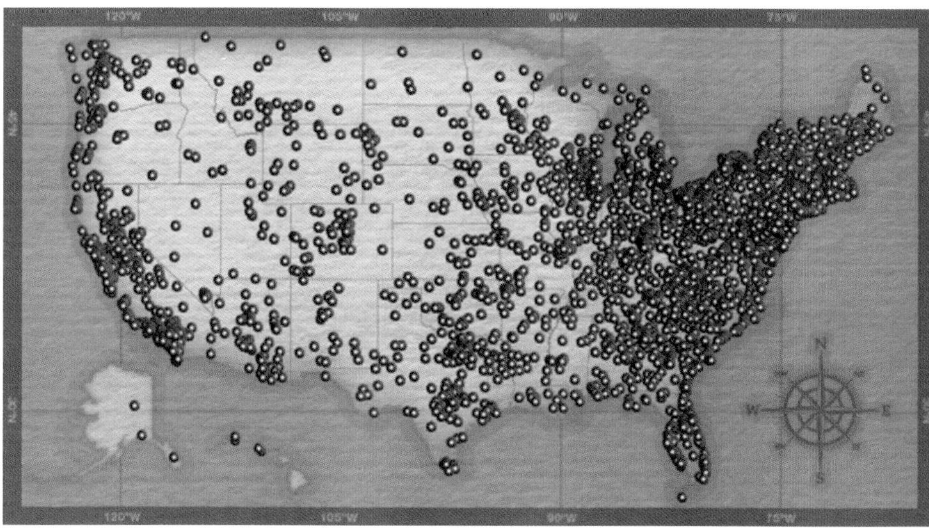